M. Sue Benford

STRONG WOMAN

Unshrouding the Secrets of the Soul

by M. Sue Benford

Foreword by Gregg Braden

Strong Woman - *Unshrouding the Secrets of the Soul*

M. Sue Benford

"Wisdom must become an ideal for us, born out of the periphery of the cosmos and capable of filling us with great strength, with the strength that enables us to fulfill our own destiny and to achieve our own cosmic ideal. With this strength, we shall also be able to realize the human ideal that awaits us in the future."

Rudolf Steiner

Strong Woman - *Unshrouding the Secrets of the Soul*

M. Sue Benford

STRONG WOMAN:
Unshrouding the Secrets of the Soul

Copyright © 2002 M. Sue Benford
Cover art copyright © M. Sue Benford
Cover design by M. Sue Benford and Precise Graphics, Inc.

ISBN: 0-9665312-2-1
Library of Congress Control Number: 2002095870

ALL RIGHTS RESERVED

No part of this publication may be reproduced in whole
or in part, or stored in a retrieval system, or transmitted in any
form or by any means, electronic, mechanical, photocopying,
recording, or otherwise, without written permission of the author.

Source Books, Inc.
P.O Box 292231
Nashville, TN USA 37229-2231
1-800-637-5222
(615) 773-7652
www.sacredspaces.org

Printed in the U.S.A.

∞

Strong Woman - *Unshrouding the Secrets of the Soul*

M. Sue Benford

ACKNOWLEDGMENTS

Just one person does not write a book of this nature, even if that person's name is in the byline. Without the extraordinary contributions of my family, friends, and supportive colleagues, you would not be reading this book right now. Although it is impossible to name everyone who has entered my life and contributed in some fashion, I would like to mention a few. First, my loving parents who always did their best with what life had given them — their constant support is unending. To my beloved late brother, Steve, whose unconditional love while living is surpassed only by his never-ending spiritual support and affirmations. To my children who have endured their mother's countless hours of "soul searching" and far too many distractions from "real-world" events. To my spiritual and life partner, Joseph Marino, whose contributions in terms of both everyday life and of providing essential Shroud information has been invaluable. Without him, much of my work would have remained incomplete. To Gregg Braden, who graciously has given of his time, energy, and expertise to assist me on many occasions. He is a true champion of the spiritual path! To Susan Gray who tirelessly helped me edit my first manuscript and to Heather Froeschl, of Quilldipper, Inc., who edited and reviewed the book you are about to read. Both have provided much needed support and encouragement throughout the process. A big thanks to you both! To my best friend throughout the past several transitional years, Carol, you have made life a pleasure. Everyone should be so lucky as to have a friend like you.

As important as all these people, and many others, have been in my quest to bring you the truth of my experiences, I would be remiss to not recognize the true source of my inspiration. To Jesus and John – this book is for you.

NOTE: Some proper names of living individuals have been changed to protect individual privacy.

∞

Strong Woman - *Unshrouding the Secrets of the Soul*

"This book by M. Sue Benford is one of the most unique, innovative, groundbreaking works on the Shroud of Turin published to date. She discusses and incorporates in her research physical phenomena and events that few scientists have attempted and even know about. Her work on pyramids and the Shroud is a first and may give us a breakthrough in how the Shroud body image was produced. Her personal life stories are touching and emotional reading. Sue puts her heart and soul into this book and few will remain untouched after reading it. She has given Shroud research a new direction for the 21st Century. This book is a must for any person interested in or researching the Shroud of Turin — truly a pioneering and courageous work."

John DeSalvo, Ph.D., Director
Great Pyramid of Giza Research Association

Dr. DeSalvo is a biophysicist and former college professor. He is Executive Vice President for the Association of Scientists and Scholars International for the Shroud of Turin (ASSIST), the largest and oldest Shroud research organization in the world. He was also a research consultant to the Shroud of Turin Research Project (STURP). He has been involved in Shroud research for over 20 years. He has lectured nationwide and the 'International Platform Association' designated him as one of the top 30 speakers in the nation in 1980. Dr. DeSalvo is also the Director of the Great Pyramid of Giza Research Association.

"I really think you are on to something that will advance our knowledge of these issues."

Edgar Mitchell, Sc.D.,
Former Apollo Astronaut,
Founder of IONS

"I am delighted to learn of your results and I congratulate you and your colleagues for what sounds like a major contribution."

Larry Dossey, M.D.,
author, Editor of Alternative
Therapies in Health and Medicine

"By general agreement one of the star presentations at the Orvieto Congress was that by Joe Marino and Sue Benford on the topic 'Evidence for the Skewing of the C-14 Dating of the Shroud of Turin due to Repairs.'.... the hypothesis should certainly now be set on a par with the more plausible explanations..."

From Ian Wilson,
author and world-renowned Shroud expert in the
***British Society for the Turin Shroud Newsletter*,**
No. 52, November 2000.

M. Sue Benford

"Thank you once again for your excellent paper, 'Evidence for the Skewing of the C-14 Dating of the Shroud of Turin Due to Repairs.'…The fact that you used an independent textile expert who had no idea that he was dealing with the Shroud makes it all the more significant."

**From Rev. Albert R. Dreisbach,
Executive Director of the Atlanta International Center
for Continuing Study of the Shroud of Turin.**

"Kudos on the verification of your Orvieto paper by Ray Rogers. I said it at the time that yours was the best delivered there and time has proved it to be a correct analysis."

**From Rev. Albert R. Dreisbach,
Executive Director of the Atlanta International Center
for Continuing Study of the Shroud of Turin.**

"Your paper was one of the highlights of the conference…"

**From Rev. Frederick Brinkmann,
President of the Holy Shroud Guild, Esopus, NY.**

"You two are moving rapidly into the forefront of Shroud research."…

**From Dr. Daniel C. Scavone,
Shroud historian,
University of Indiana-Evansville**

"If proven true, this evidence [Marino/Benford patch hypothesis] would provide the simplest explanation for the medieval age of the cloth arrived at by the three C-14 laboratories that performed the tests. I think you will find this paper fascinating and food for thought, no matter what your point of view on the authenticity of the Shroud."

**From Barrie Schwortz,
former STURP photographer and owner of
the preeminent Shroud website www.shroud.com.
See the paper at: www.shroud.com/pdfs/marben.pdf**

Strong Woman - *Unshrouding the Secrets of the Soul*

TABLE OF CONTENTS

PART ONE

Chapter One - In the beginning 1

Chapter Two - Early scars 5

Chapter Three - And the weak shall be made strong 11

Chapter Four - The transformation begins 17

Chapter Five - The first of the soul mate trinity 23

Chapter Six - The second of the trinity 29

Chapter Seven - Talking with angels? 37

Chapter Eight - The spiritual door swings wide open 41

Chapter Nine - The last of the trinity 47

Chapter Ten - The letter 51

Chapter Eleven - So you're John! 57

PART TWO

Chapter Twelve - A truly personal relationship with Christ 63

Chapter Thirteen - The apple is much more than just red 73

Chapter Fourteen - Heaven's library 81

Chapter Fifteen - Please, God, not again! 87

Chapter Sixteen - Where did I come from? 91

Chapter Seventeen - Who was the Apostle Paul? 97

Chapter Eighteen - What is a soul mate? 103

TABLE OF CONTENTS

PART TWO cont.

Chapter Nineteen - "The answer is always Love" 109

Chapter Twenty - Read Thomas! 115

Chapter Twenty One - John's Secrets 121

Chapter Twenty Two - Why do bad things happen to good people? . 133

Chapter Twenty Three - Who was Jesus Christ? 137

Chapter Twenty Four - The invisible truths 147

Chapter Twenty Five - Graduation day 157

PART THREE

Chapter Twenty Six - It's not Margaret! 163

Chapter Twenty Seven - In His image 169

Chapter Twenty Eight - The Shroud, the Grail and Magdalene 173

Chapter Twenty Nine - Spiritual soul mate 177

Chapter Thirty - A plate in the hand 185

Chapter Thirty One - But it's medieval! 189

Chapter Thirty Two - Finding the soul 193

Chapter Thirty Three - A "Shroud" for the 21st Century 207

Chapter Thirty Four - Timing is everything 223

Conclusion - Only the beginning 231

M. Sue Benford

FOREWORD

Occasionally, a book comes into our lives whose power transcends a simple summary or endorsement, and can be known only through the direct experience of the reader. *STRONG WOMAN: Unshrouding the Secrets of the Soul* is one of those books. Within its pages scientist, researcher and sindonologist* M. Sue Benford offers a rare glimpse into the adversities, and rewards of her lifelong journey that has led to what may become one of the landmark discoveries of the Twenty First Century. Through her experience, we are given insight into a possibility of such hope that its message lingers long after the book's cover has been closed.

Conventional wisdom has traditionally separated the very personal experiences of spirituality, from the scientific understandings of our world. *STRONG WOMAN* invites us to move beyond such tradition, demonstrating how the marriage of direct experience and science offer a strength in their union, that is greater than each individually. For Susie Benford, her path of spirituality actually paved the way for her professional accomplishments, while opening an entirely new paradigm of scientific study! Through her story, we are shown how the most formidable challenges of our lives, and our greatest contributions to our world, may go hand-in-hand. As we allow a similar process in our own lives, we become living examples demonstrating the power within each of us to make a difference in our world.

At the dawn of a new millennium, we find ourselves in a time of technological achievement unparalleled in recorded history. While we may have coaxed from creation her secrets of energy, matter and the building blocks of life, a great mystery still remains. When solved, this puzzle may, at long last, identify the elusive "missing link" bridging the seemingly disparate worlds of science and spirituality. The mystery is this: conventional science has failed to explain the origins of, or process, creating the image on what is now recognized as the most studied artifact in history; *The Shroud of Turin*.

In 1898 the mysterious 14' 3" long by 3' 7" wide linen sheet, known as the *"Shroud of Turin"*, was photographically documented for the first time. Already the source of tremendous controversy, the focus of the cloth is the faint and life-like image of a crucified man that appears to be scorched into the fibers of the cloth. Matching nearly item for item the Biblical description of Christ's crucifixion, the validity of the Shroud has been in question since it appeared in Western Europe in 1353, far from its suspected origins in the Holy Lands early in the First Century.

To the surprise of the photographer, as well as the scientific community of the day, these early pictures led to the discovery that the image of the man emblazoned upon the cloth functions as a "negative," becoming "positive" only when the light values are reversed through the process of photography. Since the time of the first photographs, improved techniques of image analysis, forensics, and new discoveries in quantum physics, have offered fresh insight into the man in the Shroud and the source of his image.

In the decades of the 70's and 80's, studies were initiated to determine the age, and confirm the presence of human blood, upon the Shroud. It was hoped that these investigations would bring an end to the speculation of the relic's origins, and questions of its authenticity. Making worldwide headlines, the studies concluded that there were no significant amounts of human blood on the cloth and that the Shroud dated to medieval times, preventing it from being the burial cloth of Christ. Serious questions regarding the methods, protocol and conclusions drawn from these studies have since developed. While the studies remain cloaked in controversy, it was not the first of its kind, nor was it the most extensive.

In 1978, an unprecedented effort to unlock the mystery of the Shroud began, as 40 researchers embarked upon a study that would last for five years. Composed of scientists employed by the most sophisticated laboratories of the time, including the Los Alamos National Laboratories, Sandia Laboratories, and the Jet Propulsion Laboratories (JPL), the investigators were given rare access to the Shroud following the public display of that year. Working in shifts around the clock for five continuous days to gather their data, the Shroud of Turin Research Project's (STURP's) investigation was completed in 1983. Disclosed through specialized scientific committees, technical journals and books authored by individual team members, the STURP findings received relatively little attention from mainstream media and the general public. Though several elements of the STURP findings appear to be in direct conflict with the previously mentioned studies, including the discovery of significant amounts of human blood, neither study conclusively solved the mystery of the image upon the cloth.

As of this writing, it is impossible to conclude with 100 percent certainty whether or not *The Shroud of Turin* is, in fact, the actual burial cloth of Jesus of Nazareth. While much of the evidence may appear to support the Shroud's authenticity, there is no scientific test for Jesus, per se. What is available, however, is a growing body of circumstantial, chemical and historical evidence accumulating through an ever-improving array of advanced analytic technologies. From this evidence, we can state the degree of probability, *as a percentage basis*, of the Shroud's authenticity.

M. Sue Benford

The focus of the Shroud studies may be described through five primary areas of investigation: dating, forensics, image formation, chemistry and botanical (leaf and pollen grain) analysis. Of these areas of study, four of the five, or 80% of the study results, support the hypothesis that the Shroud of Turin is the burial cloth of Jesus. For the moment, the greatest point of contention appears to be the dating of the cloth itself. Although select Shroud fibers were subjected to Carbon-14 dating in 1988, the discovery of mildew-like microorganisms and scorching from the fire of 1532, have created a lingering uncertainty concerning the results. Each discovery, alone, could possibly skew the dating process. Additionally, Benford's astounding revelation that the samples dated were from medieval patches used to mend the Shroud, coupled with advances in dating techniques, will almost certainly lead to the new dating of Shroud samples in the near future.

In the presence of so much speculation regarding the Shroud's authenticity, there is one fact that can not be overlooked. With the exception of questionable results from the dating procedures, no scientific evidence has been produced that *prevents* the Shroud from being the burial cloth of Christ. While we may never know precisely whose image is emblazoned upon the ancient linen, one fact remains clear: the man in the Shroud experienced a process that Twentieth-Century science failed to explain. Recent discoveries in quantum physics and subtle-energy research now offer fresh insight into the original findings of the Shroud research. Each suggests that the Shroud of Turin offers evidence of a process that may be understood only by expanding the way we view our relationship to creation. The principles supporting such an empowering perspective have been recently rediscovered, and validated, by late-Twentieth Century science.

The intuitive insight afforded Susie Benford through her personal triumph over adversity, focused through the impeccable use of the best science of our time, gives new meaning to the man in the Shroud for each of us, our families, and loved ones in the Twenty First Century. In a very intimate and non-technical format, *STRONG WOMAN: Unshrouding the Secrets of the Soul* offers the first viable scientific theory, complete with a replicable process, to reveal the secret of the most studied artifact in recorded history. With her explanation, Benford may have solved a mystery that has baffled Shroud researchers for nearly one and one half millennia. At the same time, she offers a legacy of hope to future generations, assuring us that our lives are more than the boundaries of our flesh, and greater than the limits that we create from our beliefs.

Gregg Braden, Author of the best-selling book, *The Isaiah Effect* (Crown/Harmony Books, 2000); *Walking Between the Worlds* (Radio Bookstore Press, 1997); and *Awakening to Zero Point* (Radio Bookstore Press, 1992) www.greggbraden.net (505) 424-6892

Footnote [*] *One who studies the Shroud of Turin*

Strong Woman - *Unshrouding the Secrets of the Soul*

M. Sue Benford

A SPECIAL INTRODUCTION TO
STRONG WOMAN:
Unshrouding the Secrets of the Soul

by Joseph G. Marino

To say that some of the events described in **STRONG WOMAN: Unshrouding the Secrets of the Soul** radically changed my life would be a gross understatement. I am a former Roman Catholic Priest and Benedictine Monk. Like Saul of Tarsus, my theology and life had been established and thought to be firmly in place for the future. Like Saul of Tarsus, I would never be the same after life-altering experiences, some of which are described in this book. I can only give a cursory summary here, but I hope it will be enough to explain why I think this book is so important.

Until I met Susie, I believed I would spend my whole life as a Benedictine monk in a monastery, where I cultivated a special interest that would eventually be affected by the events described in <u>Strong Woman</u>. Even before I entered the monastery where I was based for over 18 years, I had a fascination for the Shroud of Turin, the reputed burial cloth of Jesus. The Shroud played a significant role in transforming me from an agnostic into a Christian and my subsequent entry into the monastery. I always had a deep sense, almost mystical in nature, that the Shroud would continue to play a significant role in my spiritual life. While in the monastery, I wrote and lectured about the Shroud, produced a newsletter about it, and discussed it on television and radio. Over the years, I had various religious experiences connected with the Shroud that helped convince me that it was authentic. Even after the infamous Carbon-14 dating test of 1988, which purportedly showed that the Shroud dated only from the Middle Ages, my belief that the Shroud was the actual burial cloth of Jesus never wavered. I still strongly expected to keep my appointment with my destiny, which significantly involved this mysterious linen.

In 1997, I received a call from the author of this book, who had recently become interested in the Shroud. She told me that she had only learned about the relic through some revelations she claimed to have received from Jesus. She revealed that Jesus said that the cloth was authentic and called the image his "fingerprint." One obviously has to be cautious about such claims, but one also just cannot outrightly dismiss such claims just because they sound too fantastic. My own previous religious experiences convinced me of that. She had written several papers dealing with the Shroud and other spiritual and scientific matters, which she asked me to read. As one who makes a point to read everything on the Shroud, I agreed to read them. I found her work, including the theology and science in them, to be quite erudite. In addition to discussing the Shroud, we also talked about other spiritual matters, including the difference between our perceptions of Jesus and the reality of Jesus. You will read about these incredible insights in this book. You can decide if they are fantasy or reality. The reasons that we come to believe something, especially in the area of religion, are complex, but our beliefs are easier to hold if they are confirmed by actual life experiences.

Early on, she told me that she had a message from Jesus for me. The message was that I should put down my umbrella because truth was raining down all around me. I asked her what that meant. She said that if I believed that Jesus was actually speaking to her, I would start seeing "signs." While I was initially uncomfortable with some of the ideas she was proposing, her points were always convincing, and in my heart I found myself feeling less and less secure in my theology. Within days of the putative promise of signs, I started receiving them. They came almost every day for the next four months, and consistently after that for another six months. They usually occurred via the well-known phenomenon of "synchronicity," which is an unusual convergence of meaningful events. The Jesuit religious periodical *America* published an article titled, "When Is Synchronicity a Sign?" in the midst of my own synchronicities! Sometimes, a precise answer to a thought or a prayer based on my conversations with Susie would be answered in a matter of seconds, from a reading during prayers, seeing something in a magazine or newspaper, or a comment from individuals. I have kept track of all the signs as documentation through handwritten notes and e-mails.

Other unexplainable events were constantly occurring in this period, which cannot be detailed here. It will literally take a book to tell my whole story. Susie was also getting similar signs, sometimes even on the same matter. All of the signs, much to my dismay, pointed me in the direction of leaving the monastery, something that was unthinkable for me. Even though leaving was unimaginable, the signs were seemingly unmistakable.

M. Sue Benford

With great anxiety and fear, I started discussing these experiences with my spiritual director, a trusted priest friend whom I had known for over 20 years. He suggested that I needed to be cautious about my signs, knowing that the mind can play tricks on us. At least one other close friend in whom I confided advised the same. My spiritual director, Susie and I met periodically, and I continued to meet with him separately as well. I even asked him if he thought that my experiences could be attributed to an evil spirit. Susie herself had been skeptical of her own experiences and when she questioned Jesus about them, his reply was, "You are right to be skeptical. Believe no image, including mine, that steers you away from my one true message." When Susie asked what that message was, she was told, "The answer is always love. Any other answer is not of God no matter who says it." My spiritual director did not believe I was being deceived. My other friend, in whom I confided, a very wise and spiritual person, also met Susie and became very supportive of us. My own heart, but more importantly, my conscience, convinced me that God had a special mission for me, which would include the Shroud and more, and had used Susie as an instrument for my instruction.

I did leave the monastery, the priesthood and the Catholic Church, and I am now not only collaborating with her on the Shroud and other spiritual issues, but we have become life partners. Our union facilitates spreading the message we believe we have been given to impart to the world. Many people did not approve of my decision, and I can truly understand why people feel that way. Being in relationship with God always entails risk and surprise, even when one believes that life is grounded in an unalterable tradition. One is obligated to seek the will of God, even when decisions based on His will leads to alienation from others. God would seem to have more in mind than using Susie just as an instrument in my own life. There are far-reaching implications to her revelations, including a new understanding of what role the Shroud will play in God's plan for humankind.

We have already presented at a Worldwide Congress in Orvieto, Italy in August 2000 a significant Shroud paper that explains why the 1988 C-14 dating of the Shroud of Turin produced medieval results. This paper, which indicates that the Shroud is indeed the burial cloth of Jesus, resulted from a revelation that Susie had been given. We also wrote two follow-up papers on this theory, which now has the support of the original scientists on the team from 1978 that studied it, based on Shroud samples he still has in his possession. We have also written various other articles that are possibly setting the stage for this new understanding of God's plan for humankind. I truly believe that I am now fulfilling my long-standing Shroud-based sense of destiny.

None of this would have been possible had I not left the monastery. It was a risk, as there was an obvious chance that Susie and I were both somehow deceiving ourselves. The main criteria for judging an authentic prophet of the Old Testament was that what he predicted came true; he would thus be imparting a divine message.

Like many researchers, Susie and I both thought that the C-14 results were affected by some sort of radiation that had thrown the dating off. However, after Susie received her revelation that it was actually a repair, our subsequent research and scientific support by the only scientist able to validate our theory proves that a divine source was at work.

Although being a world-champion powerlifter and getting spiritual and scientific revelations might, at first glance seem unconnected, the author believes that there is a connection. She believes that the physical world mirrors the spiritual world. Thus, God can make incredible things happen in the material world to indicate His power just as He can make incredible things happen in the spiritual world to manifest His power. Her weightlifting power, despite her handicap, is an example of God displaying His strength through a human's weakness. Her lack of knowledge regarding the Bible enabled her to be, in her words, a "clean slate" in whom God could more easily work.

From having cancer as a young child to picking up the pieces after two failed marriages, Susie Benford's life story is a tale of unbelievable courage and tenacity as well as continual marvels. Those who accept the traditional ideas about Jesus will not likely accept her portrait of him from her revelations. Although Christians profess that Jesus was fully human, many Christians cannot even conceive of Jesus laughing, much less of having done something that people considered "bad." Susie reveals a Jesus who is indeed fully human, to the degree that it will make some readers uncomfortable. But was not that the effect of Jesus among most of his contemporaries? She offers a different slant on what constitutes sin and our present and ultimate relationship with God.

Many readers will probably think or believe these types of views are heretical. However, it should be remembered that theologians and exegetes are constantly uncovering new insights. Throughout history, new theological ideas have generally been initially rejected or viewed with suspicion. Then over the course of time, previously-rejected ideas can become part of the accepted theology. Even Thomas Aquinas, a theological giant in Catholicism, experienced significant rejection in his own day.

Each succeeding generation tends to see itself as the most theologically enlightened, but the world even today still experiences unspeakable horrors done in the name of religion. After almost 2000 years of Christianity, one has to wonder whether we have progressed much at all. The 20th century was the bloodiest time in human history. Regardless, new theological ideas flourish. The mystery of God always presents ongoing challenges. All new theological insights have to be judged on their merits.

What constitutes "supernatural" for theologians constantly changes. Susie believes that mankind has actually been given the ability to understand much of what many consider to be "supernatural" and thus unknowable. Whereas most people think of the world in terms of what is natural and what is supernatural, she believes that what people tend to term as supernatural are in reality little-understood natural phenomena. Although it should be understood that God's design and presence in the natural is no less real or significant.

Some renowned scientists in history who made some great discoveries have attributed them to spiritual inspiration. These include Nikola Tesla: alternating current; Albert Einstein: general theory of relativity; Jonas Salk: polio vaccine. However, their particular human gifts also played roles in the development of these discoveries. Such is the case with Susie. Although she attributes her revelations to divine inspiration, her own insights also play a role. God does not take away a person's humanity even when he/she is a direct instrument. This should not be surprising even from a purely religious view. Very few people would hold that Matthew, Mark, Luke, John, Paul and other New Testament writers did not leave their personal handiwork in their documents.

There is a popular saying that "truth is stranger than fiction." This saying definitely applies to the book you are about to read. It would be difficult for a fiction writer to spin a more incredible story. Who could ever believe that a small, handicapped woman under 100 pounds could become the world champion in powerlifting? Who could believe that this skeptical woman, who knew next to nothing about the Bible, could be getting revelations from Jesus that could turn the world upside down again, just as he did when he came almost two millennia ago. How could a woman with a cursory scientific background produce mind-boggling scientific discoveries that are amazing top-notch scientists?

Many who read this book likely believe that nothing could be added to our understanding of Jesus that we have not already acquired through the New Testament. However, it could be that the life of Susie Benford is a shining example of God's penchant for using the weak to spread His message. I know my life will never be the same again because of Susie. Regardless of your beliefs, it will be one of the most significant and powerful stories you will ever read.

Strong Woman - *Unshrouding the Secrets of the Soul*

M. Sue Benford

PREFACE

"What would convince me of the existence of God?" I had asked myself this question numerous times — as a child suffering the wretched treatments of experimental cancer drugs, as a nurse burying hundreds of innocent children plagued with the same disease, and, ultimately, as a skeptic defiantly disavowing any spiritual involvement in a series of unbelievable "coincidences." Even though I had somewhat miraculously obtained world-class physical strength, I had little, if any, reason to believe in the existence of God, spirits, angels or soul mates. If anything, I had ample evidence to demonstrate that a truly loving and almighty creator did not exist as, certainly, the pain and suffering I had endured and observed would not have been permitted.

I marveled at how the blindly faithful worshipped the invisible without a shred of proof that there was anything valuable to worship. More than once I chuckled at the various religious rituals that seemed to fly in the face of basic common sense. Certainly levelheaded and practical people could see that they were putting their faith in something that simply did not exist. Or were they?

Few things teach as well as experience. In late 1994, this truism was never so real. Stunned by the remnants of a disastrous and life-changing series of events, my world was turned upside down, twisted and contorted, shattering my very perception of reality. Crashing into my once practical and measurable world was the mystical and unexplainable. Unwilling to accept the "spirits" on faith, I set out with a vengeance to prove that the spiritual world did not exist. I was bound and determined to oppose my slide into the herd of docile believing sheep. I would demonstrate, using all the tools and techniques of modern science, that these faint whisperings and subtle mysterious circumstances were, in fact, fully explainable — the make-believe of a woman in distress.

Of all things, my path led to the television set and to a documentary about the presumed burial cloth of Jesus. This revered relic, known as the Shroud of Turin, was steeped in controversy. Many believing its etheric full-body image was indeed an authentic portrayal of the crucified Christ while many others believed it was nothing more than a medieval forgery. Of course, logic dictated that it was a clever hoax but, something deep inside me, refused to let me dismiss it so easily. Something, or someone, kept pushing me to pursue this ancient artifact. It all seemed so futile – no one in history had unraveled the mysteries inherent in the cloth's image. The most studied artifact in history remained a categorical mystery. Who was I to come along to answer the most profound questions about the Shroud?

Perhaps, however, this would be my chance to answer my pressing life question — what would convince me of the existence of God? Psychics, mediums, channelers and the like are all handicapped by the fact that they obtain information that is known elsewhere – the sitter, a living relative, a book. To me, this invalidates the claims of proof of a supernatural origin of the information. After all, maybe they were just reading someone else's mind. But if information was provided to someone for which NO ONE else alive knew, then this, to me, was proof that something, or someone, existed beyond the visages of our material world. This, to me, was proof of God – evidence of the soul. Could the final understanding of the Shroud of Turin provide me with such proof? Was the very essence of the soul being revealed in such a way that it was now scientifically testable? It seemed preposterous, outrageous, unbelievable and unimaginable but it happened.

M. Sue Benford

PART ONE

"All the evidence we come across in real life is faulty to a greater or lesser extent; and the only question of importance is how good the evidence is; not whether it is perfect or imperfect. Evidence is a matter of degree."

G.N.M. Tyrrell

Strong Woman - *Unshrouding the Secrets of the Soul*

Chapter One

In the beginning . . .

. . . things were not quite the way they should have been. In August of 1962, one month after my fifth birthday, I was diagnosed with cancer. My parents were told that I had a "Wilms' tumor," which is a malignant tumor of the kidney. At the time, the survival rate for children with this disease was less than ten percent — no exceptions.

As fate would have it, I was referred to Columbus Children's Hospital, one of several hospitals participating in a revolutionary new study for treating these types of cancers. Although still early in the experimental stages, my parents felt it was worth a chance and agreed to the new treatment, which consisted of surgery, radiation, and chemotherapy. I was only the thirteenth person at the hospital to receive the new combined therapy.

The treatments and their side effects proved grueling. If ever there was a torture for a young child this had to be it. In 1962, the way doctors and medical professionals treated patients and their families was still quite archaic. Instead of today's open and therapeutic communication, signs hanging in the cancer patients' waiting rooms read, "Do not talk with the person sitting next to you, they may not know what they have."

Patients were not informed of their disease, the treatments they would have to endure, or their prognosis. There were no support groups for parents, siblings, or patients. Even basic comfort measures, such as anti-nausea medication to help relieve the nausea and vomiting associated with chemotherapy, did not exist.

In addition, parents were not allowed to spend the night in the hospital with their child as they are today. Visiting hours were from 11:00 a.m. to 8:00 p.m. Although I could not tell time, I had memorized those hours. I knew that the time between the hours of 8:00 p.m. and 11:00 a.m. would be a living hell.

It was hospital policy to reserve patient procedures for times when parents were not around. The prevailing logic was to keep parents from witnessing their child's agony, thus expediting the procedure with no parental involvement or interference. Therefore, most of my chemotherapy medication was administered when I was alone. This might not have been so traumatic if there had been comforting support from the hospital staff; however, this too did not exist.

I remember many nights watching my parents walk out of my room, then lying awake waiting for the doctors to come in with my "shot." The injection of the poison (which is a good description of chemotherapy) was often painful, especially when some of the fluid would leak from the vein into the surrounding tissue causing severe "chemo burns." My hands, arms, and feet where the injections were given were covered with burnt flesh from the medication. The scars still exist today.

Even worse than the shots themselves was the overpowering nausea and vomiting that would ensue shortly after the drug was injected. I recall nights of sleeping on my pillow because my bed was completely soiled with vomit. My nurse's light sometimes went unanswered until the following day just before my mother arrived.

Although the injections I received were often very painful, I never protested or cried. The nurses and doctors told me that if I were not a "good" girl, then it would hurt all the more. For two years I laid stoically quiet and still throughout the numerous procedures. When the treatments were completed the staff awarded me with a ribbon that said "Best Shot Taker." I learned early how the World rewards those who are "good", with superficial things like ribbons and trophies.

Two weeks following my first surgery, which removed my left kidney and adrenal gland, I developed an intestinal bowel obstruction. Still extremely weak from the surgery and chemotherapy I had to undergo yet another operation. My parents were informed that the doctors would be "fighting for my life." I was weak and emaciated, weighing a mere 32 pounds.

I vividly remember one particular day following this surgery when I was in the Intensive Care Unit (ICU). As you might expect, in 1962, the ICU was off limits to parents. I remember thinking that ICU meant, "I see you" because there was a large glass window where, at certain times, the curtains would be drawn back and parents could look through to see their children.

One time I recall looking through the glass at my very depressed mother and feeling sad that she was so unhappy that I could not make her happy. One tiny tear rolled down my cheek. It was the last time I would ever cry in the hospital or in front of my mother. I had to be strong because she was so weak. She had told me that she could not endure the trauma of my illness if I was not "strong and brave" — an overwhelming responsibility for a five year old. I knew that from then on I could not risk revealing any painful emotions.

The first act of my young life's drama was complete. I knew my role very well, do whatever it takes to "save" my loved ones' and make them happy even at the expense of my own self. Be the good girl because if you're not all would be lost. It was like putting on a pair of tight shoes. They hurt at first but soon your feet are numb and you cannot feel anything. That was me. With both of my parents caught up in quests to slay their own demons there was little energy or will left to help slay mine. I was a co-addict in the making, oblivious to the many times I would repeat this ill-fated pattern until I finally awakened to the lesson I was meant to learn.

Chapter Two

Early scars

It was clear that my physical and emotional self would have an uphill climb in life. Although I survived the major battle of the cancer I was left with many devastating side effects. The radiation used to kill the cancer does not discriminate between cancer cells and healthy, rapidly dividing, growing cells. Both are equally affected. In a young child this means that bones, muscles, and other tissues are stunted or destroyed.

The left side of my torso was radiated from the middle part of my ribcage down to and including my iliac crest (hipbone region). The left side of my spine was radiated including all of the surrounding muscles in the area. The bones and muscles in this area would never grow beyond the size of my tiny five-year-old body.

Emotionally I was scarred as well. Unconsciously I had buried any real feelings of love and replaced them with whatever would make other people happy. But even by being good I was not successful in making my mother a happy person.

One of the most traumatic days of my young life occurred when I was only seven years old. I had struggled through two years of chemotherapy, radiation, and surgeries and was on the road to recovery. My hair had just started to grow back and, during second grade, I was finally able to forego my wig for the first time in two years. Things were starting to look up until one especially dreary winter day.

I remember vividly how different things seemed after school that day. Like always, I rode the school bus to and from school. Only, on this particular day, when I got off the bus and looked over at my house I sensed something ominous. My house had transformed from its usual cheery green color into a death-like gray — almost as if I were seeing it in black and white instead of color.

A cold chill ran down my spine that was beyond the impact of the weather. I froze in my tiny tracks, unable to move. I saw one of our neighbors standing on the street corner. She motioned to my brother and I to come over to her, which somehow I found the strength to do. She said that we would be staying with her for a while. I asked her why but she refused to say.

Intuitively, I knew the answer — an answer I did not want to think about. In her sadness and desperation, my mother had, only hours before attempted to kill herself. Her pupils had been fixed and dilated and she was thought to be dead by the emergency squad workers who found her.

I stayed with this neighbor for what seemed to be an eternity. She was a devout Catholic who attended church daily to worship and assist the parish priest in the administrative office. She had a daughter my age who attended a school operated by the church. For some unknown reason, she never seemed to like me.

I remember one Sunday being taken along with them to church. I had passed their church many times but had never been inside. I was excited to finally see what the inside of St. Michael's church looked like. As we walked up the impressive concrete stairs leading into the church building, we suddenly stopped. My neighbor turned to me and said that I could not go in because I did not have anything to wear on my head and had barely enough hair to show respect. I would have to remain outside on the front steps until they returned.

My mother survived the suicide attempt but was hospitalized for weeks. I thought I had in some way failed. Had I not been good enough or strong enough to save her? I would have to try harder.

My experience demonstrated that if I loved someone I would only get hurt. For most of my life I was doomed to seek out alcoholics and emotionally unavailable partners to "love" into recovery and happiness. Something deep inside told me that I had to save them, both body and soul.

My early spiritual life was practically nonexistent. Our family did not attend church nor do I recall seeing a Bible in our house. Occasionally my mother would mention something about Jesus or God but the communication in this area was minimal. We were taught prayers for dinnertime and bedtime but I never paid attention to what I was saying.

Oddly enough my parents had a picture of Jesus hanging on the wall in their bedroom. I was scared of it because it seemed out of place and foreboding. I tried to avoid looking at it whenever I could because it appeared as if his eyes were watching me no matter where I went.

The only time I can remember praying to God on my own accord was when I was seven years old. I had just lost another one of my little hospital friends who was also seven at the time. It seemed as if many of the children I was getting to know from having been around the hospital for two years were now dead or dying. Even our baby-sitter who had suffered from leukemia was now dead.

I asked God if He was taking all the seven-year-olds and would it soon be my turn? And if I was not going to die then why was I going to live? And, finally, I wondered silently, what kind of a God was He to allow little children to suffer and die? I did not get answers to my questions until much, much later.

In high school I hung out with the good girls. One of the activities the good girls participated in was a youth group fellowship at the local Protestant church. In typical peer pressure fashion I decided to join the group. For the most part it was a social function for me. I viewed the religious aspects as a necessary evil. To be confirmed as members of the church we had to take classes but I never paid much attention since I had a crush on one of our pastor's sons. He was perfect for me — a budding alcoholic!

I was busy being a good girl in other ways as well. I started volunteering my services at a local Convalescent Center when I was twelve years old. The program was offered through the Red Cross and I earned more hours over the four years I worked there than anyone else at our facility. I was happy in dedicating myself to serving the needs of others — pouring myself in to their misery to avoid my own.

I met many precious souls in those early years but none could penetrate my veiled heart, which had been sealed and rusted over like an old steel door. Following the Convalescent Home experience I volunteered at a local hospital until close to my high school graduation. I then entered nursing school, still intent on providing tireless service to others. As I would later learn, God gave me many opportunities to remove the veil I held ever so tightly across my heart but over and over again I refused.

One such opportunity arose upon graduating from nursing school. I was asked to work on the same cancer unit where I had suffered so much as a child. Although I did not originally plan to return to this particular unit in the hospital, it was the only opening available at the time I was looking for work. Medical care and nursing services had improved dramatically since I was a patient on the unit.

Chemotherapy was a routine practice, parents were staying in the rooms with children, support groups flourished, and honest, open disclosure was the rule instead of the exception. Children were treated with kindness and respect. It was all very refreshing and a perfect setting for me to make a difference in people's lives! After all, I was living proof that children could survive cancer. But, heartbreakingly, many more still did not.

The old questions I had asked God began to resurface, only now I was angry. In the three years I worked on this pediatric cancer unit, I knew and cared for over 250 children who ultimately died. For the most part, my emotional veil stayed strong and intact. I was the perfect person to work in this emotionally charged environment. When people would ask me how I could handle the stress I would honestly reply that it takes a certain unique attitude to deal with dying children.

They thought I meant a belief in God and the afterlife but I actually meant the total blockage of all emotions. Everything was working as planned until I met Nikki.

Nikki was two years old when I met her and the brightest child I had ever encountered. She could recite the "Pledge of Allegiance" and, amazingly, could name each one of her chemotherapeutic medications. We clicked immediately and formed a strong bond. We did publicity related things together including a television commercial for the American Cancer Society, or as she said, American Cancer "Ascites." I even spent some time away from the hospital with her family. My nickname for her was Nicodemus.

Nikki hated intravenous transfusions (IV's) more than anything, so I bought her a little stuffed monkey that she immediately named "Baby Nicodemus." Baby Nicodemus would stand guard, propped under her wrist, while I started her IV's so she would not have to watch. Emotionally I felt secure in letting my veil down a little and loving this little girl. After all, she had the same type of cancer I had overcome and now the survival rate was nearing 90%. I was sure that she would not leave me. I was dead wrong.

One of the darkest days of my life was the day I got the phone call that Nikki had died suddenly of an overwhelming brain infection. She was four years old and cancer free. The day before her sudden death, she asked her mother out of the blue, "Does Jesus love me?" Rather surprised, because Nikki had not ever been to church and the family was not religious, her mother responded, "Of course he loves you." Nikki just said, "Good, 'cause I love him too!" She went into a coma and died less than twelve hours later.

I had never attended a funeral for one of my patients before Nikki's. It was a two-hour drive to her small town and my two colleagues and I were a half-hour late and were afraid we had missed the service. When we reached the large hall, we saw her petite white casket far up in front of hundreds of people sitting in metal folding chairs. They were waiting for us to arrive.

My chest tightened and I could not breathe while we searched for empty seats in the back of the room. As we surveyed the room her parents came to greet us and lead us to seats in the front row. Before we sat down they insisted I come, alone, with them to view her body in the casket. I saw my precious little friend lying "asleep" in the child-sized casket with a blue bandanna covering her bald head. Under her right wrist was Baby Nicodemus standing at attention watching out for any harm. Her parents said that they knew she would want it that way. She would want to take a part of me with her. And she did.

Soon after Nikki died I left the hospital for a safer, less emotion filled position. The veil had been dislodged, briefly, but effectively. I decided that I would not risk another emotional involvement. Little did I realize that God had other plans. I would continue to lose those I loved until I had learned the lessons I needed to learn. What I would find out later was that, in order to wake us up, God will first whisper in our ear. If we do not listen he will shake us on the shoulder. If we still do not listen he will roll us completely out of bed. It would be a long time and I had a lot of losses ahead of me before I finally woke up.

M. Sue Benford

Chapter Three

And the weak shall be made strong

As my emotional life spiraled downward from one destructive relationship to another, my physical life followed suit. Multiple abdominal surgeries for bowel obstructions and a ruptured incision left my midsection weakened and scarred. The wire sutures used during the closing of my first incision continued to poke and prod their way through the outer layer of my skin, causing constant irritation and pain. Much to my dismay, I became constantly aware of the "T" marking formed by the intersecting scars on my abdomen.

My activity level in 1983 could best be described as slightly less than a sedentary couch potato. I had gained a significant amount of fat, actually I was 36% bodyfat, and I knew I needed to do some type of exercise.

I joined the local YMCA with a co-worker of mine and we went to an aerobics class during our lunch breaks. I was married at the time and my husband forbade me to go to any type of exercise class, afraid that I might attract the attention of someone better than him. Needless to say, this was one of my many dysfunctional and unhealthy relationships. Every morning I had to sneak my clothes and tennis shoes out of the house so that he would not see them and become abusive.

I began to notice improvements in my aerobic capacity and flexibility but I still wanted to tone my body as well. That is when I met Jake. At the time he was the Physical Fitness Director at the facility who assisted people with their workout programs. He was a big, strong man. At five feet nine inches tall and 200 pounds of solid muscle he was very intimidating considering my slight pushing five-foot height. He was confident, witty, charming and soon to be my personal physical fitness trainer and second husband.

Originally I thought he was a bodybuilder but, actually, he was a "powerlifter." Powerlifting, he explained, was an amateur strength sport measuring how much people can lift in three different events: the squat, the bench press, and the deadlift. The squat involves putting a bar with weights on your upper back and "squatting" down and back up. The bench press involves lying on a bench and pushing the weight from your chest back up until your elbows are fully extended, and the deadlift involves pulling a dead weight off the floor and standing up with legs fully erect.

Although lifters compete against others in their own weight class the true adversary is the force of gravity. Overcoming this mighty earthly force was the challenge and goal for every powerlifter. On the lifting platform there was only one contest at stake — human strength against the force of the World. Nothing else was relevant at that moment. Either the lifter succeeded in controlling the opposing force or failed. It was a very basic and simple equation.

Jake told me that short people could do very well in the sport and that I was a natural. Since I had trimmed my body weight to 102 pounds from all the aerobics, I would compete in the 97-pound weight class. The only thing I needed to do was train and get strong. There was only one problem — I had barely more than half a back, an underdeveloped left hip, and practically no abdominal musculature of any kind on my left side. This sport depended almost exclusively on those muscle groups and mine were the size and strength of a five-year-old child.

When Jake first tested my base strength he was shocked. He asked me to lie face down on an elevated board with my legs dangling at a ninety degree angle and to raise my legs to parallel as many times as possible. I could not even lift my legs up one time. My back strength was virtually nonexistent. He quickly changed his prediction that I was a natural. He said that mine would be a long road to gaining any significant strength, if it was even possible, let alone winning against healthy competitors.

I went to several doctors to see if the stunted muscles could grow and get stronger but no one was encouraging. Many even suggested it might be dangerous for me to stress my weakened body with so much additional weight. Not only did I risk injuring my torso but also I still was at increased risk for bone fractures as a result of my depleted skeletal system. Successfully competing in the sport of powerlifting was certainly a long shot, to say the least.

Lifting seemed to be a perfect sport for me though. The complete focus on the development of physical strength was ideal for someone closed off to the other parts of life. It was non-emotional and non-spiritual — completely objective and measurable.

My marriage to Jake five months after my divorce from my first husband was also ideal for me, as I continued to hide securely behind my emotional veil. When Jake asked me to marry him on our second date, I was stunned. He had been my knight in shining armor, rescuing me from an abusive husband. He seemed to want me and, after all, he did not drink so that was an improvement over my other relationships. Or was it?

Since love had not been a part of my relationship equations for a long time I could not assess whether I loved him or not. I had forgotten what love was, if I ever knew what it was in the first place. It seemed good enough that I was comfortable with him, he wanted to be with me, and he did not have any overt addictions.

I can recall making a list of Pros and Cons to marrying him since logic and objective evaluation were the only tools I had to work with. I had found a haven of non-emotional tranquility. A life partner totally and solely consumed by the growth and strength of his physical body — no more accidental slipping of my veil. I was safe, never having to risk frightening emotions or failing to save a loved one again.

When I began lifting I looked upon the reigning World Champions as more gods than mere mortals. They were so incredibly superior to me in every way. They were gifted with genetic potential and blessed with healthy bodies — neither of which I could claim.

I could not relate to these strong women so, instead, I idolized them. I elevated them so far above me that a gulf existed between where they were and where I was. Their world of strength and achievement seemed light years from my own world of weakness and imperfection. Who was I to think that I could ever compete along side of these great champions?

I recall a time, following one of my early meets, talking with two of the strong women in the locker room. I congratulated them and told them how impressed and in awe I was of their achievements. I asked them how they had gotten so strong?

As we were discussing their lifting techniques one of them inquired, "What's the matter with your back? I saw you twisting during your squat." I felt a rush of embarrassment to realize they had noticed my weakness and imperfection. I explained that it was a permanent disability I had on the left side of my torso.

They looked at each other not thinking I could see their expressions. After a couple moments of silence the second one responded, "You <u>do</u> know that powerlifting is dependent on strength in the back and hips don't you? Maybe you should try something you could be good at like running or tennis."

My heart sank. I knew they were probably right. Of all the sports I could have chosen, this was, most likely, the worst one for me considering my limitations — my very permanent limitations.

I left the locker room on the verge of tears. I momentarily propped myself up against the wall in the outer corridor to gain some composure. When I closed my eyes to blink away the tears, in my mind I saw a slight glimmer and heard a faint voice. A tiny whisper that said, "Arise to the challenge. I am with you." I had absolutely no idea where such an inspirational thought had come from but it was a flicker that, against all reason, could not be extinguished.

Of course, the idea of someone like me daring to think such grandiose thoughts of great strength was so incredulous that to verbalize them would have seemed insanity. I wanted to be strong just like my idols but I kept it to myself. I wanted to overcome the challenges life had dealt me and be a strong woman like the champions who had led the way before me.

Unfortunately, during the first three years I competed I managed to finish dead last in every competition. The joke became that I did not have to even see the roster of lifters, because no matter who was on it, I would always finish last. I did not even need to compete.

One time, on the drive home, following yet another dismal performance, my husband groped for some positive words of encouragement. With as much enthusiasm as he could muster he said, "Well, at least you're going in the right direction."

Then, oddly, something came over me and I said out loud, "Someday I will deadlift 300 pounds and be the strongest woman in the world." I surprised both Jake and myself with these crazy predictions. I did not have a clue how I was going to achieve these goals.

And of all the lifts, the deadlift was the one that most represented sheer brute strength — beyond skill, beyond experience, beyond lifting technique. It depended on two things only – back, plus hip strength and the intestinal fortitude of the lifter to take on the challenge. It was truly human against the World!

But Jake's comment had made me think — little by very little I was heading in the right direction. I started to realize that the more I struggled against the weights the stronger I was becoming. With every lift I made and with every training session I completed I grew stronger. In the world of weight lifting the phenomenon is called "progressive resistance training."

Indeed, by persisting in the right direction I was making headway. Gravity was most certainly still my foe but I also now saw it as my assistant — a kind of necessary evil. Without this force of the World I would not be able to grow stronger.

With Jake's coaching and prodding I started to make some noticeable gains in year four. My first World Championship title came in late 1986 on the island of Maui, Hawaii. From my humble first meet lifts of 165 pounds (squat), 82 pounds (bench), and 214 (deadlift) I now lifted 245, 130, and 300 respectively. Goal number one had been obtained; I dead lifted 300 pounds. I improved steadily from there, slowly inching my way up the *Women's Top Twenty List* that was published every year in Powerlifting USA magazine.

Miraculously, I began setting world records at almost every contest I entered — becoming known for my deadlift. I broke my own records in the 97-pound weight class and even climbed to the 105-pound weight class one time and broke the deadlift record there. In a two-year time period I had broken more records in the deadlift than any other lifter — male or female. Against incredible odds my outlandish predictions were coming true.

By the time I retired from the sport in late 1991 I had set world records in every lift and held the all-time best total (combined lifts) of any other 97 pounder in history. My final record lifts were 308 pounds (squat), 173 pounds (bench), and 339 pounds (deadlift) with an unprecedented total of 798 pounds.

More surprising than these accomplishments was the translation of my efforts compared to all the other women in the world. Using a standardized formula, comparisons can be made between lifters from various weight categories. In November of 1993 I received a fax from the President of the World Powerlifting Congress. In it, he compared all the World Champions for the years 1991 to 1993 — incredibly, I was first. Not only this, but the results for the all-time 97 lb. lifters for the 20th Century named me as number one.

Years after I retired from the sport it dawned on me that something very amazing had taken place. Almost insidiously I had surpassed my former idols, which I had once envisioned as beyond mere mortals. In fact, I had surpassed everyone who had come before me in the sport.

In many respects I had become the strongest woman in the world — at least, physically. No other lifter my size had ever accomplished these feats and certainly not anyone who was considered handicapped. How was it humanly possible that such a weakling could become the strongest woman in the world?

Chapter Four

The transformation begins

If ignorance is bliss, then knowledge is hell. The only bad thing about hiding your head in the sand is that eventually you have to come up for air and when you do you might not like what you see. I was quite successful in burying any emotions I might have for Jake and our marriage for seven years. We were much more like roommates than husband and wife. I knew at some level that this was not what a real marriage was like but it was too scary to think of actual intimacy with someone. After all, that would involve the things that I feared most. It would mean risking being close to another human being and then possibly, and in my experience most probably, losing that person. No, I had the right idea. Play it safe, keep that head in the sand.

My plan might have been successful had a friend of mine not pulled my head up suddenly one day. Although Jake never showed any affection towards me, I never thought that he was paying any special attention to anyone else either. I just reasoned that he was not the type of person to be romantic or emotionally involved. I realized how wrong I was when one of my lifting partners pointed out how interested Jake had become in one of our fellow competitors. On the surface I scoffed her insinuations that they were having an affair but I had an uncomfortable feeling deep inside that would not go away.

Of course he denied any extramarital involvement and accused me in return of being jealous, petty, and paranoid. But still, I felt a sense of unrest and uneasiness about the whole situation. Thinking back on our seven years together there were many times I had felt this sense of uneasiness about his attention to other women. Was a pattern being revealed?

I had long ago refused to listen to my intuition. After all, intuition was just the overactive imagination of a non-analytical person. Certainly there was no real scientific evidence that gut instincts or strange voices in our head had anything to do with reality or future happenings. At least that is what I had convinced myself.

In March of 1991 my veil was once again yanked down. My greatest fear had become a reality — my husband was having an affair. My instinct had been correct. Worse of all, he claimed to be "addicted" to her. There was that evil word again rearing its ugly head in my life. A word I thought only went with other words like smoking, drinking, gambling, and drugs.

I had long ago tried to forget the word, which had caused me so much pain in my past. I felt safe with a husband who did not have any of the addiction vices that I had come to recognize in so many other people who crossed my life's path. But he, too, was an addict. Addicted to the sexual high of infatuation. I was sure that I had been right about all the other women as well.

My head was out of the sand and I was devastated. My life had been a delusion and now that I saw the truth I could never go back to the same fantasy.

Jake pleaded for another chance claiming that this was a "one time occurrence" and that he never intended to leave our young daughter or me. He admitted that he had a problem and wanted to seek counseling to overcome it. I truly wanted to make our marriage work and thought he was being sincere in wanting to deal with his own issues of self-esteem and addiction.

But the trust was gone and it would take years to rebuild. I was bitter, vengeful, and jealous. I detested the "other woman" and blamed her for our problems. My reactions fluctuated from rage to despair. I was the typical woman-scorned.

We both began counseling. We met with separate counselors and together in joint marriage counseling sessions as well. I started to see myself a little more clearly. I learned how we are products of our past and how we repeat patterns in adult relationships that were created in our childhood. We do this in an attempt to get it right. Until we learn what it is that we should know from a particular relationship or situation we are destined to repeat it — a "karmic" repeat in this lifetime.

After a year of counseling sessions Jake announced that he was cured. He felt that he had gotten everything he possibly could get from the sessions and that further investigation and psychological work was fruitless. I, too, felt much better and now looked optimistically at our new relationship. I had put the past behind me and was ready to move on.

We both wanted to have another child, and so in July of 1993 our second daughter was born. Life was back to what it had been before the affair. Gradually, and unconsciously, my head started inching its way back into the sand. Once again, I began to deny any uneasy feelings I was experiencing.

M. Sue Benford

Now I had even more reason to repress any potential problems in our relationship because the stakes were much higher. We now had two children, one still a baby. My businesses were experiencing legal problems, turmoil and setbacks. I had already been betrayed once and nearly had not recovered. I had tried to forgive and was trying hard to forget.

Three days before Christmas 1994 my life changed completely, dramatically, and forever. My husband and I shared office space for the operation of our two small businesses. Although he did not occupy any offices himself, since this was more of his hobby business, we did jointly employ a secretary to perform routine office tasks for our separate businesses. We had shared space for five years without incident.

On December 22, 1994 our secretary called in sick. This was the first time she had been ill since working for the two of us. When the mail came that afternoon, one of my other long time employees sorted it and put Jake's business mail on the secretary's desk and brought me mine. Normally the secretary put all of Jake's mail in a sealed envelope for me to take home to him each night.

Work was slow due to the holidays so I found myself sitting at my desk mentally going over what I still needed to do to prepare for Christmas. Out of the blue I heard a voice say to me, "*Go into his office and look through the mail.*"

Where had that "thought" come from? I assumed that maybe a check might have come for Jake that he needed right away so I went into my employee's office and asked him if anything important had come via the mail for Jake's business. He said "no" and that he had specifically looked for anything important that Jake might need right away. I was satisfied with his response. Anyway, the secretary would be back the next day in case something had inadvertently been overlooked.

I went back into my office and resumed my mental Christmas checklist and, once again, only this time more emphatically, the voice said, "*Go into his office and look through the mail.*" What was this all about? In over eleven years time I had never had any urge to review my husband's mail, business or otherwise. I could not just walk into his secretary's empty office and look through his company's mail without a reason.

I continued to sit still when a third time I heard the same message. I finally figured that even though it was a waste of time I would do what the voice commanded. I walked into the office but did not put the lights on so that I would not draw attention to my unexplainable behavior. There were over thirty pieces of mail in a neat stack on the secretary's desk. Clearly, my employee had reviewed everything and placed it in an organized pile. I was feeling more ridiculous by the moment.

One by one I looked at each piece of mail. Nothing was out of the ordinary. Then I came to one particular business size envelope addressed to Jake in care of his company that was marked "Confidential." Receiving confidential mail was very typical for his business since they dealt with many companies that were going out of business and did not want others to know. His name was spelled incorrectly on the envelope so I was sure it was not a personal note of any kind.

I proceeded to put the letter back in the pile when the same voice said, "*Open it.*" Now I was appalled. I could not just randomly open another company's mail! I was not a partner or in anyway connected to his business. How could I possibly explain why I had illegally gone through another business' mail and, for no reason at all, randomly opened one unremarkable piece? No, I could not do this and I would not do this.

Once again I set the letter down in the stack and once again the voice commanded, "*Open it.*" At this point I gave in realizing that for some unknown reason I was supposed to go through with it. Looking around to make sure no one was watching me, I opened and read the letter that would change my life forever.

It was a love letter from yet another one of my lifting colleagues claiming her undying passion and devotion to my husband. My husband who had attended counseling sessions for one year and claimed he was "cured." My husband who had begged for a second chance because he had only strayed "just this once."

The letter provided plenty of documentation of their affair and even described a vacation trip they had taken when he first told her he loved her. But most peculiarly at the end of the letter was a quote that said, "*The message of a true angel of God is like an apple; always sweet, refreshing, and nourishing.*" What in the world did angels or God have to do with this affair?

I was numb. I could not move and I could barely breathe. Through the haze of shock I heard that same voice say, "*It is over.*" I believed that to be a fact but I did not realize until much later exactly what it was that was finally over. I only knew in my heart that my life, as I had known it, was ending. I could not see beyond the steel door that was being closed and locked behind me.

When I finally confronted my husband with the letter on Christmas Eve, he denied ever knowing the woman who wrote the letter (even though we all worked out together). He then recounted and stated that she was crazy and just trying to harm him for some reason. Finally, he admitted that, yes, the letter was true but he had not seen her in six months. Unbeknownst to me, he disclosed that he was preparing to ask me for a divorce as soon as Christmas was over anyway because he just "was not happy." It had nothing to do with me. In fact, he claimed that I was the perfect wife but, well, you know the story.

The letter had given me the upper hand and thwarted any plans he might have had to leave me in an uncomfortable situation financially and emotionally. He conceded to all my requests — a minor victory in a lost war. Jake vehemently denied to friends and family that any third party was involved in our divorce. He even claimed that I wanted the divorce as much as he did. Nothing could have been further from the truth. I always just wanted the status quo.

Gradually as the shock of the situation wore off, reality of the situation set in. I flashed back to four years earlier when I had found out about his "first" betrayal. I vividly relived the anger, hurt, rage, and depression. This time it was much worse. I had trusted, and allowed myself to care for, this man again. I even had another child with him. How could I ever recover from this emotional devastation? The veil was down and I felt as if I had been mortally wounded.

About a week following Christmas as I lay in bed trying to make some sense out of my dismal situation, I heard that same voice that I had heard the day in my office guiding me to the letter. But this time the voice said, *"You will see him as God sees him and have the forgiveness of Christ."* I had no idea what that meant but, within a couple of days, everything changed.

Since I was not familiar with Jesus' perception of wrongdoers or his ideas on forgiveness I was not anticipating anything in particular. But literally overnight my entire perception of my husband had suddenly undergone an amazing transformation. I saw him as a troubled individual worthy of sympathy and not disdain — like a wounded animal in a way. An image kept flashing in my mind of a person in a wheelchair. We would not expect that person to walk so why would we expect emotionally and spiritually "disabled" people to perform loving tasks outside their capabilities? He was spiritually and emotionally challenged, incapable of performing at any level other than where he was.

I had learned from my counseling sessions that it is one thing to hear what we need to learn and quite another to feel and assimilate these lessons. That was the truly amazing thing about this new awareness I had been given. It was not just an appreciation for an addict who was not in recovery but a deep, ingrained, and complete feeling of peace and understanding that could only come from a higher power. Was this how Jesus envisioned and felt about those who betrayed him? Was this what was meant by true "forgiveness?"

Along with this inner peace came a certain understanding about my new situation. Intuitively, I became aware that I was on some sort of new journey. I had no idea what that journey was or where it would take me but I knew it would lead me to new paths that would greatly benefit me. Strangely, I became almost happy at the prospect of the divorce. In fact, I was so enthusiastic that my own father inquired as to whether or not I was the one actually having the affair instead of Jake!

As the weeks went on, this feeling of peace and forgiveness did not go away. The true test came only three days after our dissolution was final on March 1, 1995. While attending a large public event one of my friends came up to me and asked if I had seen Jake with his new girlfriend. At first I was surprised that only three short days after our divorce he was out with someone else when he had so vehemently denied a third party involvement. But that was not to be the most shocking part of the story.

As my friend had learned, this woman was from one of the countries that had participated in the World Powerlifting Championships, which took place and were directed by my husband in November of 1994. The event lasted four days and, his now girlfriend, had been one of the lifters. In that brief period, he had apparently decided to leave me for her and they had planned for her to move to the United States and take up residence with him. This was not even the woman who had written the love letter to him in December!

I looked around the crowded arena and finally saw them standing together and talking with several people. As I watched my former husband and his mistress I waited to see if my feelings would change from peace and forgiveness to anger and rage. Remarkably they did not.

The true test would be in confronting her face to face. I walked up to her, introduced myself, and welcomed her to our country. I asked her when she had arrived, which turned out to be two hours after our divorce court hearing was completed, and how she liked America.

At first it did not dawn on her who I was until she looked down and read my nametag. Her face grew pale and her eyes wide. Sheepishly she asked, "Oh, so you are okay with this?" My answer surprised even me. I responded, "I just want you to know that although I have no respect for either you or Jake, as long as you treat my children well you will never have any problems from me." With that I smiled, bid them both a good day and walked away.

To this day, some six years later, I have never spoken an unkind word to my ex-husband or his now second wife. More importantly, I have never felt anything but those loving and forgiving feelings given to me by Christ. Something very important was starting to occur in my life, but what was it?

Chapter Five

The first of the "soul mate trinity"

If the definition of love is as M. Scott Peck stated, "The will to extend one's self for the purpose of nurturing one's own or another's spiritual growth," then I truly loved and was loved by the three soul mates I became involved with following my second divorce. I call them the "soul mate trinity" because the combined and sequential effects of being intertwined with these three men literally induced my spiritual birth and awakening.

What is a "soul mate?" At the time of my meeting with the first of these three men I had no real understanding of that term. In fact, I believed it to be the mystical mumbo-jumbo of some Buddhist monk or New Age fanatic. I had never before experienced any special recognition of another person's soul or even vaguely felt like I really had any special connection to someone, except maybe chemically in an infatuation type circumstance. I did not believe in past lives so it would have been impossible for me to remember someone from one of them. To me, things seemed pretty clear-cut, definable, objective, and explainable by modern science.

As I now describe these three post-divorce relationships, and their context within my spiritual journey, it would be that, the first of the trinity soul mates, forcefully and quickly thrust open my spiritual steel door, which had been jammed shut. The second slowly and methodically opened the door wide enough so that I could pass through; and, the third of the group held my hand and gently coaxed me through the spiritual threshold. I did not realize it at the time but very soon I would start believing in soul mates, plus a whole lot more.

It had been a long time since I had dated. I was not even sure if the same rules of courtship applied and, to be honest, I do not think I ever knew what a healthy courtship was in the first place. Still feeling as if I had been given a new lease on life I also assumed that I had learned enough about failed relationships via both counseling and experience that I could successfully connect with someone in a healthy way. Of course, at this point I was thinking only in terms of physical and emotional connections since the spiritual realm was still a nonexistent component for me.

After my divorce and the incredible happenings that led to the discovery of the love letter and the forgiveness of my husband, I thought it might behoove me to start attending church to learn more about Christianity and Jesus. At a minimum it would provide a new post-divorce activity and a new group of potential friends. At most, perhaps, I would gain some understanding and insight into these strange voices and occurrences. Did these types of things happen to other people as well? I was on a data-gathering mission to try to find out.

A friend told me about the wonderful experiences she had in the organization of Parents Without Partners (PWP). More than just a place to meet other unattached people, it was a support group and opportunity for family activities for both my daughters and me. My oldest daughter had struggled with her father's and my divorce. Her most profound fear was that she would lose me. As a highly sensitive child, from the day she had been born she had needed extra reassurance that I loved her. Somehow I must be failing to provide that comfort and security she most desperately needed. I thought that joining PWP might be a way for our new little nuclear family to become closer as a unit, but all the while I realized this would only be a start.

I convinced another one of my divorced friends to attend an upcoming orientation meeting with me on April 19, 1995. The meeting was being held at a member's house. Although her family room was large, we quickly were overcrowded with people wanting to join the group. An enthusiastic article about PWP had run in our city's newspaper the day before so many people were anxious to find out more. Fortunately, my friend and I had gotten to the meeting early and found seats on the couch along the wall.

With over 25 people in attendance and the starting time already delayed by fifteen minutes, the meeting commenced. About fifteen more minutes into the speaker's presentation we heard the front door open and close. A man came running into the family room looking disoriented and embarrassed for being so late.

I could only see him from the side as he dashed into the room. He could not see me at all. By all practical standards he was not particularly remarkable. He had dark brown hair that was graying, thick glasses, a somewhat large nose, and was of medium height and build. So why did I get a shiver down my spine and a weird feeling that I not only knew this man, but also was somehow deeply connected to him?

I was certain that I had not met him before but equally as certain that somewhere I had. It did not make sense, was not logical, and yet it was such a strong feeling that I could not concentrate on another word the speaker was saying.

After what seemed to be a decade, the speaker finally stopped talking, which allowed us to get up and mingle. Never being assertive in talking to strangers in the past, I surprised myself when I made a beeline straight for the kitchen where "he" was standing.

I do not even remember what we said to each other that night in the kitchen. I just remember looking at him and him looking at me in such a way that we both knew something was strange and yet familiar about our "relationship." He said his name was Mark but beyond that I could not remember much else.

As my girl friend and I were walking out the door to leave, one of the other male members at the meeting asked us if we were going to attend a dance that the organization was hosting that coming Saturday night. Although my friend had already told me that she could not go, and I certainly would not go by myself, something made me turn around and say, "Yes, we'll be there." At that moment I noticed Mark looking at us. Had he heard what I had said? Would I ever see him again?

When Saturday night came around I started to panic. I knew I needed to go to that dance just on the outside chance I might run into Mark again but I did not have anyone to go with and I would not dream of going alone. Finally in desperation I coaxed my very dear and fun-loving nineteen-year-old AuPair (nanny) from Germany into going with me. I even suggested that she might meet some guys near her age. She did not really believe me but she went anyway.

At first it did not look promising. We had been at the dance for over an hour and there was no sign of Mark. I had almost decided to call it a night when I saw him walk through the door. That same feeling I'd had at the meeting was there again. I knew that it was not a fluke.

I shouted and waved at him but he didn't see me. He was swooped up by a table of members eager to meet the new initiates. Eventually he detached from them and headed for the table with refreshments. Now was my chance.

After we finally connected that evening I can remember little else. A couple of times people came up to us and made some comment about how we were not being social and circulating like we were supposed to. Neither of us cared. I even totally forgot about my young AuPair, who, as I learned later, had been entrenched by a 30-year-old man who wanted to take her home and show her his etchings.

Nothing else in the world existed as it had before. I felt as if I had found a long lost friend. It was such a noticeable "reunion" that others came up to us and asked if we had known each other before meeting that night. They were surprised when we honestly answered "no."

Things heated up rapidly between Mark and I. We began spending almost all of our free time together and as a result we began to learn a lot about each other, our families, and our backgrounds. The more I learned about him, the stranger our "coincidental" meeting became.

Mark was originally from a large suburb outside of Cleveland, Ohio. I had been born and raised in Columbus and knew only a few of my father's relatives who lived in the Cleveland area. The one family that my parents stayed in contact with was my dad's brother and his wife. Although most of their contact was through telephone calls and letters, once a year my aunt and uncle came south to visit my parents. In 1995 their annual visit occurred two weeks after I met Mark and two days after I told my mother about him.

During their visit, my aunt inquired how I was doing since my divorce. My mother was happy to report that not only was I doing very well but that I was also starting to date again. She told my aunt that I had met a man named Mark at a PWP meeting. She did not know too much about him except for where he worked and that he had just been transferred to Columbus from Chicago. Mom also thought that he had grown up somewhere in Cleveland but she did not remember where.

At first my aunt did not say anything in response to my mother's story about my new boyfriend although she seemed somewhat distracted and distant during the rest of the conversation that quickly progressed to other issues. When the topic shifted back to me, my aunt asked my mother if this Mark had been married to a girl named Sarah and was his last name Stankowski? Mom said she did not know.

As it turned out, my aunt had worked with a Mark and his second wife Sarah for over seven years. In fact, she had attended their wedding and the baby shower of their first child. Not only did she work with him but my uncle and cousin worked with him part time as well.

It seemed impossible that in two big cities like Cleveland and Columbus this type of incidental overlap in people and circumstances would occur. After all, I only had a few living relatives in Cleveland to begin with and of those, my parents only spoke to one of them. The timing of that visit was oddly placed only days after my disclosure to my parents of my relationship with Mark. Could we be talking about the same person? And what did it mean if we were?

My mother called me after my aunt and uncle left and asked me if Mark's last name was Stankowski. I was speechless. How could my mother have known his last name? Especially since it was not a common Anglo-Saxon name that you might hear in everyday conversation. When she told me what my aunt had said I was flabbergasted. I knew he was from a suburb of Cleveland but it was not the suburb where my aunt and uncle lived. Was there something to our meeting that was more than just a freak accident? I started to look deeper at other significant factors of comparison between the two of us.

Mark and I had similar family backgrounds in many ways. He had been closer to his mother, who was now deceased, than his father whom he barely spoke to because of his emotional distance. His father was from a large, first generation immigrant family, in which he had lost his father as an infant the same as my father had.

As a child, Mark played in a park near the house where his family had lived for a short time. The park was rich in Indian Folklore. He told me about games that he and his siblings would play along the characteristic railroad tracks that marked the entrance to the ancient Indian grounds.

As his stories became more descriptive I could feel something stir inside me of a distant recollection. When I asked him about the exact location of the Indian park, I was shocked at what I heard. Ironically, this was the very same park that was adjacent to my Grandmother's back yard! The same park where my brother and I played whenever we visited my Grandma. This was odd to say the least but it still did not convince me that anything other than sheer coincidence had brought us together.

Other unlikely parallels started to pop up as well. Mark and I had both been married and divorced twice. The total duration of our two marriages was the exact same number of years. His second divorce was final exactly one week prior to mine and also involved infidelity on his spouse's part. We wore the same eyeglass frames with nearly the same prescription for nearsightedness. We each had two children with the oldest born on the 31st of the month and the youngest children born on the 26th of the month. We even had the same exact family room sofas! All in all there were over 18 "coincidences" that I knew of between the two of us and I had only known him a month.

Other odd things began to happen on a feeling and intuitive level. One night when we were out dancing I had a strange and unexplainable feeling of total happiness and contentment. It was as if I was finally "home" and exactly with whom I needed to be with and who I wanted to be with. I had never had that feeling before.

Almost as strange was the first time we made love. Instead of the usual feelings one might have after such an experience I had the undeniable feeling that we were not just making love with each other for the first time but that we were both making love for the very first time period! I <u>knew</u> we were both virgins! This was obviously ridiculous since we clearly were not even close to still being virgins. But that feeling was as real as any I had ever experienced before.

One day when we were talking about our future, I said that I wanted us to be together for 52 years. After I said that he looked at me very quizzically and asked why I had said 52 years. I had no idea where I had dreamed up that unusual number. It would have been more logical to say 50 years or some other well-known anniversary year. He said that 52 was a significant number of years to him because when he married his second wife, at the age of 30, he told her that she had a contract with him for 52 years since he suspected he would die at age 82 like his grandfather.

Mark also acknowledged that our relationship was highly atypical. One night when we were discussing the series of strange similarities between us, he coyly admitted something very interesting. He told me that the first evening we met at the PWP orientation he had heard a strange voice. After our initial discussion I'd left the kitchen to rejoin my friend. Mark said that he heard a voice from behind him ask, *"Can you believe how well they know each other and they only just met?"* When he turned around there was no one standing there. The voice had sparked a deep recollection in his soul and prompted him to attend the dance. He knew that we had to meet again.

Devastatingly, within three months of meeting Mark our relationship ended. It had been too soon for him to consider getting seriously involved with another person. He had major issues remaining from his divorce that he still needed to resolve. Being in a relationship was not possible for him at that time. Holding back tears he told me it was time for me to "move on."

I was despondent. What was I to "move on" to? How could he be leaving me? We were souls that had been brought together for a purpose; of which I was now convinced was more than coincidence. Were not "soul mates" supposed to marry and live happily ever after? Who could help me make some kind of rhyme or reason out of my experiences and my distress?

I knew of a psychic in our town that had a very good reputation for being accurate in his readings with both routine issues and with "past life" issues. I had been to him before, at the insistence of a friend of mine who wanted me to inquire about my husband. Did Mark and I truly know each other before in some past existence and if we did what did that have to do with me now? I needed some answers. I needed some more data.

There was a long waiting list to see this particular psychic. I scheduled my past life reading a month in advance. Prior to the session, I was required to read the book <u>Many Lives, Many Masters</u> by Dr. Brian Weiss in order to gain some basic knowledge of the subject of reincarnation. I found the book fascinating and Dr. Weiss to be a very credible professional. Apparently, there were certain scientists who had researched this topic and found evidence of past life existence. I still was not thoroughly convinced, but my curiosity was piqued.

The once jammed steel door to my heart and soul had been forcefully opened, such that a little ray of light peered through the tiny crack were the door was slightly ajar. My brief, yet intense, love relationship with Mark had forced the spiritual door open and I wanted to see more.

Chapter Six

The second of the trinity

While I was waiting for my appointment with the psychic, the second of the soul mate trinity entered my life. Although I had worked out in gyms for over ten years I had never considered it a place to meet people and establish any lasting connections. My workouts were always serious and never for social entertainment. I paid little attention to the other people in the facility and rarely made any attempts to strike up conversations. That was, until I met Jeff.

Although I had seen Jeff in the gym I never gave him much thought. He was nice looking but seemed quiet and somewhat of a loner. He was never with anyone nor did he make any attempts to socialize. Occasionally, my female training partner would point out that he was staring at me when I was not looking. Sometimes I would briefly catch his gaze as he was quickly trying to look the other way. We would chuckle at his unintentional obviousness.

About two weeks after Mark and I stopped seeing each other I ran into Jeff in the gym's parking lot. He drove a shiny new black sports car and, uncharacteristic of me, I told him I liked it. He made a witty retort about trying to constantly keep it clean and I saw that he had some personality after all. A couple of days later, when I saw him working out again, we introduced ourselves and talked briefly about mundane things. He had never been married and had no children. I thought he was nice and certainly attractive but I was still reeling over Mark so I felt unavailable emotionally for a new liaison.

The next time we ran into each other marked the real beginning of our relationship. Oddly, although he saw my training partner and I come into the gym on this particular day he made no overt move to come over and talk to me. I thought this was slightly peculiar since we had talked recently and gotten along very well.

When I approached him to say hello I noticed that he had a strange, very serious look on his face, almost as if he had seen a ghost. He said, "We have a mutual friend in common." I was curious. Who was our mutual friend and why was he so disturbed by this fact?

He explained that after he heard my name the other day he could not get it out of his mind. He knew that he had heard it somewhere before. When he went to work the next day it came to him. A business associate had told him about me two years earlier and had tried to bring us together in a business deal. I vividly remembered this person and his ardent desire to match the two of us professionally. My business card had been sitting on Jeff's desk for two years and his had been on mine. But the time had not been right for us to meet.

Jeff looked pale when he stated somewhat ominously, "I do not believe in coincidences." He already suspected what I was yet to discover. This was the start, or rather the completion, of a saga that had begun a long time ago. It would prove a soul changing experience for both of us.

He asked me out to lunch to discuss "business" but it turned into much more than I expected. He seemed to be quite different outside the gym environment. It was almost as if he were two different people. At lunch he was outgoing, flirtatious, enthusiastic, and very funny. He was like a little boy who had found the new bicycle he wanted under the Christmas tree.

He seemed enthralled with me. There was a certain eerie compatibility between us from everything including life values to hobbies to work to sense of humor. It was like we had found a matching person with all of our likes and dislikes wrapped in a separate body. We went out two more times that week and even more similarities began to be uncovered.

He told me on our third date that he was a recovering alcoholic. He had been sober for several years but no longer participated in Alcoholics Anonymous. He was from an alcoholic family the same as me. His father and one of his brothers were both recovering alcoholics as well. As with both Mark and I, his father had also lost his father in childhood and had suffered emotionally as a result.

The only way to describe our third date is to depict it as some corny seduction scene from a grade B movie. It had all the usual come on lines, premature attempts at emotional intimacy, a candlelight dinner, music, and the "come back to my place to see my etchings" ending scenario. Having been out of the dating scene for many years, and looking for an easy escape from the pain left by Mark's departure, I fell hook, sleazy line, and sinker.

I had always been considered a bit gullible and naive but this had to take the cake! I truly believed that Jeff had fallen madly in love with me at first sight and we were going to be a couple from that night on. After all, Jake had proposed to me on our second date.

The following week, I enthusiastically made a visit to the counselor I had seen following my husband's affair. I thought she would be pleased to learn that I had found someone so quickly after the disastrous ending of my recent relationship. She was not quite so enthusiastic.

I described my dates with Jeff and the fact that he had not called me as planned the next day. In fact, he had not called me twice when he said he would. I excused his behavior as just an unintentional oversight. She sensed from everything I described that he might be what was called a "dry drunk." Apparently, this was someone who had stopped their particular addictive behavior but who had not fully dealt with the issues that lead to the addiction in the first place.

She described our relationship as "all sizzle and no steak." She said that love did not happen like this and that it took time to build true love and intimacy. The only way I would know for sure was to see if there was a pattern to his irresponsible and unpredictable behavior. Unfortunately, her perceptions would end up being right.

After the third time Jeff told me he would call but failed to do so I confronted him with his lack of regard. I told him that I could not tolerate that behavior in a relationship and that if he could not keep the dates he had set then we could not date anymore. I was extremely proud of my new assertive behavior and I was sure that he would "see the light" and tell me he would respect my needs from then on. But he did not. In fact, he quickly said, "Okay, let's just be friends." I was stunned but happy that I had seemingly averted yet another dysfunctional relationship with a dependency-prone individual. My optimism about the victorious end of our relationship was short lived.

Although we had definitely ended our budding relationship, God had another plan in mind. For one reason or another Jeff and I kept getting pulled back together. Whether it was to train together in the gym or to work on some mutual business opportunity, our paths seemed destined to cross. No matter how emotionally uninvolved we tried to be, we each had a strange feeling that there was more to be learned and to be resolved between us.

I finally got to meet with the psychic and by that time I had a lot of additional questions about Jeff as well as Mark. The psychic was exceedingly accurate in his descriptions of both of these men. He said I lived past lives with each of them before and even described in some detail several of these lives. One with Mark involved us marrying as teenage virgins back in Russia with all the ornate wedding clothes worn in the 12th century. I had not told him about my feeling that Mark and I were both virgins when we slept together the first time.

The most dramatic past life that I had spent with Jeff was one in which I had been a young English girl named Mary Louise. I lived in early 19th century England with a stringently religious Protestant family. I was the youngest of four children and was not extremely close to either of my emotionally distant parents, although I loved and respected them very much.

My feelings for my father, who was a successful insurance salesman within the boating industry, changed dramatically when I found out he had a mistress. I saw that my mother was devastated. I was 15 years old at the time and did not tell my parents that I had, unbeknownst to them, found out about my father's affair.

At the same time of this discovery about my father, I met a young Irish boy named Kevin (now Jeff) who worked in our town as a leather smith's apprentice. Kevin had red curly hair and lively brown eyes. He was Catholic and from a lower class Irish family. He was witty, charming, enthusiastic, and an alcoholic.

I made several secret trips into town to try to run into him by "accident." My parents were disapproving about any relationship I might have outside our church, let alone one with a poor Irish Catholic boy.

I fell in love with Kevin and got pregnant. My father, who already blamed poor Kevin for my change in attitude towards him, detested the mere mention of his name. I married Kevin and we moved back to Ireland where he hoped to run his own leather goods shop. I was ex-communicated from my family, friends, and church.

After our first child was born we sent word to my parents and several other friends and relatives. No one responded. My destiny was to die never seeing my family or friends from England again. Kevin felt guilty about my loss. Even though I assured him that I was happy and loved him regardless of the circumstances, he never could believe me. He could not control his drinking and never was able to fulfill his dream of starting his own business. He thought he had failed me because we lived very humbly with few luxuries for either our four children or us.

As the psychic spoke about this lifetime I had shared with Jeff, images kept appearing in my mind. I could picture Kevin's eyes gazing at me, smiling with a childlike wonder. I saw our house with a wood-burning stove and above it a large black kettle cooking our evening meal. I recalled telling him I was pregnant with our fourth child and sensing his disappointment and concern about possibly not being able to feed another child.

Some things were very clear while other aspects of that life remained outside of my grasp. I sensed that there was something more, something left unresolved from that lifetime. A certain anxiety lurked deep within my soul. But what was it that made me feel so much dread and why couldn't I remember?

Almost insidiously, Jeff and I became steadfast friends. He announced to his family over Thanksgiving that he had a new best friend and "It's a girl!" He had never had a best friend who was a female before and never anyone whom he felt comfortable enough with to share all his deepest and darkest feelings and thoughts.

Even more than sharing our feelings, thoughts and fun times together there was still something else very special about our relationship. We knew intuitively that we had something of critical importance to learn from each other. Unfortunately, neither of us could put our finger on what that "something" exactly was. Because of this insurmountable gut feeling we both took everything the other said as gospel. I taught him things about certain weight lifting techniques and he taught me about scuba diving. I guided him in certain business decisions and he assisted me in marketing and networking. And then, around Christmas time, our lesson started to become clearer.

Although we had verbally agreed that we were not dating each other exclusively, we came to realize that the heart doesn't always agree with the head in these matters. One day when I was picking up some advance tickets at the local movie theater I "coincidentally" saw him with another woman. I did not think he had seen me since I was in my car and at some distance but I was wrong.

I thought I was going to have a heart attack. I could not breathe at first and do not remember driving home. I had not felt this way since the time I learned of my ex-husband's first affair. Why did I have this dramatic of a reaction to someone whom I was not even dating steadily?

It did not make any sense. After all we were "just friends." When he called me at 9:00 the next morning he was visibly shaken. He claimed to have had the same heart attack feeling I had experienced. I realized that he meant more to me than just a friend. I concluded that if we were not going to change our relationship to reflect this realization then it would be better if we did not see each other anymore. He said he was not ready to settle down to dating one person. We stopped seeing each other mid-December 1995.

I was forlorn over losing the strong connection I had with Jeff. My whole world had to change. I lost my best friend, my training partner, my business colleague, my confidant, my children's friend, and the most inspirational and witty person I had ever known.

I sensed that there was much more to his not wanting to be in a relationship with me than appeared on the surface. I knew he felt the same way about me that I felt about him but for some reason we were both holding back. Beyond being best friends he had told me that he would move "heaven and earth" if there was ever anything I needed and I knew he was telling the truth. So why could we not be together?

Three days prior to Christmas 1995, while I was cleaning my kitchen, I heard a voice say, *"He filed for bankruptcy and feels unworthy. He lost his fiancé because of this and fears losing you."* There it was again! Exactly one year ago to the day that same voice had instructed me to find the love letter sent to my husband, which had drastically changed the course of my life. Why was it back again now?

I knew instinctively the voice was referring to Jeff but logically it did not fit his situation. He lived a very comfortable lifestyle, had a lot of valuable possessions, had a good job, and had a college degree in finance. It did not fit his picture at all. Yes, he had been engaged once before and it did break off prior to the wedding but money was not the reason he had given for it not working out. Plus, what did any of that have to do with our now ended relationship?

I could not shake the feeling that there was something important about this message. As a member of our local Credit Bureau it would be easy enough for me to find out if Jeff had ever filed for bankruptcy. I had to know the truth so I put in a request for the information. What I received back astounded me.

The voice had, once again, been correct. Jeff indeed had filed for bankruptcy in 1992. Shortly after this his relationship had soured with his fiancé. He was still climbing out of that hole and feeling the strain on his self-esteem. Even so, the question remained, what was the purpose for me to know this?

My answer came that night. While lying in bed just before falling asleep I received another message. The voice said, *"The truly bankrupt person is not someone without coins in the pocket but someone without God in the heart. That person is spiritually bankrupt."* I also was told that I would tell Jeff about this revelation but that he would tell me about his own bankruptcy.

The voice also said that Jeff and I were not only training our physical bodies together but our spiritual bodies were training together as well. It was an example of how the physical world mirrored the spiritual world. This would be the first of many examples of this "mirroring effect" that I would be given. I was shown the image of the two of us climbing ladders side by side. When one needed assistance the other would stretch out a hand to help. The definition of soul mates was becoming clearer to me now.

Oddly, ever since I had been in college I had been drawn to the image of the time 11:11 on the face of digital clocks. It seemed as if I would routinely look at the clock whenever this time appeared. I used to say to myself that this would probably be the time I would die. But after I was given the image of Jeff and I climbing the ladders, I immediately looked up at my clock and saw the time was 11:11. I sensed it was the "two ladders" I was seeing all along.

The voice then continued with, *"The true meaning of Christmas is not about giving it is about receiving."* Then I saw a picture in my mind of God as a bright shining light beaming down into two people's hearts. I then saw Jeff and I standing back to back and some "Being" standing above us. This Being put one hand on each of our shoulders and gently turned us around to face each other. Once we were eye to eye I saw this white light, that had been previously radiated from God into the two human hearts, begin to stream from my heart into Jeff's and vice versa.

This was all very foreign to me. How was I supposed to give this type of "message" to someone I did not even see or talk to anymore? I made a deal with God. I told Him that I would pass on His message to Jeff if He gave me the opportunity to talk to him about it.

I got my chance in about two weeks when Jeff called out of the blue to ask me a question related to business. When I nervously relayed the messages I had received, he was stunned. I sensed that he recognized their significance in his life. The topic of his past bankruptcy did not come up but within two months he did explain everything to me as the voice had predicted. I never told him that I already knew all about it.

Chapter two of our relationship was about to begin. My spiritual door was starting to slowly edge a little further open. The true meaning of our relationship was now starting to crystallize.

Within a month of these revelations, Jeff and I were dating each other exclusively. We had both accepted the fact that, for whatever reason, we belonged together at that point in our lives. Things could not have been better. Since we were practically identical in our likes and dislikes it was not hard for us to find things we wanted to do together. We spent most of our time together and I even attended one of his business expos.

One night, as we were discussing our feelings for one another, I commented that he had not yet told me that he loved me. He thought for a moment and then responded rather profoundly, "What we have is much deeper than love." I understood immediately what he meant and I knew he was right. Our connection was at a level that neither of us could explain with words.

In May of 1996 things began to change. Our relationship had started to take a serious turn and we were talking about marriage, houses and kids. His past insecurities and unresolved issues began to surface and take over. Our paths would soon diverge. He told me, "This is the path I must be on now. This is where I need to be." I did not understand what he meant.

The ironic part is we both were content and strangely excited about our new directions. Somehow it seemed different than all the other break ups I had endured. There was a sense of rightness about it and also a feeling that there was still much more to be gained from our relationship.

Initially I thought my calm acceptance of the situation signified it was not truly over between us. After all, we had broken up twice before and gotten back together. Deep inside, however, I sensed that even though the physical interaction between us had ceased there was more to be gained spiritually.

Jeff knew this too. In a letter he wrote me at the time of our break up he said, "You have been and presently are the best friend I have ever had. We have grown in so many areas together. Half of which I am probably yet unaware!" He went on to say, "You are truly a soul mate of mine and I am confident that God will do for us what we cannot or will not do for ourselves. He will make all things right. That I am sure of." How right he would prove to be on all accounts.

Chapter Seven

Talking with angels?

    Jeff and I stayed in contact until the day before my birthday in mid-July when he told me he was seeing someone else. He said that his relationship with her was a path he had to take. I had no idea what he meant by that statement but I knew I had to move on with my own life as well. I decided to make a return visit to the psychic I had seen for the past life reading the previous year. I thought it would be fun to get a birthday prediction or two.

    When I called the psychic's number to set up an appointment his recorded message gave the names of two other people to call for readings because he was booked solid. One of the names, Lillian, stood out from the other so I decided to give her a call.

    I was pleasantly surprised when she said that she could see me the next day, on my birthday. When I arrived she ushered me into her kitchen. I had never met her before and all she knew about me was my name. She said that she liked to first tell clients what she was picking up from her "guides", and then I could ask questions at the end. This sounded perfect since it would give me the opportunity to assess her psychic abilities prior to disclosing anything personal about myself.

    Without me ever saying a word Lillian accurately described my 11 year marriage, exactly when it had ended, my ex-husband, our marital relationship and difficulties, my relationship with Jeff, our three break ups and various other amazing facts that were impossible for her to guess. In addition, she predicted that, by the coming autumn, I would meet yet another soul mate. He was an attorney and born under the sign of Gemini. I would recognize him and click with him immediately. There would be something very special about his smile.

I was amazed. How did she do that and who were these "guides" she credited with knowing my life's story? Lillian explained that we each have angelic guides that assist us personally and give us information to help guide others.

Unlike me, she had been raised a strict Catholic where the belief in angels was prevalent. Although I had heard of various angel-related stories, I had never experienced their presence in my life. Or at least I did not think I had.

As luck would have it, Lillian was offering a workshop on how to "Talk with your Angels." Being a curious person by nature I decided to attend the workshop and gather data on how all of this was possible. Somehow she had been privy to detailed information about me that was unobtainable elsewhere. It was worth finding out.

About twenty people attended that first workshop on July 23, 1996. When we went around the room at the start of class to introduce ourselves and share the reason we had attended, I decided to be totally honest. I explained that I was skeptical of supposed angelic encounters and I wanted to see exactly how Lillian was able to learn information about people. I was not expecting much from that evening's class and certainly not the life altering changes that were about to take place.

The major thrust of what Lillian shared with us was meditation and visualization. I had never tried meditating before, mostly because I kept myself very busy and did not think I had the time. It also had some negative connotations to me reminiscent of the hippie generation that preceded mine. To me they were "anti-" everything that I tried to excel at business, home, family, sobriety, being good and living life for the benefit of others. I had never wanted to associate myself in any way with that particular group.

Lillian asked us to relax and try to visualize ourselves in a lush green meadow. In that meadow we were to picture what our "angel" looked like. I was very disappointed by what I saw in my mind's eye.

My angel looked like a regular guy. He was a rather nice looking man and appeared to be about 30 years old. He had short, dark hair, brown eyes, deep dimples and a beautiful smile. He was average height and had broad shoulders. He wore a long white robe with a tie around the waist. He introduced himself as "John."

When we went around the room to report what we saw, I became embarrassed. Everyone else had these truly angelic looking images complete with wings, halos, and glowing lights, etc. The names ranged from the exotic to the descriptive like *Angel of Light*.

When it was my turn to describe my angel the class all giggled. John sounded more like a "dream man" than a "dream angel." Even his name was commonplace and unexciting. I thought I had failed.

We then were instructed to ask our angel guide for a message. My message was confusing to me: *"We provide the love you seek."* What was that supposed to mean? At first, I interpreted it to mean that these guides were in charge of finding me men to date, a kind of cosmic dating service, so to speak.

But the message and my interpretation troubled me. Somehow I knew my superficial explanation was not the end of the story. Somehow I could sense that I had only just started to define what this simple phrase would mean in my life and what it meant in everyone's life.

Before we ended the class, we each randomly selected an angelic message from a box that held dozens of little pieces of paper. Lillian called them "angel whispers" and claimed that she dictated them from what her guides told her. We each would be directed to the message most important to us at that particular time in our life. My angel whisper proved eerily prophetic, *"In your search for a loving partner, use this criteria, does this person promote my emotional and spiritual well-being and my growth as a soul?"*

Lillian also taught us a simple technique to ask "yes" or "no" type questions to our guides. For the next couple of weeks I continued asking John all types of yes or no questions. Amazingly the predictions proved right, nine out of ten times. I practiced on one of my friends who had not taken the class but had several personal and business matters up in the air. She, too, was curious how I could continuously "guess" things that would happen in her life before they happened.

By this time, my curiosity was really piqued. I decided to learn more about the concept of psychic phenomenon and angel guides. I purchased a book called The Psychic Pathway by Sonia Choquette; it provided yet another series of tools to help those interested in enhancing their psychic abilities.

One of the things Sonia taught was to become aware of all the psychic miracles that happen in everyday life. She recommended that we keep a journal of all unexplainable happenings that relate to our growing abilities and God's miracles. One of the most profound things I learned was that miracles do not always represent large dramatic events but, in most cases, they are small and barely observable unless we are paying attention. Many times we are tempted to pass these events off as coincidence or luck. Becoming more aware of what was happening in our daily lives was the first step to becoming more psychic.

Like Lillian, Sonia believes that everyone has the ability to become more psychic in his or her everyday lives. It was not a rare gift for only a few to harness and use. Nearly everyone has had intuitive thoughts that have come true or gut feelings that later proved to be accurate. Most of us had just stifled these less than analytical thoughts in order to not seem weird or unusual to those around us. Especially for people like me, who always strove to "fit in" and not deviate from the norm, these psychic skills had been kept off limits.

Sonia also focused on meditation as the means of getting in touch with our "Higher Selves." This Higher Self includes our unconscious mind as well as the superconscious realm, supposedly inhabited by angels. She taught other tools for communicating with these "guides" through automatic writing, tarot cards, and the like.

I decided to test these tools to see what might develop. Like a good scientist, if I were going to accurately assess the merit of these psychic happenings, I would have to learn the trade, then gather as much data for documentation as possible. I began to keep a journal and also began my remarkable spiritual journey.

M. Sue Benford

Chapter Eight

The spiritual door swings wide open

One of the most devastating experiences of my life was the loss of my only brother, Steve, to AIDS in January of 1991. It was not only devastating because he was a bright, ambitious, caring, and highly productive individual but because he, through it all, was there for me. He, like nobody else before or since, worshipped the ground I walked on. He loved me unconditionally.

Our childhood had not been easy for either one of us. He had always felt guilty that perhaps an accidental kick to my stomach, while we were playing in 1962 had caused me to develop cancer. His feelings of guilt quickly became intermingled with a sense of loss: both from his fear for my life and for the attention he lost from our already overly stressed parents. Moreover, he suffered from sensing at an early age, that he was somehow "different." It would be much later before he could put a word on what that difference was — gay.

As we grew up, he became the rebel of the family while I played the role of the good child. He constantly battled with our parents and as soon as he graduated from high school, he left home permanently.

Steve was an excellent student. In only four years he earned four undergraduate degrees and became the Executive vice-president of his university's student body in his senior year. He personally went from door to door to meet each student and campaign for votes. He loved people and they loved him.

After earning a Master's Degree in Advertising from Northwestern University, he went to work for a large corporation in Los Angeles. He quickly moved up the corporate ladder, but all the while, doing it through helping those who needed his assistance instead of climbing over top of them. Over four hundred of his co-workers and friends would eventually pay their respects to him at his memorial service.

There was no one in the world I was more proud of or respected more than my big brother. He was my hero; the person I pointed to most often to describe success in both physical and emotional terms. He had challenged his own demons to become who he really was, regardless of what other people might unlovingly think.

But my reality changed with a cataclysmic bang when he told me he had AIDS. I was the first one in our family to know about his illness. He had come to me because he knew I would "be strong" and help the other family members accept him and his diagnosis. He knew he could count on his little sister, the only person, whose picture graced his large executive desk, to be there for him and to love him unconditionally, as he loved her.

But could I be there for him? I was devastated by his news and secretly resented him for snatching away the only rosy picture I had of our family — a picture that I had planned to take with me long into the future. I pretended that I accepted his lifestyle and his fate, but I lied. I lied to him, I lied to our parents, but I could not lie to myself.

Two months before Steve died, I took my mother to California to see him in the hospital. It was Thanksgiving Day — how ironically inappropriate I thought. A day to "thank the Lord" for all the many blessings he had bestowed upon us. I could find nothing to be thankful for. There, lying weak and emaciated was all that was left of my once strong and vital brother.

As we all said what were to be our final good-byes, I found myself standing alone in his room after everyone else had walked out. I never will forget the look on his face. He had always had saucer-sized, dark, penetrating brown eyes but now they looked abnormally huge in comparison to his sunken cheekbones.

With what little energy he had remaining, he reached out his hand to me. I put my hand in his and he said, "I love you and always will." For years without fail, my brother had consistently closed our conversations by telling me that he loved me. I had never reciprocated the sentiment.

On this occasion there was an unmistakable look of anticipation in his eyes. He wanted something back from me at that moment. He was waiting — one last chance for me to respond. I wanted to tell him how much he meant to me, how I loved him too, how his unconditional love and support had meant everything to me. But I could not. The words stuck in my throat. Something in me still stubbornly refused.

I never saw or spoke to my brother after that final good bye. Shortly after our visit he slipped into a coma and on January 3, 1991 my only sibling passed away. He uttered one final phrase before his death. Waking from his deep sleep for only seconds his eyes opened wide in amazement as he gazed at something not visibly present. He whispered in a hushed breath, "I see Jesus!" My brother, who had renounced Christianity years earlier, shocked all of us when we learned about this declaration.

Before the wounds from his departure began to heal, my life would, once again, be turned upside down with the discovery of my husband's "first" affair. I would eventually make peace with that anguish but my only brother was gone — I could never tell him how much he meant to me. I thought I would have to live with my regrets forever. But I was wrong.

One night while I was practicing my meditation, I started to think about my brother and what he would say about my life now. What words of wisdom would he have for me? I asked John if I could talk to him. Initially, he did not respond.

That night I went to bed at my usual time but awoke at around 4:00 a.m. when I heard what sounded like my brother's voice calling, "Hey Sue." The tunnel like quality to his voice was reminiscent of when we were kids and he would secretly yell down through the register vent thinking that our parents could not hear him. I gently closed my eyes and could envision my healthy, vibrant brother in my mind's eye. I asked him to physically manifest but he said that he could not. I told him that I did not believe that I was really talking with the spirit of my deceased brother but, rather, his voice was merely a figment of my imagination.

To prove who he was, I asked him to tell me something I could verify that he would know but that I would not know. He began by telling me to go down in my basement where I kept an old filing cabinet of his but I said "No, I do not want to go all the way down there with the spider webs and everything. Plus it's 4:00 in the morning!" I could not believe I was actually arguing with myself.

Then I said, give me your address on West Knoll where you last lived. I had only been to his place twice and that had been many years before. I had no recollection what his address was but figured I could find out. He did not respond to my request but, instead, went on talking.

He said that he was there to help me resolve my past feelings of loneliness, fear, and abandonment from childhood. He showed me myself in intensive care as being a good example. He said I had only one tear because I was too afraid to cry with Mom watching. She was so weak and needed me to be strong. I had believed that, if I was not strong and under control, she would not love me and I would be left alone to die. He said that because I thought that I could not rely on anyone to be there for me consistently, I kept repeating the same pattern in the hope of finally changing the outcome.

He explained that God, my angels, and other souls like him would always be there to love me and that they would provide the human network of people that I need, when I need them. He showed me it as three separate, but overlapping, circles. The first with past friends, family and loved ones, the second with some of the same people but some new ones added (this is the present), and the third circle with a few of the past groups but still new people being brought into the circle (the future). We are given who and what we need at all times. He said that I had to learn to trust in God and know that He was always there to provide exactly what I needed, when I needed it.

He said to always be happy in the moment because it is really all that we have. He said I needed to grieve the past and finally move on. He said that he would be with me for the rest of my life to watch over me because, "Mom prays a lot." I did not understand what he meant.

The whole time we talked he laughed and was so excited that I finally asked him why he was so happy and giggling. He said he was excited about my future because it was very bright and happy. I wondered why I would have "thought" this particular happy ending scenario since I was not feeling particularly hopeful at the time.

As he started to depart I said, "I am sorry, Steve, for not accepting you completely. I am sure that you must know by now that my feelings were ambiguous and that I've hated myself for not being able to give you the unconditional love you gave me. Can you forgive me?"

His response was not what I expected. He began laughing and said with a chuckle, "Forgive you for what? That was not really me. It was just my body and the lessons I had to learn. Now you see the lessons you have to learn, too. You need to let people love you and tell them that you love them before they leave their physical life — that's when we learn our lessons. And you need to stop always trying to be 'good' to save other people. I was trying to help you then, and I am here to help you now."

It was true that I had a difficult time expressing loving feelings because, after all, I had a difficult time even *having* the feelings. I especially had a hard time accepting love from others and telling others that I loved them, too. Somehow it frightened me, made me feel vulnerable or out-of-control like the little girl behind the glass window in ICU. My life was lived by the motto: If you love, then you get hurt. I had closed off my life to love of any kind — even God's.

Steve had, many times before, tried to get me to look closer at my behavior and how I was sacrificing my own soul trying to save others. How would I break out of this vicious cycle? Was I going to be getting more "opportunities" to learn these lessons? I was not sure I really wanted to know the answers.

I went back to sleep and woke up at 7:30 a.m. I started walking down the stairs to the kitchen when I heard a voice say *"201."* I wondered if it could be the address that I had asked for from Steve. I went to my old address book to look it up. I only had his address from college, which, remarkably, was "201 W. Chestnut." I did not have his address on West Knoll.

M. Sue Benford

On Sunday August 19, 1996 I returned home from a visit with my cousin in New York. I had told her the story and suggested that Steve had purposely given me the address on Chestnut because he looked like he did during his college days or perhaps because he knew I did not have his most recent address. I was groping for answers. She said, "But, still, why wouldn't he give you the address on West Knoll?" I could not figure it out.

I called my mother and told her the story of Steve's "visit." She confided that she no longer had my brother's old address either so it looked like the issue would remain a mystery. She also revealed that one of her prayers every night was for Steve to still be allowed to watch over his little sister. What he had said about our mom praying a lot, now made sense.

Later that night my mother called me back to report that, while she was in the spare bedroom of their house, she accidentally knocked into Steve's glass-top table where a large pile of papers and miscellaneous materials of his were kept. Unbelievably, the large jolt to the table had caused only one thing to fall off — a luggage label with my brother's West Knoll address. The address was also "201."

Chapter Nine

The last of the trinity

According to my single friends, the thing to do in the 90's was to join a dating service. I had mixed feelings about these types of services but one of my best friends had been a part of one a few years earlier and claimed to have met some nice people. There was a certain logic about them, especially considering the fact that my social circle consisted of mostly married or otherwise ineligible men.

Ironically, I had never been solicited by a dating service until the day Jeff and I permanently separated — July 9, 1996. It was the eve of my birthday and the phone rang. I made it a habit to never purchase anything over the phone and rarely did I even let someone get away with a complete sales pitch. But, for some unknown reason, this time I listened.

The sales woman offered a free introductory "date" with no obligation to join. I astounded myself when I actually scheduled a meeting at their office to select a potential suitor. Later, when I was getting cold feet about the whole deal, my friend surprised me by revealing that this was the same organization she had joined years earlier. I decided to give it a shot.

With my friend's encouragement, I joined the service. We had fun taking pictures for their book and completing the profile required. Within a couple of weeks several men had chosen to meet me. I went out with a few guys but no one attracted my attention or interest.

On August 24th, John told me during one of my meditations, that I had a "hole in my heart" which I must fill before being able to fully give or receive unconditional love. This was one of my life's missions. He said that I was beginning to fill it now through my new spiritual awakening.

He said that Jeff's soul, and mine, had chosen parallel paths of addiction and life trials to get to the point where we could learn these lessons. He said that I was not yet destined to meet a soul mate who was not struggling with these issues; in other words, someone emotionally healthy, because then I could not learn what I needed to learn in this lifetime.

My relationship with Jeff was as much for my learning experience as for his. We had been separated to focus on our individual growth. By me staying true to the path of spiritual growth, self-love, and love for others, I would encourage others in my life to choose that same path as well.

John said that my challenge would be to remain true to my new spiritual path in the presence of worldly temptations. Then he gave me several affirmations of what I would see in the next day's newspaper to prove what he was saying was true. I asked constantly for this empirical data and told John that I would not believe him if I did not get tangible evidence immediately.

In light of John's morose revelation about my love life, by the end of August I had decided to forego the dating scene altogether. Men kept calling but I had decided to tell them that, for personal reasons, I was not seeing anybody at this time. I figured that if I did not date anyone, then no one unhealthy could enter my life. Everyone seemed to understand and let it go; everybody except Dan.

One Sunday afternoon while I was in the middle of cooking dinner, I was interrupted by a phone call from a rather meek sounding man who claimed that he had gotten my name from the dating service. I told him that I was making dinner, could not talk, and did not feel like dating anyone at this time.

Rather comically he retorted, "Well then I guess I better find out what you're making for dinner so I can avoid that dish in the future!" He had caught me off guard and I started to laugh. There was something oddly comforting about his voice that I could not put my finger on. Before I realized it, I had agreed to meet him for a drink the next evening. I could sense that Dan was not going to be so easily discouraged.

Between the time of our date and the phone call I had become more resolute about my decision to not date anyone. I decided I would meet him, have a quick drink, and give him my routine story about dealing with other issues — nothing personal — just other irons in the fire.

When I got to the restaurant and looked around in the lobby area, I did not even see him standing there. He was so nondescript that he practically blended into the wall. He was on the short side with prematurely gray hair, glasses, and was about 30 pounds overweight with most of it resting in his midsection. He was not at all like the other men I had dated. But when he smiled the whole picture changed. His smile was the warmest, most genuine and loving thing that I had ever seen. Why did this seem so familiar?

We made our way to a table and began to talk. I liked him immediately but there was something else about him that I could not quite put my finger on. I discovered that he was new to Columbus. He was originally from Minnesota but most recently had transferred to Columbus from Chicago. He was an attorney by profession and worked at a large corporation in a small town east of the city. He did not know many people in Columbus and, in fact, had only one local contact phone number that had been given to him by a girl friend who had also been his next-door neighbor in Chicago.

His friend's father was a businessman who worked in Columbus but lived outside the city; in fact, he lived in the same small town where Dan worked. Her father did not spend much time in town because he commuted between Ohio and California. Dan had tried to call his work number several times but had not been able to reach him.

Something in the back of my mind was beginning to click. I had heard this story somewhere before. I only knew of one other person who lived in the small town where his friend's Dad lived — Jeff's boss and mentor. I asked Dan the father's name and was stunned at his response. It <u>was</u> Jeff's boss and the number he had been given was Jeff's! The only connection Dan had to Columbus went through Jeff's small, four-person office.

I could feel my face starting to pale. Cryptically, I asked him when he was born. He was a Gemini. Lillian's prediction rang in my head, "attorney. . .great smile. . .by autumn. . .soul mate. . .Gemini." I was beginning to feel like Ebenezer Scrooge.

On September 1, 1996, while in meditation, I asked what the purpose was for Dan to be brought into my life and John said it was so that I could experience what those "special" feelings were like. They would, in some way, help fill part of the "hole" John had said was in my heart a few nights ago. There would be other lessons that I would learn as well but John would not specify what they were. He also said that I would be helping Dan in the process of my own growth. I did not know in what way I could help him.

As it turned out, Dan was a devout Christian. He had been raised in a strict fundamentalist family that had their heritage in the Amish-like Mennonite denomination. He had graduated from a small Christian college in Minnesota. His parents had been distant and unaffectionate towards him growing up, which left him emotionally scarred.

On our second date, our life stories poured out in almost one long run-on sentence. I told him more in one evening than I had confided to anyone in a lifetime. I felt an all encompassing love and acceptance from this total stranger. No matter what I told him he never took his adoring gaze from me.

And he told me things that challenged him, too. John had been right — apparently I was not destined to meet anyone who was not struggling. Dan had never had a healthy, intimate relationship with any woman he dated. He had yet to tell a woman he loved her and did not think another person had ever truly loved him.

Like me, he had compartmentalized his physical, emotional, and spiritual lives so that they never overlapped. He did not know how to love someone and allow himself to become intimately involved with her at the same time. He claimed that he did not believe in premarital sex; yet, he had slept with numerous women where there was no emotional, and certainly, no spiritual connection. He had yet to join with someone who truly cared about him, about his soul.

We were so different that I knew I would never marry him; therefore, theoretically, we should never sleep together. But the attraction between us was extremely strong. I could not imagine, knowing the circumstances, how physical or emotional intimacy could benefit either of us. Everything about our lifestyles was incongruent. What could we possibly learn?

Dan's strength was in research of difficult legal cases. He prided himself at finding the answers and facts within hopelessly difficult to discern situations. He also prided himself at knowing the Christian religion. He had not only practiced it all his life, but history and Bible study were also his extracurricular hobbies. He would prove to be my human guide and mentor through some very tough religious fact finding missions that were about to begin.

Chapter Ten

The letter

Around the time I met Dan I started to have strong feelings about Jeff again. It was the oddest of times to start feeling reconnected to a past flame but I could not shake the feeling that something was very wrong in Jeff's life. I asked John to show me what was happening to him and, first, he sent me the most riveting dream I had ever experienced, then, a few days later, a vision to complete the picture.

On September 7, 1996 I experienced an overwhelming feeling that Jeff needed to hear what I had learned from John about his life. I asked John if it was the appropriate time for me to write Jeff a letter describing my experiences and he said *"yes"* and that I should go get my Bible because I was going to be shown quotes for the letter.

I did not know where my Bible was since I had not opened it since I purchased it nearly a year earlier, when Jeff, for some unknown reason, had suggested I buy one. I never could understand Scripture and I was intimidated to start trying to read it now.

When I found my Bible, I sat down at the table with paper and pen in hand and John said, *"Go to the computer to type the letter."* I said that I did not think I would have that much to say and he said that he would guide me. This is the letter I sent to Jeff that same day:

"Dear Jeff,

The Bible says, "It was he who gave some to be apostles, some to be prophets, some to be evangelists, and some to be pastors and teachers, to prepare God's people for works of service, so that the body of Christ may be built up until we all reach unity in the faith and in the knowledge of the Son of God and become mature, attaining to the whole measure of the fullness of Christ." Eph 4:11-12. That is why I am writing to you. As unlikely as this may seem, God is using me, as his pastor, to get some very important messages to you. These past two months have been extremely miraculous for me in terms of my spiritual awakening and how it has impacted my life. I have been blessed with understandings far beyond what I ever imagined. Your statement that, "You are very intuitive" is now a gross understatement. With this new awakening from the slumber we all must endure, I have been given the opportunity to help God awaken others— most specifically; his messages have revolved around you, my soul mate.

He wants you to come home, Jeff, to re-member with him as a spirit of the Light. He has sent detailed instructions on exactly how you can do this. Do you recall in the letter you sent to me on May 17th saying that, "you are a soul mate of mine and I am confident that God will do for us what we cannot or will not do for ourselves. He will make all things right. This I am sure of." He heard your prayers and is now answering them. "For it is light that makes everything visible. This is why it is said: 'Wake up, O sleeper, rise from the dead, and Christ will shine on you.'" Eph 5:14. Listen to what he has told me.

So much has come to me in the form of visions, dreams, etc. that I began writing everything in a journal. I am going to try to summarize as best I can in this letter. First, He has asked that you remember "who you are." By that He means that you are a spiritual being who happens to be inhabiting the human form of what you call your body. This is very important. Understand that as a spirit/soul we have chosen the path for our lifetime, which will give us the types of experiences we need to understand and rejoin with God.

He has said that you and I are "soul mates of the highest order." At first I thought this had something to do with our closeness but that is not all it means. It mostly is referring to the paths we have chosen. Some souls choose "easy" paths in that the focus is on simple lessons of survival such as finding their next meal. More evolved souls, or souls of higher orders, choose more difficult life quests. The highest understanding is that of giving and receiving unconditional love and diminishing fear. "I sought the Lord, and he answered me; he delivered me from all my fears. Those who look to him are radiant; their faces are never covered with shame." Ps 34:4-5.

We, my friend, have chosen this highest life lesson with, of course, the most difficult life experiences. I have reached this point of awakening before you for the simple reason that your path has been more difficult (you chose the high road, I chose the low road or something like that!) Either way, we are being used, and have chosen to be used, to help each other obtain this insight and be reawakened to Christ.

I must tell you, I asked God to let me, "walk a mile in your shoes" and experience your trials and tribulations. He brought to me the most riveting dreams and visions I have ever experienced. I have never felt fear, like I did that night. I woke up feeling as if I was in a Stephen King movie. I am so in awe of your courage to take on these life challenges. Your rewards will be equally as awe inspiring when you have rejoined and reawakened with God. Now I can see why you were given the "high road;" I simply could not have handled what you have.

When I asked God to help me outline for you what he wanted most for me to tell you, he literally, took the pen I held in my hand and began writing (I know this sounds bizarre but believe me I have received many affirmations that this is really God speaking - I will share those with you if you want). Here is what he wrote:

Revelations for Jeff
1. *His quest was predetermined as a struggle to experience the highest truths of love and fear.*
2. *You are soul mates of the highest order seeking highest truths.*
3. *Fear must be faced then embraced for if it is left unseen it dominates all.*
4. *Love and fear cannot exist together. Love is eternal between soul mates and comes from God. Fear is of man and material things.*
5. *We are spiritual beings first. Be proud of your courage to choose the tough path. He and you are destined to train and support each other to re-membering with Christ.*
6. *He must choose the Light to have what his soul seeks. Only there will he find peace and unconditional love.*
7. *Tell him of your dreams and visions, Sue.*
8. *We all know him and love him. We will answer if he will ask. Look up into the Light.*

God has spoken, hear His words and find your peace.

According to #7 above, I should attempt to relay to you my dream, as I was walking in your shoes, and then the follow-up which was more of a vision sharing the "how to find God" message for you. The dream was full of symbolism. In this dream I was you and Mariah, (another world champion female powerlifter), was me.

The dream begins with me walking into a large room filled with caskets. One casket, the newest one, still had the lid open. I knew it was a good friend of mine, and a strong ally in the fight I was in against the "Unseen Evil One" and his followers. I was heartsick as I walked up to the casket and it was Mariah. Even though she was in a casket, I knew she was not completely gone. I asked her if she would still be there for me helping me and, through closed lips she said "yes." She then added, "There are a lot of good souls here." I knew by that she meant all the others that had died in my battle against the Unseen Evil One.

At that point I had to run because I am being chased and the fight must continue. I run, trying frantically to alert innocent bystanders and recruit them in my battle. I kept looking around, so scared but never seeing whom I was running from. I came up to a tall chain linked gate with a heavy padlock on the other side. I know my path is beyond the gate but it is too big to climb and I couldn't reach the lock. I looked up and Mariah had come down from the sky to the other side of the gate. She karate chopped the lock and it broke off. She opened the gate for me. I noticed that she has blood on her hand from trying to help me and I feel bad but she shakes it off and says she was just glad she could help.

She disappeared and I begin my run through the unlocked gate. I came upon a hill, and stopped to think about my direction. I know the Unseen Evil One is getting closer so I have to do something, start formulating my plan of attack. I started up the hill and saw Mr. Spock from Star Trek (he is very strong, logical, smart and has telepathic abilities). I felt a ray of hope because I did not know I had this strong of a resource at my disposal. I asked him if he can use his telepathic abilities to steer the Evil One away from me. He says, possibly but he might be detected since the Evil One is very powerful. My second plan is for Spock to get the "followers" to veer off their path, which would leave the Evil One on his own and more susceptible to defeat.

I woke up feeling hopeful that this plan will work. Jeff, the fear I felt from the Unseen Evil One was like nothing I have ever felt before and I hope never to again!

Although this dream is full of symbolism I think you can figure out and relate to what it means. I can contribute more of my understanding of it if you wish. The second part of the dream was actually more of a vision. I asked God to show me what happened next and what your choice should be. This time you were you and I was me. Here is what he told and showed me.

M. Sue Benford

You finally defeated the followers (minor fears) but were told you had to actually see and face the Unseen Evil One in order to conquer it. You agreed to do this with God's help and waited on the hill for the Evil One to finally appear. When it did, it was you as a little boy. You were shocked that it was just yourself and in such a non-fearful looking form. You said that you wanted to see me but were afraid I would not come back. The boy said I would and to be honest and tell me where you were in facing your fear. The boy told you to call for me and you did.

After a slight hesitation, a ray of light shown down from the heavens and my own image was in the middle of the light. You explained to me your situation and asked me to come over to get you and bring you into the Light. You said that you were weak and I was much stronger. I said that if you give your fears to God to carry, it will lighten your load and make you stronger too. I told you that you were as strong as I was because we were mirrors of each other, only your burden was far greater than mine was so I reached the Light first. In order to come to the Light you only need to choose to be there. It is as close or as far as you make it.

You seemed to comprehend that but still felt you had nothing to bring to me in the Light. You said, "You are all Light now, I have nothing to give you." I said that is not true, look closely. You saw one dark, non-lighted spot in my heart. It was the hole in my heart I needed to fill with unconditional love, which is my soul's journey. Then I told you to look at your heart. When you did you saw a glow of light. It was a glow of unconditional love. God had put it there.

You mustered up the courage, grasped the boy's hand, and chose to come into the Light. When you got there you noticed that the boy stood on the outside of our lighted circle. Fear cannot exist in the realm of Love. You also noticed that my girl of fear also stood outside the Light but close at hand. I showed you how to toss your fears outside the Light to the little boy. I explained that you must always embrace the fear because unseen fear becomes unmanageable fear, as you had experienced.

You said you were afraid I would leave and take the Light but I showed you that now, even when you walk away or if I leave, the Light will remain because it is attached to God. You look up and see that it is true and the Light doesn't go away. You said, in the past, the Light had gone away as you feared but I explained that was because it was not the pure unconditional love Light of God that you have now experienced. You then moved away from my Light and continued to practice giving away your fears, embracing the boy, and testing that the Light would not go away even when we were apart.

There is so much more I would like to share with you, my soul mate. I was instructed not to contact you until these messages were clear and I could express them well to you. I have chosen to write to you instead of calling because there is so much and I did not want to leave important messages out. We have both been so richly blessed to have this chance for an awakening with God. What we built together and struggled through this past year was no accident. It has led us to this point.

You have free will to choose your path, Jeff. That is God's promise to us as his children. I will continue to pray that you will hear his words and choose the Light. I have experienced the peace promised by God and the miracles now come to me as I ask Him for them. I have truly evolved.

"This is the message we have heard from him and declare to you: God is light; in him there is no darkness at all. If we claim to have fellowship with him yet walk in the darkness, we lie and do not live by the truth. But if we walk in the light, as he is in the light, we have fellowship with one another, and the blood of Jesus, his Son, purifies us from all sin." 1John 1:5.

Hear these words and join me in the Light.

In God's Name

I felt a sense of relief after I mailed that letter. It felt like I had completed a very important task. Whether I ever heard from Jeff again or whether I learned if this letter had any significance to him, seemed unimportant.

Still, deep inside I knew that I had unfinished business with Jeff, I was sure of that much, but I still did not know exactly what it was. It was an uneasiness that I could not shake, like an itch in the middle of your back that you just cannot reach to scratch. But what was the unfinished business and how would I ever resolve it so that I would be free to move on?

M. Sue Benford

Chapter Eleven

So <u>you're</u> John!

I became curious about the dream that John gave me about Jeff and, further, about what he had said regarding interpreting them with the help of Scripture. Never having read or studied the Bible before it seemed unlikely that I would somehow be able to dream and imagine in terms related directly to specific Biblical Scripture. Although the two "revelations" had been remarkable, as my dreams and visions usually went, I still pictured them more in terms of psychological significance than of any religious significance.

I began looking through the Bible and searching for any text that seemed related to the stories. Incredibly, I began finding numerous references. In the process of recording all the Scripture text that seemed related, I noticed something interesting. While writing down some text from 1John it occurred to me that most of the Scripture was coming from one of the Books or letters attributed to the Apostle John.

Half jokingly, I chuckled to myself, "What, did I used to be the Apostle John in a past life?" Then a voice answered back, *"No, but I was ."* It was my guide, John! John proceeded to tell me that he was once in the body of Christ's beloved disciple, John, and that Jeff and I were a part of that soul group. He said that one of his tasks is to bring us back to the Light.

John showed me many of the following verses that related to my dream and vision; most were Scripture verses attributed to him:

"We know that we are children of God, and that the **whole world is under the control of the evil one.**" (1John 5:19)

"Dear friends, let us love one another, for **love comes from God**. Everyone who loves has been born of God and knows God." (1John 4:7)

"No one has ever seen God; but if we love one another, God lives in us and **his love is made complete in us**." (1John 4:12)

"There is **no fear in love**. But **perfect love drives out fear**, because fear has to do with punishment. The one who fears is not made perfect in love." (1John 4:18)

"**I am the gate; whoever enters through me will be saved." (John 10:9)** My command is this: **Love each other as I have loved you**. Greater love has no one than this, that **he lay down his life for his friends**." (John 15:12-13)

"**Love never fails**. But where there are prophecies, they will cease; where there are tongues, they will be stilled; where there is knowledge, it will pass away." (1Cor 13:8)

    John continued to explain to me that higher order souls seeking highest truths are most challenged by the Evil One. This term, *Evil One*, that I had never heard before my dream, was something John, and sometimes Jesus, used almost exclusively to describe Satan in the Bible. The irony is that, to gain the perfect truth of God, one must travel the roughest roads on Earth, which leave us prey to the Evil One who challenges us with worldly forces. Christ and his followers work diligently to assist souls and coax them back from the clutches of the Evil One/ World; especially those of higher orders because they have already come so far in their development and obtained the greatest degree of spirit and knowledge.

    I asked John to explain to me exactly what a "soul mate" was and he led me, point blank, to a particular greeting card at the supermarket. The card said, "What is a friend? A single soul dwelling in two bodies." Aristotle had made the observation many centuries before.

    He showed me how soul mates had once been connected to one another, by God, in a single spiritual unit but, on Earth, they were separated in different physical bodies. There was an eternally strong bond that pulled the souls back together during physical lifetimes. This "reunion of the souls" served to propel the souls into enlightenment. Advancement by one soul led to the advancement of the other. Spiritually, we would be "stuck in the mud," so to speak, without our soul mates. In essence, soul mates are spiritual training partners!

    I still had many questions about my dream and vision that I could not explain. One question was, why did I appear as my friend Mariah instead of myself in the dream? My answer came months later when I learned the truth about the significance of Mariah.

He told me that there was no greater expression of love than that of a person willing to risk or extend their worldly self, either emotionally or physically, to enlighten another's soul. He told me that God had demonstrated this lesson in the story of how Abraham was preparing to kill his beloved son Isaac to show his appreciation and reverence for God's unconditional love over love of the flesh or the World.

At first I did not understand what he was talking about. The only Isaac I had ever heard of was Isaac Washington, the bartender on the old television show *The Love Boat*. Jesus told me to go get my Bible and look up Abraham. I found references to him and a son Isaac in the Old Testament. I knew even less about the Old Testament than I did the New Testament — which meant I knew nothing.

I turned to the Book of Genesis and was shown this passage: "Then God said, 'Take your son, your only son, Isaac, whom you love, and go to the region of Moriah. Sacrifice him there as a burnt offering on one of the mountains I will tell you about.'" (Ge. 22:2) I was amazed and startled to find the connection between my dream of "Mariah" and this Moriah. I read on and discovered that Abraham had been willing to comply with God's request and choose God's unconditional love of spirit over his worldly love of flesh for his only son.

Later, King David was told to build a temple to God on this same mountain at Moriah instead of on Mt. Sinai to reflect the message that our willingness to make a worldly sacrifice for the love of God was His paramount Law. When Jesus came to Earth incarnate and subsequently attached us to God directly, our own bodies then became the region of Moriah where God's temple dwells. The original temple, he said, will never be found because it now dwells within our souls.

That is why I appeared as "Mariah" in my dream and why I was portrayed as being nearly dead in a casket after trying to help Jeff. I had been willing to give up any worldly "loves" for the chance to give and receive the divine unconditional love within our hearts.

Our individual willingness to accept God's love into our bodily temple and sacrifice worldly love for spiritual love is the cornerstone of our relationships with each other. By unconditionally loving ourselves, and others we are, in essence, achieving God's paramount Law.

We are given many soul mates throughout our lifetimes to assist us in our spiritual development. I had recently been sent three.

M. Sue Benford

PART TWO

The whole outward, visible world with all its being is a signature, or figure of the inward spiritual world; whatever is internally, and however its operation is, so likewise it has its character externally; like as the spirit of each creature sets forth and manifests the internal form of its birth by its body, so does the Eternal Being also.

Jacob Boehme
in *The Signature of All Things*

M. Sue Benford

Chapter Twelve

A truly personal relationship with Christ

One of the most baffling things to me that Christians referred to was having a "personal" relationship with Jesus Christ. How was it possible to personally know someone who had died nearly two thousand years ago? I understood the concept of prayer; I was beginning to understand and believe we could communicate with angels, but how could we interact with, and personally know, Jesus?

One night, at the beginning of my meditation, I relayed my desire to meet Jesus, to John. He nodded his head, gave a big smile, and moved back to one side. Behind him stood the most magnificent being I had ever encountered. His image was bathed in a brilliant white light. I knew it was Jesus Christ, the Son of God. Being in his presence was so powerful and awe inspiring that I literally began to cry and shrank to the level of a small infant.

He asked me to come walk with him. He led me to a pond of still water where he sat on a rock at the shore. I sat on the ground in front of him. I took special notice of his leather sandals and reached out to touch them like a baby does when it wants to examine something new.

Oddly, I found myself talking to him in child-like sentences and he kept referring to me as his "child." I asked him why he called me a child since I was an adult and he said because I was just beginning to learn the Word of God and I was a "newborn in Christ." I asked him to perform a really big, observable miracle to prove to everyone that I had spoken to him and he said, *"I am your Counselor, Teacher, and Savior but I am not your magician."* He assured me, though, the affirmations and miracles would continue.

He said for me not to hide my light any longer but to shine it where others could see it. He said, *"Tell them what our Father has done for you."* I did not understand whom I was supposed to tell or what it was that I should tell them.

I was also told by Jesus that I substituted earthly things, or things of the World, for the love I truly need. He said that unconditional love was given by God. It was this love that I sought and must learn to fill up the hole in my heart with in order to find peace. Perhaps, this was what they had meant the first night at Lillian's when I heard, *"We provide the Love that you seek."* As we parted I heard the song, "Jesus loves me." I had not heard this song since childhood and even then I was not sure where I might have heard it since I never had attended church. Remarkably, as I put my oldest daughter to bed, I was able to sing her that song in its entirety.

The next morning, for the first time in the nearly two years since I had attended my church, a short parable about Jesus loving little children was spoken, and it was followed by the "Jesus loves me" song on bell chimes! In addition, the sermon was on what Jesus had told me the previous night — that we are born into Christ as naive infants and are nurtured and matured in the ways of the Lord for the rest of our lives. Was this another affirmation or another wild coincidence?

My curiosity was once again piqued. How could my non-religious brain have conjured up all of this? A few minor connections, maybe, but all of these intricate relationships seemed highly improbable.

Soon after learning the identity of John, who had told me that he was John, the Apostle, I had an unbelievable conversation with Jesus. While in my nightly meditation, he told me that he was sending back the spirits of his Apostles to physical bodies on the Earth in order to pave the way and ready the world for his second coming! I asked him, "Why them?" He said, *"Who better to teach the Gospel than my Apostles?"*

I asked him why he was beginning this process now and he said that he was not just beginning now. He said that the spirit of the Apostle Peter was in Rev. Billy Graham and the spirit of the Apostle Paul had been in the late Rev. Martin Luther King, Jr. He continued to say that I would be involved in helping *"to awaken these coming souls to remember who they truly are"* through the secret teachings he would be giving me. Apparently, even the Apostles were born into physical bodies in a state of slumber, needing to be awakened.

Stunned, I told Jesus that I did not believe any of what he was saying and that I was now convinced that I was just making all of this up in my imagination. As I began to depart from his presence, declaring never again to eat pepperoni pizza before bedtime, he said solemnly, *"Matthew was Thomas' father."*

My first thought was Thomas who? Ridiculously the first person to pop into my mind was Dave Thomas, the well-known local founder of the Wendy's hamburger chain. But Jesus said patiently, *"No, the Thomas in the Bible."* I had never heard of someone named Thomas in the Bible before. He went on to say,

"No one alive today knows this mystery." What mystery? Then he directed me to, *"Read Thomas."*

He then did something I did not understand. He called to an angel named Michael to appear before us. This angel, who towered above Jesus, was naked from his waist up. His upper body was lean and muscular. He had a leather-looking strap over his right shoulder descending crosswise down to his left side. Attached at the back I could see an arrow holder with multiple arrow tails sticking up from it.

Jesus said, *"Command your angels to watch over her and her soul mates. They are to be protected from all harm."* Michael replied in a resounding voice, *"As you command."* Then he disappeared. He looked to be a no nonsense type of angel! I felt immediately safe and reassured that I would be fine in whatever was about to take place.

The next morning when I awoke I remembered the weird discussion from the previous night and went to my Bible to prove that there was no one mentioned by the name of Thomas. I was surprised to find that there was such a person mentioned in the Bible and even more shocked to see that he had been one of the twelve original Apostles.

Interestingly, his name was linked to Matthew's several times throughout the Bible. In Matthew 10:2, where the names of the Apostle's were discussed, the brothers Peter and Andrew were together, James, and his brother John were together, and Matthew and Thomas were together. The relationship between the two was not identified.

Also, in Luke 6:12-15, this same type of linkage of related individuals occurred when the Apostles were listed. Here, although James and John are listed together, their relationship was not identified.

In a third instance, Mark 3:13-19, the names of Matthew and Thomas were also next to each other and were the known to be related Apostles. Only this time, the relationship between Peter and Andrew was overlooked.

Clearly, relationship descriptions were not always systematically included when discussing the Apostles in the Scripture texts. Could it be possible that the relationship between Matthew and Thomas was omitted or overlooked in the Gospels and if so what did Jesus want me to learn from this new knowledge?

I decided to call my minister to find out what he knew about Matthew and Thomas in order to put this issue to rest. I was curious about the second part of what Jesus had told me: that no one living today knew about this relationship.

Astonishingly, my minister concurred. He claimed that no one really knew for sure if there was any type of relationship between the two Apostles in question. He told me to call the public library if I wanted further information. The people at the public library were unable to help me with my search but they gave me the number to call at the Pontifical College Josephinum Library. Next I called Dan, certainly after his years of Bible study, he could answer my questions about the two

Apostles. Because his forte was research he was extremely helpful in guiding me in the right direction to attempt to prove, or disprove, as he liked to say, this assumption. He came up with some excellent suggestions for me to pursue: look for sources that showed where the two Apostles were from, their ages, who else knew them and their relationship to the others. As almost an afterthought, he told me to look in the *Book of Thomas*, which did not appear in the Bible.

I was confused. Why were there writings that did not appear in the Bible if they were written by one of the Apostles? Who determined which writings made the Biblical "cut?" Dan was not clear on this either but thought that there were probably some very good reasons why some of the Apostolic writings had been excluded from the New Testament. In any case, he was sure he had heard of a *Book of Thomas* somewhere before.

Although I had heard of the Josephinum most of my life, I had no idea what type of college it was outside of the fact that it had something to do with religion. I decided to make a visit and ask for assistance from their librarians in piecing together the facts of this story.

As I approached the library building on the campus complex, a feeling of regal awe overcame me — reminiscent of the time I had walked up to the Catholic church when just a child. For a moment, I hesitated remembering the once strong feelings of unworthiness.

Once inside, as I was walking towards the library, I saw a large oil painting hanging on the corridor wall of a religious man wearing a beanie-type cap. The picture looked familiar but I could not recall where I had seen him before.

The library itself was large and grandiose. Thousands of books lined the multiple shelves that extended hundreds of feet into the distance. The information desk stood in the center and two librarians, a male and a female, stood dutifully awaiting questions. I approached the tall middle-aged man who immediately asked me if he could be of some assistance. I explained that I was looking for information on the relationship between Matthew and Thomas.

He raised an eyebrow in a quizzical fashion and said, "I do not believe there was a relationship between Matthew and Thomas. What is this information for?" I could feel my heart beating faster. I did not want to tell a lie but, at the same time, how could I tell the truth, which would seem insane? I compromised and stated, "I'm a student and this is for a project I am doing." At this both of his eyebrows raised and in a sardonic manner he replied, "Well, unless the Pope decided to admit women to the priesthood while I was at lunch, you are not a student here!" Frightened I looked around the large room. For the first time I noticed that everyone was male and most were dressed in priestly attire. The Josephinum must be a Catholic school for priests! Now I recognized the man in the oil painting that I had just seen — it was the Pope!

M. Sue Benford

My mind flashed back to the cold front steps of the Catholic Church where I had been denied entrance into the sacred realm of the orthodox Christians. Once again, I was that little girl alone and was being turned away from what some Christians called God. The long ago forgotten feelings of sadness and exclusion swept over me.

I managed to muster up the courage to explain that I was a doing an independent study. I asked if he would help me find some information linking the two apostles. He once again claimed that there was not any information describing a relationship between the two apostles because there was <u>not</u> a relationship between the two apostles! With that, he turned around and began to walk away.

As he departed a strange feeling of empowerment engulfed me. I surprised myself when I rather loudly and confidently projected, "Are you sure about that?" The words rang like cymbals permeating the silent hush of the solemn library. Heads from nearby tables, previously bowed in quiet study, raised up to see where the unusual disturbance originated.

The librarian stopped in his tracks, slowly turned around and stared at me. My confidence somewhat waned but I continued to explain, "Well, I mean, their names are linked together several times in the Bible. Maybe, if we just looked for some general information we might find out why that is the case." Something must have awakened inside of him because from that moment on the librarians at the Josephinum became my willing assistants.

I learned more about the history and significance of this Pontifical College as well. The Josephinum, as it is locally known, was founded in 1888 by Joseph Jessing, a German immigrant who established a Roman Catholic seminary for orphans who wanted to study for the priesthood and then minister to German-speaking congregations. The Vatican granted the request in 1892 that the Josephinum become a pontifical institution, which made it the only pontifical seminary outside of Italy. It remains as such even today. It now serves students from around the world and contains a library reflective of its status.

I spent several days at the Josephinum Library working with their librarians to research this story. I discovered some remarkable information that started to support what Jesus had told me. I was becoming more than a little uncomfortable by the prospects.

I was not sure what I wanted more — to prove that I was receiving some "insider" information from God or to disprove it and live happily ignorant ever after. Let us face it, if this wild tale proved to be true then what about everything else I was being told?

I had not applied for the job of prophet. Many others were better suited and more qualified to receive these messages than I. Was I even strong enough to carry such a heavy burden?

Tediously, I pieced together facts from numerous documents — all bona fide articles sanctioned by the Catholic Church. Every now and again I would hear a whispered voice leading me to a certain piece of crucial data among the stacks of books I was given.

For days I sat shoulder to shoulder with seminary students and ordained priests in a reverent silence. There I was, with all the religious knowledge ascribed to a newborn, researching things that these wise and learned men did not have a clue about.

They gazed at me in wonder. It was obvious that I did not fit in — a woman among men, ignorant among wise, newborn among mature, and weak among strong. How ironic it was all beginning to seem.

On the final day that I had prepared to go look for information at the Josephinum, while walking into the building, I heard a voice say, *"You will find what you seek today."* I was excited by the prospect of finding the answer to this mystery regardless of what it turned out to be.

I began the day in my typical fashion, pouring over books and papers, when one of the librarians handed me a large textbook. She said, "I think you might find this interesting." The thick book was opened somewhere in the middle. I looked down and saw at the top of the page, *Book of Thomas*.

Somehow, in all my excitement, I had totally neglected to pursue Dan's suggestion about reviewing this alleged book. My heart began to beat faster. This was it. Somehow I felt it. This would contain a crucial piece to the puzzle.

I read the first passage of the Book and gasped, "The secret words that the Savior spoke to Judas Thomas (also known as Thomas) and which I, Matthew, wrote down. I was passing by and heard them speak with one another." What was Matthew doing writing another Apostle's secret Book? I knew the answer. It fit with everything else I had discovered. As much as I did not want to believe it maybe, just maybe, Matthew <u>was</u> Thomas' father!

I documented the complete story that I had received both from the historical references and from John and Jesus. As my understanding grew, mysteriously, so did the knowledge I had of these two Apostles, but especially, of Thomas. The story follows with the items in underline representing documented facts:

<u>Matthew was a tax collector</u>. He and his family, including his son Thomas, <u>lived in Capernaum</u>. When Jesus called them to be his disciples, Thomas was in his late teens and, obviously, Matthew was older. <u>He had been called later in life.</u> <u>Thomas, a fisherman, grew up knowing the Apostles John</u>, his brother James, Andrew and Peter. <u>The four, excluding Thomas, were friends who had formed a fishing business together. John and Thomas, although they shared the same trade and hometown</u>, were not close friends. <u>John was a positive, charming, insightful, and witty person; whereas, Thomas was pessimistic, moody</u> and often times seemed

to have "a chip on his shoulder." During their youth, John often called Thomas "the twin" because of his seemingly moody nature and dual personalities.

Being a tax collector, Matthew suffered from the disdain of many Jews. As a result of his father's dishonest and disreputable job, Thomas also suffered. Matthew had built quite a bit of wealth by the time Jesus called him but it was at the expense of others — even his son. More than anything, Matthew desired respect and admiration from his fellow man. He hoped his discipleship with Jesus would "redeem" him in other's eyes. He was so thrilled that he and his son, Thomas, had been chosen as part of the twelve, he celebrated with a feast at his house honoring Christ.

Matthew was an intelligent and well-educated man. He loved his son but felt guilty that he had caused him to suffer shame and ridicule. He also felt ashamed that Thomas had been outcast by his peers. Matthew realized that Thomas was not especially gifted in intelligence or in personality. He watched as his son interacted with the other Apostles and with Jesus. None of these interactions proved to redeem either his (as a parent) or his son's position as he had sought. He felt ashamed of Thomas' doubting of Christ's resurrection. This is one of the reasons he does not recognize Thomas as his son in his Gospel but merely places their names together as he does the brothers'. Matthew's shame also keeps him from recounting the important story of Thomas' doubting in his Gospel. This story was described in the *Gospel of John*.

Matthew was deeply concerned that Thomas' doubting would keep him from the Kingdom of God. In the *Gospel of John*, Jesus says to Thomas, "Because you have seen me, you have believed; blessed are those who have not seen and yet have believed." John 20:29 Matthew interpreted that as a sign that Thomas would not reach the Kingdom of God unless he could learn and could prove that he had "unquestionable faith in the unseen."

After Jesus' death, the spirit of the Son of God appeared to Thomas. He gave Thomas many revelations of great importance. Thomas was elated to be chosen to receive Christ's words and went to share his good fortune with his father. Matthew listened intently as Thomas recounted what the Lord had told him.

Matthew saw this as an opportunity to document Thomas' transformation, or "birth," and demonstrate Thomas' unquestionable faith as a result of the transformation. Therefore, in an unprecedented move, Matthew wrote the *Book of Thomas* on Thomas' behalf. Both Matthew and Thomas knew that Matthew was the better writer, better communicator, and more intellectually respected of the two. In no other case had one of the Apostles written an entire Book for another Apostle. The Book begins with, "The secret words that the Savior spoke to Judas Thomas (also known as Thomas) and which I, Matthew, wrote down. I was passing by and heard them speak with one another."

If the words were truly secret, then why was Matthew privy to them? Also, why did Matthew feel he had to justify how he came to hear the words? Did he think readers would believe he could hear and record an entire Book of detailed information just from merely "passing by?" Most importantly, why would Matthew not choose to claim this encounter with Christ in his own Book or in a separate writing of Matthew like the other Apostles did? Clearly, Matthew wanted it remembered as a story about Thomas and Thomas' redemption, and not about him. He was a father celebrating his son's second birth.

The *Book of Thomas*, that Matthew hoped would be respected as one of the revered documents of Christianity, represented the brightest picture ever portrayed of Thomas. In this Book, Thomas appears transformed into a deeply insightful, wise man, and most of all, a person of unquestionable faith. In one quote, when Thomas is talking to Jesus, he states, "You have indeed persuaded us, O Lord. We have reasoned in our heart and it is clear to us that this is so, and that your word is free of envy." No doubting in this Thomas!

Considering I had never before known of a Thomas in the Bible, let alone linked him in any way with Matthew, it seemed highly improbable that I could explain the creation of such an intricate story using current earth-based explanations alone. Imagination was one thing but this had now gone far beyond a mere dream or vision that could be explained away, at least entirely, by rational psychology. If only I had something tangible to rely on — a physical miracle.

One of the things I had always questioned were the so-called "medical miracles" people reported. Being a registered nurse who had seen more than her share of crackpot remedies that did nothing but delay appropriate medical care, I bristled when someone claimed God would cure them. Not that I had anything against prayer when it was combined with adequate and appropriate medical treatment. As a result of my intense skepticism, I felt this type of physical miracle would be out-of-the-question as a device for Jesus to prove what he was saying was true. However, within a week, I would be once again be proven wrong.

Having been extremely nearsighted since college, I always dreamed of a time when I would be able to see more than two feet in front of my face without glasses or contact lenses. Up until May of 1996, that was not possible.

I had gathered up the courage to undergo Radial Keratotomy (RK) surgery to correct my nearsightedness. The initial surgery consisted of "in-cuts" into the cornea of each eye with small scalpels. The procedure was not a picnic and the recovery was even less fun. But the worst part was that my eyes regressed — they became nearsighted again, following the surgery.

This was a rare occurrence, which could, supposedly, be corrected with surgical enhancements. This additional surgery was less involved but, unfortunately in my case, did not work either. On September 16, 1996 my doctor concluded that after three enhancements had failed, he would need to re-do the original in-cuts to both eyes. On that day my eyes were tested as having 20/70 vision.

The surgery, to the extent I would require it, was somewhat radical and carried an increased risk of corneal perforation with possible loss of vision. But it was the only hope remaining to improve my eyesight. My surgery was scheduled for September 24, 1996.

I had prayed quite a bit about my eyes and each time I got a rather confusing answer. John had promised me that everything would be fine. My eyes would not be harmed. What did that mean? I did not know what he meant except that I should not worry about it anymore.

The day prior to my surgery, I had lunch with a friend who worked in downtown Columbus. Driving had become difficult for me, especially in the afternoon and evening hours when my vision always got progressively worse. But this day turned out to be different.

On my way home after lunch at about 2:00 p.m., I noticed that suddenly I could see the street signs very clearly. In fact, everything looked perfectly clear. As it happened, I was passing the exit for my doctor's office at the time I noticed the dramatic improvement. Almost concurrently a voice said, "*Go to the doctor's office and have your eyes tested.*" I did as the voice suggested.

When I got to the doctor's office parking lot I heard the voice say, "*I perform miracles on even the highest of Jewish Holy Days.*" I did not understand what that meant. I had no knowledge of Jewish Holy Days or Jesus' perceptions of these holidays.

I went into the office and requested an eye exam. The receptionist claimed they were booked and could not see me. I informed her that I was not leaving until the doctor examined my eyes, which had seemingly made a remarkable recovery. I began to recite all the license plate numbers in the parking lot some 50 feet away! She worked me in immediately.

Sure enough, when they repeated the same exam they had done only a few days earlier, my eyes were a perfect 20/20. The doctor and his staff were amazed and said they had never seen instantaneous improvement like this so long after surgery. Obviously, my next day's surgery was canceled.

When I got home I looked on my calendar to record the date in my journal and saw the strange words "Yom Kippur." I immediately called Dan and he told me that Yom Kippur was one of the highest of Jewish Holy Days. He told me how Jesus had been condemned by the orthodox Jews for performing miracles on the Sabbath, which was a Jewish holy day. Jesus claimed that God never rested in helping his children and neither would he.

When I hung up the phone after talking to Dan I sat at my desk in a stunned silence. Had Jesus waited until this day, September 23, 1996, to make a special point? As I began recording the day's events in my journal I heard a voice proclaim,

"Know that I am Jesus Christ, Son of God the Creator who has been talking to you. Have faith until you have knowledge." I was not sure what the last part of his statement meant but I would soon find out.

Incredibly, my eyes remained 20/20 for only two hours. During subsequent visits, my doctor and I agreed that the surgery I would have undergone on September 24th could have led to severe corneal perforations and irreparably damaged my vision. He was spooked by the strange course of events and refused to perform any more surgery on me.

I remembered Jesus' earlier command to the angel, Michael, to protect me and my soul mates from harm. Did this have any relationship to that command? Is that what John had been referring to when he said my eyes would not be harmed?

Even though this miracle had been one of prevention, instead of long-term visual improvement, Jesus now had my complete attention. What did it all mean? Medical miracles? Matthew and Thomas? Jesus assured me that I would soon begin to see the bigger picture. He and the others would continue to spoon feed me information, as I became ready to accept and digest it. This had been my first test at interpreting what they told me — a practice run, a beginner's workout. The process had begun. The spiritual door that had been merely cracked now stood widely agape before me. With little baby steps, I tentatively walked through the spiritual portal.

Chapter Thirteen

The apple is much more than just red

The most pressing question on my mind at this point was "why me?" It just did not seem to make sense. Why give me, a virtual nobody in the world of religion, these tidbits? I took my concerns to Jesus one night in meditation.

He told me that I was being given certain understandings because I, like a child, was willing to listen and accept. He showed me some Scripture that said, "I praise you, Father, Lord of heaven and earth, because you have hidden these things from the wise and learned, and revealed them to little children. Yes, Father, for this was your good pleasure. All things have been committed to me by my Father. No one knows the Son except the Father, and no one knows the Father except the Son and those to whom the Son chooses to reveal him." (Mt. 11:25-27)

He said that for anyone to obtain the knowledge of the Kingdom of Heaven they would have to approach the lessons as an open-minded, receptive "child." Jesus used the example of trying to teach an older person, who had spelled the word "house" like "hous" all their life that the real spelling is "house." That person would be reticent to believe any alternative spelling was correct, but a child, who could not spell at all, would be accepting of the missing "e" which seemed strange and wrong to adults.

He said I was such a child in God's word. This was why I was being shown more of the "truth" than a lot of people. He said it was available for everyone to see who had the eyes to see it and the ears to hear it.

Jesus said that he was also telling me these truths for the same reason he told me the mystery about Matthew and Thomas. So that I would become more knowledgeable in lessons to be taught to, and eventually taught by, his returning

Apostles. As he said, where the Bible might teach that "an apple is red," although this is quite true, it is not the complete description of an apple.

A fuller understanding of apples would demonstrate that it is a fruit, it is edible, and it also comes in other colors. He said that without the full understanding of the apple we cannot fully appreciate its value to us. I was being given more knowledge about "spiritual apples" so that we may grow, become wise, and understand the truth as Jesus taught it.

Jesus also stressed to me that <u>all</u> of his teachings are important, not just those selected for the Bible. Without understanding all of his teachings we cannot hope to fully understand the truth; thus, we are destined to be in the dark. He asked me, *"who among you, living or dead, is worthy of judging which of my words has meaning and which does not?"* I did not have an answer.

He explained to me that, as early Christianity formed, there were many more teachings of his being taught by his disciples. These teachings had been hidden because it was not time for them to be revealed. He told me a story about someone named Constantine who had been a Roman Emperor in the early days.

He said that the Emperor Constantine had supported the early church's omission of certain teachings from the Bible partly because of a vision Christ had sent to him but also because of his own desire for worldly power. Constantine saw that increasing numbers of early Christians were leaving and disavowing societal life, which included paying taxes and producing progeny; both were needed to support the Roman Empire. These "monks" believed in pious and separate lives from the mainstream community. This threatened both the structure of the organizing Christian church and the Roman Empire.

Constantine shared his concerns with early church leaders who also were beginning to fear loss of control over parishioners, which in turn diminished their worldly control. They believed most of the problem stemmed from certain Christians' belief that they were a part of another world — a spiritual realm more powerful than the Earth realm in which they resided. These renegades also believed that they could communicate directly with Christ without the assistance of church authorities; thus, threatening the control and influence of the fledgling church.

These radicals, who claimed to follow several of the early Christian teachers like Apostles John, Thomas, and Paul, also believed that they had many opportunities to atone for their sin through reincarnation. In fact, the concept of "purgatory" stemmed from their early views and was so prevalent among all Christians that it lasted into the orthodox Christian era after the belief in reincarnation was officially denounced by the Catholic Church.

Jesus told me that many early Christians believed in all the teachings of his, including some secret teachings. Often times these secrets were only verbally transferred from one "all knowing" Christian to another — such was the truth of the story about Matthew and Thomas' relationship. A special initiation ritual was held to bring new Christians into the realm of those privy to the secret teachings, not in the attempt to exclude others, but merely because it was their time to "be born."

These all-knowing Christians had developed ears that could hear — they were no longer among the deaf. This growth had occurred through use of their sight, in seeing that the physical represented the spiritual, and through their mind by means of meditation, visions, and dreams.

But, why me and why now? I had not asked to participate in this new understanding. Jesus claimed that I had. He told me that this had always been my selected course. He said that even before I had been born into this life the seeds of my destiny had been sown. Jesus showed me this verse from one of the Psalms: ". . .All the days ordained for me were written in your book before one of them came to be." (Ps. 139:16) He said I would awaken within the light and then lead others to it as well. He claimed that I was destined to arise from *"one of the weakest to one of the strongest"* as he defined it.

What did my physical strength accomplishments have to do with this new spiritual discovery? How could one thing be compared to the other?

Although I had never recognized any type of spiritual calling in myself before, deep inside me I had an odd feeling that I was forgetting something that I never altogether knew. I began to recollect long forgotten times when I was a child and used to write poetry to express my inner thoughts. Jesus told me that these had been inspired by my angels as prophecy of things to come.

He led me to my old childhood journal where I had hand written my long forgotten poems. The journal's pages had become worn and tattered. The ink and pencil marks were fading but still revealed the large child-like script that I barely remembered putting down on the pages. I turned to one of the poems that had caused great trauma in my life. I had written it when I was only twelve years old as a part of an assignment for school.

I remembered the day my teacher passed back all the graded class poems. Mine was not with them. He said he wanted to talk to me about my poem. He said he could not grade my work because he did not believe a child my age could have written it.

He asked me where I had found it. I felt faint. My life goal was to be good. I never would have dreamed of doing such a bad thing as cheating. I told him it was my own work.

He said he would hold the poem until the end of the grading period while he searched literature to find the name of the true author. If he found it I would receive an "F" for the class. If he did not find it I would receive an "A." Since it truly was an original he never found the poem. Was there really some deeper insight in that poem that foretold of my destiny and perhaps gave insight into the destiny of humankind? Was I seeing beyond the mere physical into, perhaps, the spiritual? This was my ungraded poem:

Deafman, have you listened?

Deafman, have you listened,
To the songs the young birds sing,
Or to the wind against the sky,
To the sounds of early spring?

Deafman, have you listened,
To the quiet of the night,
Or to the falling leaves against,
The ground in Autumn light?

Deafman, have you listened,
To a herd of cattle lo,
Or to a child's laughter,
In a deep December snow?

Deafman, have you listened,
To the squeaking of a gate,
Or to the crackling of a fire,
Burnt in the night so late?

Deafman, you can listen,
Through your sight and through your mind,
And then someday you will hear,
The sounds of all mankind.

    I had no earthly idea where I had gotten the insight for that poem. I had never known anyone who was physically deaf. Did this have something to do with me having "the ears to hear" and teaching others that they, too, could hear? Why, at that particular age, was I being inspired with this type of spiritual insight?
    There were other unexplainable things that I wrote as a child. Things that seemed divinely inspired in one way or another. I began reading my old journal with a renewed interest and insight. One of the more interesting poems I had written, still only twelve, was written from a third-party perspective:

M. Sue Benford

The Worth of Life

Swing high, my child, swing high,
And pump to your life's goal,
Do not slow or stop on the way,
Or naught will be thy soul.

Ropes of twine are built to lift,
You to the heavens sky,
Bring your goals to their full,
Swing high, my child, swing high.

What "goals" was I referring to? I had no goals or at least I did not know of any at the time. There was a strange connection made in this poem between the physical "ropes of twine" being somehow designed to lift us into the realm of "heaven." Was this what Jesus was trying to explain to me about how the physical world propels us forward into the spiritual world both in lessons learned and by its very representation of the spiritual? And what was the symbolism of slowing or stopping our development leading to the nonexistence of our souls?

Then there was the poem I never had understood. When I reread this poem after more than twenty-six years I, still, only barely grasped it's meaning. It was strangely apocalyptic in nature. Did it somehow reflect the "unawakened," the living dead, those who had "stopped pumping the swing of life?" Was it a prophecy of what was to become of unenlightened souls?

I recalled sitting at my desk, barely thirteen at the time, and "recording" these words - words that seemed to come from elsewhere. A meaning so deeply hidden that I consciously could not understand it.

Death

If the sky was filled with emptiness,
And no heaven resided in its domain,
And hell was but a poet's thought,
In the imagination of his brain.

If the world's speck of time were to perish,
And the causes of the earth were forlorn,
And the people were but nothing,
In their grave of death and mourn.

Their mind, their conscious not aware of their state,
And the existence of reality lying immobile in time,
The world now unyielding to their senses,
And the senses unyielding to the mind.

When all are gone who have built the earth,
And the graves have vanished from within the ground,
And with time now sleeping idly without a cause,
Darkness moves in without a sound.

And then, I came across one of the final poems in my journal. It ominously supported what Jesus said about me having agreed to this particular "mission" that I was now beginning. A poem written during the brief two-year period I attended church. It was a prayer. A prayer, written prior to my high school graduation, which represented a turning point in my life- a prayer that eerily depicted my journey to come.

Graduation Prayer

Dear Lord, give me strength to break away,
And help me to see the good in leaving here today.
Prepare me to face a future full of unknown paths ahead,
Help me to see the beauty of the world.

Enable me to give myself so that others can find the sun,
And show me the way to lead them all home,
And most importantly stand by me all the way,
Until my work is done.
Amen

My childhood journal ended with the following story — an entry about, what I later came to know, were soul mates.

M. Sue Benford

Two Rainbow Geese

And once, two geese flew south. Each alone, without a flock, they encountered the unknown. But as fate would have it, the two rainbow geese met. As familiarity grew, their outstretched wings touched more often and the two found strength was in companionship.

As days passed, the wind blew harder and colder. The geese relied upon one another to provide the warmth and security they needed to survive. Times were hard, but the two colorful birds pulled through with an even stronger reliance and trust for each other.

Spring ended. The hot summer sun began to scorch the geeses' beautiful wings. Time had come to head north. Parting was hard, they knew summer was a long season and many geese did not survive. But their love was strong and steadfast. And in their hearts they were certain that as winter approached, two rainbow geese would once again be seen flying south.

    Still struggling with the question "why me," one night in my meditation, Jesus said something that, at first, I did not completely understand. He said, "*Do not make the sign of the cross, but live the sign of the cross. Look at yourself to know I am with you*"
    The next morning while I was standing undressed in front of the mirror I noticed something that I had never paid attention to before. The surgical scars on my abdomen formed the sign of the cross. Carved in my body, by the most painful experiences of my life, was the sign representing Jesus. The wire sutures that irritatingly poked through the outer surface of my flesh, and that I had long struggled to ignore, now focused my attention on a much different image.
    I went to my Bible and he showed me this passage: " . . .If anyone would come after me, he must deny himself and take up his cross daily and follow me." (Luke 9:23) I had no choice but to take up my cross daily, it had been permanently imprinted on me a long time before — maybe even longer ago than I realized.
    Jesus then showed me Paul's words to the Galatians, "Finally, let no one cause me trouble, for I bear on my body the marks of Jesus." (Gal. 6:17) Did I, like Paul, bear the mark of Jesus on my body? Had it been a mere coincidence that my child-sized, weakened torso, marked by the cross, had grown in such strength as to

defeat the very forces of the World itself and surpass those of the World? I was stunned by this remarkable possibility.

Jesus had proven his point. Perhaps I had asked for this mission in life. But what exactly was it that I would have to do to fulfill this preordained role? The picture was slowly unfolding.

Chapter Fourteen

Heaven's library

For many nights and days to come I continued to receive a plethora of insights about early Christianity, Jesus' teachings, and new understandings that clarified certain Christian beliefs. A whole new world was opening up to me that was all at once thrilling, simplistic, complex and alarming. As soon as I would be told a new "revelation" I would almost immediately be led to a source for documentation or additional insights. That is, until one particular night.

Always in the past, I "met" Jesus and John in a meadow through meditation. But one night that all changed. As I began to mentally journey into the meadow, I was guided in an alternate direction. This I found very peculiar. Jesus took my hand and, along with John, we ascended a large staircase that led to a closed door.

When he opened the door we all walked into a small room that appeared to be a library. It was very small and I could only see books on one far wall that extended from the floor to the ceiling. The room had a few rectangular-shaped wooden tables that were old and worn. The floor was hardwood. My first thought was, that if this was heaven's library they were really lacking in reading material!

Jesus motioned for me to sit at one of the table. He then approached the wall of books and started pulling several from the shelves. They were dusty and obviously had not been used in a while. He continued to walk back and forth looking for books. Occasionally he pulled one out and set it in front of me.

Nothing was said during this time and I could not see the titles on the books. The only thing I knew for sure was that I was supposed to be reading something that had not been read in quite a while. What it was, I had no idea and they would not say.

For three nights this same routine continued. I was getting increasingly confused and frustrated. Where and what were these books? Would someone tell me what I was supposed to do next?

It appeared as if I were at a crossroads. Most of the time before I was shown passages in the Bible, or related interpretations of the Bible, that helped guide my understanding of what I was being told. Now, however, I was receiving insights outside the realm of the Biblical text alone. My hard-line position was that if it could not be supported by known documentation I refused to believe it. That was the scientist in me. I refused to cast off this treasured objectiveness that I valued in my personality. Was I at a dead end with no objective way of proving any new insights or stories Jesus was teaching me?

One day out of the blue, I received a letter from an old friend whom I had not kept in contact with but whose friendship I had always treasured. It had been well over a year since I had last heard from her. We met for lunch and I told her about my recent spiritual experiences. As it happened, she was married to a Methodist minister who now worked in the church organization. I had known both of them for many years and considered Ted a wise and open-minded professional. With her encouragement, I scheduled a meeting with him to discuss the strange visions and dreams that I was having.

When we met I told him about all of the experiences I was having from ethereal voices to dreams and visions. He said that a lot of what I was describing sounded vaguely familiar to him. He said it sounded like the beliefs of the early "Gnostic" Christians. I asked him who and what were the Gnostics and he said they were the "knowing" people who felt they contained within themselves the divine spark of God.

Ted said that these Gnostics, or heretics as the orthodox called them, faded out when orthodox Christianity gained strength with the conversion of Emperor Constantine in the 4th century. They believed that everyone who had been initiated into gnosis could receive revelations from Christ. They also shunned the material world in search of more spiritual callings. They became the pious "monks" in many cases.

A shiver ran down my spine. Was the story that Jesus had told me of Constantine's involvement in the demise of certain early Christian beliefs going to turn out to be true? Were these the "all knowing" Christians that Jesus was referring to in our discussions? How would I find out more about these teachings? I had more questions than answers.

I relayed to Ted what Jesus had told me about Constantine and the fact that the monks' refusal to participate in society, especially in paying taxes, was one of the causes of the Emperor's alliance with the orthodox Christians. Ted said that he did not know if that was true, but suggested that I read about early Christian history. He was not sure it would help answer the questions that I had but it would be a start.

He also reassured me that my experiences were not completely unprecedented. Apparently, others like me were experiencing similar types of "awakenings." I felt better about that fact but was still uneasy about not being able to document Jesus' stories.

That night, as I laid in bed attempting to go into meditation, for some unknown reason, my thoughts seemed to be blocked. Over and over again I heard what sounded like one word — *"Naghamdi."* Where had I seen or heard that word before? Neither Jesus nor John would talk to me except to keep repeating that strange, indiscernible word.

Remembering what Ted had told me about the "knowing," or Gnostics, and comparing that to what Jesus had told me about the "all knowing," I saw a possible connection to pursue in the literature. The day after our meeting, I called the bookstore to inquire about any material available with the word "Gnostic" in the title.

One reference they told me about was a book written by a history professor named Dr. Elaine Pagels. The book was entitled The Gnostic Gospels. Something inside of me fluttered. I immediately headed off to retrieve it from the bookstore.

On my way I started to get a strange feeling. It was as if there was some kind of electrical current running through my body. This was something that I had never felt before. I was at a loss to explain where this weird and sudden sensation had come from.

As I arrived at the bookstore and walked up to the "books on hold" counter, the sensation intensified. The clerk was busy with another customer and stood, with his back to me, about ten feet away. There were over a hundred books on the shelves above awaiting the arrival of purchasers.

As I gazed over the groupings of indistinguishable books, I felt a swishing current go through me. Almost simultaneously, the clerk shuddered as if he were having a slight seizure of some sort. Immediately after that, one solitary book fell from its shelved position with a loud thud.

Moments later when the clerk turned to me and asked for the title of my book, I was not surprised when the book he located had been the one to fall. Intuitively I knew it was my book and I knew what the angels were trying to tell me — I was on the right track again.

The author of the book, Elaine Pagels, appeared to be a renowned authority on early Christian teachings. After receiving her doctorate from Harvard University in 1970, she taught at Barnard College, where she chaired the Department of Religion. At the time her book was published, she was a Harrington Spear Paine Professor of Religion at Princeton University. The Gnostic Gospels had won the National Book Critics Circle Award and the National Book Award in 1980.

I began reading Pagels' book and was stunned. It was starting to all come together. I was beginning to understand what Jesus and John had been teaching me. In some strange way, too, I was able to see beyond Pagels' very words.

"What Quispel held in his hand, the *Gospel of Thomas*, was only one of the fifty-two texts discovered at *Nag Hammadi*." (Pagels, Gnostic Gospels, page xv). There was that name I had heard the night before and thought was *Naghamdi*! I kept reading as lesson after lesson was revealed or, at least, hinted at.

Pagels reveals how the Emperor Constantine's conversion completely changed Christianity and gave military and political power to the sect for the first time. But instead of accepting all the Christian sects, Constantine aligned himself with the more organized Orthodox groups who supported his own political agenda, which included building Rome through added resources of more people and taxes. Sects, like the Gnostics, who denounced such a strong focus on procreation and material possession, saw their books and lifestyles crushed by the new regime.

Fortunately, not all the books were destroyed. Apparently, in Upper Egypt, a monk from a nearby Monastery took the banned books and hid them from destruction — in a jar where they remained buried for almost 1,600 years. Although Pagels does not mention the specific issues that finally drove Constantine and the Church into each other's arms, other texts I would soon discover did help confirm the answers to that question — worldly power appeared to be a central issue. These long-forgotten Gnostic gospels must have been the books Jesus had been leading me to in "heaven's library."

Jesus had said that these teachings were hidden for a reason, it was not the right time for them to be revealed. Several historians suggest that major themes of Gnostic teaching, such as the discovery of the divine within, appealed to so many that they constituted a major threat to the orthodox, Catholic doctrine. After all, the religious perspectives and methods of gnosticism did not lend themselves to mass religion since the primary focus for the Gnostic was finding spirituality from within instead of through regimented rituals and ceremonies.

For the time, the regimentation of Christianity was required to orchestrate and perpetuate the small sect's growth. Without the downfall of early gnosticism, Christianity would have perished. All of Jesus' teachings along with the message of human salvation accomplished by his death would have been lost forever. Instead, by allowing the orthodox Christians to thrive, Christianity survived and flourished throughout the centuries.

But today is a new day. Was it a mere coincidence that both the findings at Nag Hammadi and the Dead Sea Scrolls were unearthed within eighteen months of each other after having both been buried for some 1,600 years? Was it finally time to reveal the hidden truths that Jesus taught to his disciples? And how will we be taught the things that were "lost to us?" Apparently, the same way they were taught to Jesus' earlier disciples — through our "personal" relationship with Jesus and by the grace of the Holy Spirit.

Discovering Pagels' work started my new journey in more ways than one. She had written several other books that I immediately purchased but, deep down, knew I really did not have to read. I already knew what they would say and which of the Apostles would be saying it.

But more importantly, I had found the support and documentation I needed to believe my revelations. My life's work in God's service was becoming clearer but there was still work to be done on my own soul. I had already learned that we do not get out of this life without addressing both of these tasks. I was still here for two reasons and certain that I would be given still other chances to lift my emotional veil and transform my growing soul.

M. Sue Benford

Chapter Fifteen

Please, God, not again!

My mother's life story was one of challenge and opportunity, weakness and strength, lessons given and lessons learned. Her fight against alcoholism and depression took a turn in her favor in 1978 when she finally obtained treatment and medication for her illness. She started on her own road to recovery.

We, too, began to recover as a family. Our fragile and sometimes volatile relationship began to improve. We grew much closer to one another as a result. Throughout the ensuing years she became my mentor, friend, confidant, but most of all, my unconditionally loving mother. One of the few remaining people I could trust to be there for me.

One day in mid-September 1996, she asked me to look at her neck. When she lifted her head I saw a large, very noticeable golf ball sized lump on the right side of her throat. She went to a doctor, within the week, who performed an ultrasound on the area. The test concluded that there was a mass in her thyroid area but it was on her left side not right.

The growth itself was still relatively small and had not been large enough to be seen by the naked eye. The protrusion we had noticed on her right side, that had sent her to the doctor in the first place, turned out to be an "illusion." The doctor said that perhaps what we had seen was some scar tissue left over from a previous surgery. The truth was, he really did not know what I had seen as it appeared to be gone. However, surgery would be required to remove the tumor that had been discovered.

I began to worry. My mother had been a smoker since she was a teenager. I feared, more than anything, that this detrimental habit would someday take her life. I asked both Jesus and John in my meditation whether she was going to die soon. They both agreed that she would not die at this particular time but they left me with an ominous revelation: this was just the beginning, a warning sign of worse trouble ahead. What did that mean? Would she die from some new problem that had not yet been discovered?

Immediately before surgery, the doctor ordered an ultrasound to be done on her carotid arteries to determine how the flow of blood was to her brain. The report was dismal and surgery was nearly canceled. The report showed that both sides were almost completely blocked. Surgery could cause a stroke.

After much deliberation they decided to proceed. Remarkably the doctor found a benign thyroid tumor but, hidden behind it, was a small growing cancerous tumor as well. This tumor had not been seen on the ultrasound. Rarely were both types of tumors found in the thyroid at one time. She was fortunate they found the benign tumor in the first place.

All the cancerous matter plus half of the thyroid was removed. She was on the road to recovery except that now she had to deal with her occluded neck arteries. She scheduled an appointment with a vascular surgeon who sent her for an angiogram to confirm the degree of blockage in the arteries.

Remarkably, the report showed only minimal occlusion in the arteries. For some reason the prior ultrasound had been grossly in error. But the real problem had now surfaced: she had a moderately large "aneurysm," a balloon-like protrusion in the wall of an artery, in the center of her brain.

She was immediately referred to a neurosurgeon for advice. From his evaluation of the angiogram report he stated that she could do one of two things: let the aneurysm go and risk a slight chance of rupture or have surgery to correct the problem. The choice was hers to make.

Just having undergone the thyroid surgery, her first choice was to leave the aneurysm alone. After all, the doctor had said the choice was "50/50." But something inside me knew this would be a deadly mistake. This whole series of events had taken place to lead us to the discovery of this potentially deadly aneurysm. Every fiber of my being knew that this had been a fabricated series of observations, erroneous tests, phantom masses, and relatively minor surgery to lead us to this discovery. I told my mother my feelings and my visions. She opted to have the surgery.

The week of her surgery we took one of our typical shopping trips to the local grocery store. I watched as she walked ahead of me, pushing her shopping cart, for what might be the last time. Pushing a shopping cart: such an inconsequential activity to remind me of my beloved mother. .

But I realized that is what life is really made up of — numerous moments of the mundane. Moments that do not in and of themselves mean very much but when added together form a lifetime. And that was my mother. Through the bitter and through the sweet, facing death and facing life, she had always been there for me as best she could. Was this to be the end?

On the way home from that shopping trip she revealed her concerns that she may not make it through the surgery. The doctor had said the risks were high, especially considering her weakened condition. There was a chance the aneurysm would rupture during surgery and that she would never regain consciousness. She told me all the practical things I should know in case of her death.

Most of all, she wanted me to help my father and be good to him. She claimed that he really did love me although he had never been able to tell me himself. His own life had been overshadowed by a destitute childhood growing up during the Great Depression. The youngest of five surviving children from an immigrant family, his own father was killed when he was barely two months old; thus, forcing my grandmother to take two jobs just to put food on the table. My father had been left to be raised by an abusive older brother. The scars his life had created left deep and lasting imprints on the man, and father, he was to become. His fear, anger, and insecurity had kept us emotionally distant. I do not ever recall having a personal conversation with him or receiving a single word of love or encouragement. But deep down I knew my mom was right — my dad really did love me, even if he could not express it.

When I got home that night I flashed back to the other losses in my life; but I still could not cry. Could not cry for them and could not cry for me. Soon, I thought, God will run out of people to take from me. Deep down I knew I was back in that same old place where I repeatedly found myself — at the threshold of a lost love and too afraid to reveal my feelings.

The day before my mother's surgery I talked to her for what might have been the final time. She called me with one last list of things for me to do. We went over some of the basics. I started to see how dependent she had been on my father and he on her. She asked me to help him with the shopping and cooking. He also did not know how to do laundry or keep the checkbook. I could not believe we were having this discussion; me taking over her duties, maybe forever.

The list of the routine things had started to wrap up and it was time to say good-bye. My mother had never been a verbally demonstrative person but today was different. As we concluded our conversation, she said, "I love you." The words rung in my ears like the clanging of cymbals. There it was again, that phrase, that declaration of the vulnerable.

I closed my eyes and the words my brother spoke to me echoed in the darkness, "You need to tell people that you love them before they leave their physical life — that's when we learn our lessons." Was this yet another opportunity for me to redeem my soul? And then I said it, "I love you, too, Mom." And I really meant it. I cried myself to sleep that night.

My mother's surgery was long and tenuous but successful. The aneurysm had been on the verge of rupturing. There was a tissue paper thin protrusion that further weakened the structure. The doctor had not seen this on the angiogram. He concluded that without the surgery she would have been dead in a very short period of time.

As everybody claimed, it was truly a miracle that the aneurysm was found in time to save her life. But I knew that was not the only miracle that had taken place. Another life was being saved, too — mine.

M. Sue Benford

Chapter Sixteen

Where did I come from?

"Where did I come from?" It is a question that children routinely ask their parents. We are creatures born with an innate curiosity about our origins — not only of our physical self but our spiritual self as well.

How difficult it is for us as adults to explain to our young children how they came to be created! Should we tell them about the intricate details of sexual intercourse, DNA, or the stages of fetal growth? We could. But how much would they comprehend? Instead, we simplify the science in an attempt to make it as easy for children to understand within their own developmental parameters. In essence, we do for them exactly what Jesus did for us.

It is important for the young child in all of us to have a basic sense of "knowing" about his or her origins. Before we can understand our life's tasks, our inherited traits, and our soul's journey it is imperative that we know who we truly are. If we do not know what our true heritage is and what all of our gifts are then we will never be able to make full use of our talents, either for God's service or our own soul's journey. It is that simple.

I am reminded of a story our minister told during a sermon about a young Indian boy who finds a large egg that has fallen from it's nest. He takes the egg back to his tribe to let the elder's identify its species. They believe it is an eagle egg.

Since the eagle has lost its mother, the tribesmen give the egg to a mother hen to hatch and raise. Sure enough, when the egg hatches a little eaglet is born. The eaglet grows up among the chicken and comes to believe that it, too, is a chicken. It does not fly because chickens do not fly.

One day, the eaglet looks up into the sky and sees a large eagle soaring majestically overhead. The eaglet proclaims that he, too, would like to soar like the eagle. His chicken mother tells him to forget such wild thoughts because, after all, he is just a chicken.

After hearing that story, I realized why Jesus was telling me about how we, as human beings, came into existence, why we were on Earth, and what it all meant. One of the first lessons I learned dealt with the creation of our souls.

As Jesus explained it to me, similar to how the human body reproduces itself the spirit also reproduces itself once it has become "perfect." Once perfected, the soul takes its rightful place in the eternal Tree of Life. He said that as we have earthly parents so, too, we have spiritual parents. He showed me a story that represents this lesson in the Old Testament.

The story is of the prophet Elijah who transfers his spirit to his "son" Elisha. "When they had crossed, Elijah said to Elisha, 'Tell me, what can I do for you before I am taken from you?' 'Let me inherit a double portion of your spirit,' Elisha replied. 'You have asked a difficult thing,' Elijah said, 'yet if you see me when I am taken from you, it will be yours — otherwise not.' As they were walking along and talking together, suddenly a chariot of fire and horses of fire appeared and separated the two of them, and Elijah went up to heaven in a whirlwind. Elisha saw this and cried out, 'My father! My father!. . .'" (2Kings:2:9-11)

Jesus said that Elisha, who knew that Elijah was not his biological father, also realized at that point the truth about spiritual parents. Elijah had reproduced his perfected spirit into his spiritual progeny represented by Elisha.

In *The Gospel of Thomas* it states, "Jesus said, 'Blessed is the one who came to life before coming to life. . .For there are five trees in Paradise for you. They do not change, summer or winter, and their leaves do not drop. Whoever knows about them will not taste death.'"

Once a soul is fully transformed spiritually it is granted eternal life among the trees in Paradise. These perfected spirits then reproduce spiritual offspring in still developing souls and, thus, pass along various characteristics to succeeding generations. In this way, a part of them always stays alive through their spiritual progeny.

The concept of living trees within heaven or Paradise is known from other Gnostic texts as well as from the Bible: Genesis 2:9, Revelation 2:7, 22:2. ". . .on each side of the river stood the Tree of Life, bearing twelve crops of fruit, yielding its fruit every month. And the leaves of the tree are for the healing of the nations." (Rev. 22:2) Were our souls the fruits that were being yielded from the twelve crops?

Jesus likened our souls to a growing fetus in development. He showed me a long timeline with many physical bodies along the horizontal axis representing many physical incarnations. Parallel and above this physical existence was a second timeline. This timeline showed a developing fetus growing slowly across time and overlapping the boundaries of many incarnations. This represented our spiritual growth and development in the "flesh" of the soul. During one of the physical lifetimes we would be "born," and like human newborns, we would be distressed at first with our new surroundings. The bright lights, freedom of movement, and loving beings all around us would, initially, invoke shock. Dr. M. Scott Peck recognized this phenomenon, too, in his book Further Along the Road Less Traveled, when he aptly recognizes the fact that we may experience our transformation not necessarily as an "Oh joy!" phenomenon, but often as an "Oh shit!" phenomenon. (Peck, page 231)

This idea was also portrayed in *The Gospel of Thomas*, "Jesus said, 'Let one who seeks not stop seeking until one finds. When one finds, one will be disturbed. When one is disturbed, one will be amazed, and will reign over all.'" Our comprehension of the truth makes us realize that we stand beside Jesus and not behind or beneath him. We, too, are eagles.

Amazingly, other Gnostic texts seemed to also support the idea of a spiritual pregnancy and fetal development culminating in a birth. In the *Discourse on the Eighth and the Ninth* the author discloses an "order of tradition" that guides the ascent to higher knowledge. He or she explains that the disciple alone must bring forth the understanding he seeks: "I set forth the action for you. But the understanding dwells in you. In me, (it is) as if the power were pregnant." The author, acting as teacher, suggests that they both must pray that the disciple reach the "eighth and the ninth."

Did this reflect the nine months of fetal development before birth occurred? Was this the physical world, once again, mirroring the spiritual world?

Both the lessons that we learned in each lifetime plus the nourishment we received through the "spiritual umbilical cord" determined if we continued to live and thrive or if we eventually died, were "miscarried," and did not return to the Earth with more opportunities for growth and development. Growth occurred while we were in physical form.

In *The Secret Book of James* it states, "For the Father knows about desire, and what the flesh needs: the flesh does not long for the soul. For the body never sins apart from the soul, and the soul is never saved apart from the spirit. But if the soul is saved from evil, and the spirit too is saved, then the body becomes sinless. For the spirit animates the soul, but the body kills the soul." (Chapter 7:8-11)

Could the spirit of a person actually die and fail to be reincarnated into a new lifetime if it failed to embrace and accept spiritual nourishment? If the soul really could be depicted as a fetus, the analogy would be similar to a miscarriage where death occurred before birth. Fetal death, or soul death, then, could presumably occur all the way throughout the "pregnancy" regardless of what levels of development had been previously obtained.

If this were true then it would stand to reason that we must always keep growing and nurturing our souls with the "fuel" of the spirit. When left to pursue only bodily desires, or desires created by the World, the soul can not be spiritualized to its fullest extent because the focus is away from higher spiritual tasks and replaced by those of the lower body (flesh). Therefore, it is possible for the body to kill the soul and; thus, destroy our spirit. It is a death caused by the rejection of God's paramount Law — Love.

Just as blood is the life force of the body, the divine spirit is the life force of the soul. And just as a human fetus is transformed into a newborn infant through receiving adequate nourishment from its parent, so too is the fetal soul transformed into perfected spirit through receiving adequate nourishment from its parent. Both are transformed into images of the parent.

Jesus said that it was important to understand that we never truly regress in our development. Where it might appear that we "back slide" in our faith and become "doubters like Thomas," only demonstrates the *"quieting of a larger fetus ready to be born."*

It made some sense. Larger, more mature fetus' did often stop moving as much in the womb simply because they were starting to outgrow the facility. This did not mean that the fetus had lost the ability to move but, quite the contrary, had actually grown past smaller, less mature counterparts.

Jesus claimed that God had given us earth-based examples that mirror our heavenly creation. He told me to, *"Look out your window and behold the workings of heaven."* I recalled something he had told me earlier that I now recognized as coming from *The Lord's Prayer*,

". . . thy will be done on earth as it is in heaven." Was that true? Was there some connection between the way things happened in our physical/visible environment and the way they happened in the spiritual/invisible realm? I had never read *The Lord's Prayer* in that way before. My eyes were being opened to new images and understandings.

In *The Gospel of Thomas* it states, "Jesus said, 'Know what is within your sight, and what is hidden from you will become clear to you. For there is nothing hidden that will not be revealed." Apparently, once we have figured out the analogies between the physical environment and spiritual realm, we will be able to fully understand heaven. The goal is not to keep anything a secret from us but rather that we are given certain knowledge at certain developmental levels. Otherwise, it would be as futile and frustrating as giving a twelfth grade textbook to a first grader.

I found documentation that both earlier and later 20th century philosophers and scholars seemed to be pulled to these same theories of creation. One such person was Rudolf Steiner (1861- 1925). This Austrian-born scholar was renowned for his contributions in science, literature and philosophy, especially his work on Goethe's scientific writings. After the turn of the century his focus turned to psychological and spiritual phenomena. His multifaceted genius led to innovative and holistic approaches in medicine, science, education, architecture, religion, economics, agriculture and many other fields. In 1924 he founded the General Anthroposophical Society, which today has branches throughout the world.

In a book excerpting his many lectures entitled The Spiritual Hierarchies and the Physical World: Reality and Illusion, Steiner had some remarkably similar things to say about our creation. His basic premise was that during each lifetime a little, or a lot, of a person's "astral" or spiritual body was transformed with complete transformation being the long-term goal.

Steiner believed that once a person had been completely transformed or "perfected," they could transfer or project some of their self to others. What a person achieves through perfection, however, is passed on to others who have certain tasks to accomplish in the world. Thus, the spirits of earlier individuals are interwoven and assimilated into the souls of later individuals.

Was Steiner describing what I was independently learning from Jesus? Was the "sacrifice" of the spirit actually more of a reproduction process than a true loss of being?

This idea of a "progressively developing soul" was also being thought about by modern day philosophers. In his book, Further Along The Road Less Traveled, M. Scott Peck describes four stages of spiritual development ranging from the least transformed to the truly enlightened. Was there a pattern developing among all of us who had thought deeply about these issues and received lessons from our spiritual mentors? What did the Bible have to say about all of this? Would I find similar things in the Scripture?

Chapter Seventeen

Who was the Apostle Paul?

Since I knew that God was methodical and organized in his creations, it stood to reason his process for creation itself would be similar. Jesus showed me Scripture that supported some of the unbelievable things he was claiming — mostly he showed me lessons taught by the Apostle Paul. But why the focus on Paul? Was there some significance to him a part from the others?

I intuitively felt that there was something special about the Apostle Paul. Along with having "met" both John and Thomas, I had recently been introduced to Paul as well. He appeared to be older than the others. He had long grayish hair and a long gray beard. He wore the same long white robe tied at the waist that both Jesus and John wore. He was pleasant and joyful as he talked.

He told me that he was the original author of the Scripture named *Hebrews*, that it had been his final writing, and that he considered it one of his best works. I had never read the Scripture called *Hebrews*, did not know what it contained, and had no idea why this was being revealed to me now. My Bible listed *Hebrews* as being of "unknown" authorship. Why was I being told that it had been written by Paul, and what difference did it make anyway?

With the information I had been given I, once again, returned to the Josephinum Library. Looking through the biblical encyclopedias I found some startling pieces to the puzzle. Apparently, Paul had been a prolific writer whose thoughts were abundantly portrayed throughout the New Testament in the form of letters to one group of people or another. The reference material cited his career as falling between the years of 33 AD and 64 AD when the Necronian persecution began. His last imprisonment, and execution occurred soon after in 65 AD.

The writings attributed to Paul appeared to have begun with the letter to the *Galatians* in 48 AD and ended with *2 Timothy* in 65 (?) AD. I could see an image of him writing by moonlight from a dark and dingy prison cell. I saw him passing, through the cell's window, some sort of rolled up paper-like material to his disciple, named Luke. It seemed as if he was doing his writing in secret, away from the watchful eyes of the prison guards who he knew would disapprove.

The reference material related to *Hebrews* discussed its creation date as, most likely, sometime in the early 60's AD. The timing was right: Paul conceivably could have written *Hebrews* in his final days. But who did historians believe had written *Hebrews*?

Apparently, the early Christians had been convinced that *Hebrews* was written by, none other than, Paul. It was not until the time of the Reformers that the Pauline tradition was challenged by Erasmus, Luther, and Calvin who all questioned Paul's authorship.

There it was in black and white. Once again, like with the story of Matthew and Thomas, it looked like something I was being told just might be true, although few, if any, other living people could legitimately validate it. But the bigger question remained unanswered — so what?

Numerous scholars discovered that the Naassenes and Valentinians revered Paul as one of their own Gnostic initiates. Additionally, Valentinian theologians paid special attention to what they knew as Paul's letter to the *Hebrews*.

Hebrews illustrated many of the things that I was learning from Jesus, especially related to the spiritual differences that exist within the human ranks. The Gnostics also saw these elements within the Scripture they attributed to the Apostle Paul. In discussion of the Scripture of *Hebrews* 5:11-14 which says, "Concerning this we have much teaching which is hard to interpret, since you have become deaf in your hearing. For indeed, you should be teachers by now, but again you need someone to teach you the elementary things of the beginning of the words of God: you need milk, not meat. Everyone who takes milk is inexperienced in the word of righteousness; he is still immature. Meat is for the mature who have disciplined their perceptive powers to discriminate good from evil."

Gnostics would interpret this as representing the two distinct levels of understanding among Jesus' followers. The elementary level would only see what is visible before him, whereas, the more advanced student could interpret the hidden or spiritual meaning of the teachings.

In *Hebrews* 6:4-6 it demonstrates the soul's inability to "regress" once it has received enlightenment. The Scripture says, "For it is impossible for those who have been enlightened, who have tasted the heavenly gift, and have become partakers of the holy spirit, and have tasted the goodness of God's word and the powers of the age to come, to have fallen back to renew repentance again. They recrucify for themselves the son of God. . ." Is that what Jesus was explaining to me about not really "back sliding" when it may appear that we were? Similarly, once we had awakened was it impossible for us to go back to sleep?

In *Hebrews* 12:22-24 it states, "But you have come to Mt. Zion, to the city of the living God, the heavenly Jerusalem, and to innumerable angels gathered in celebration, and to the assembly of the firstborn who are enrolled in heaven, and to a judge who is the God of all, to spirits of the just who have been perfected, and to Jesus, the mediator of a new covenant, and to the sprinkled blood, which speaks better than Abel's blood."

In other words, we are born by growing our soul, to a certain level, through interaction with those ahead of us. Ultimately, however, we need to join with Christ to complete our spiritual transformation.

And what about the whole concept of reincarnation? Dan informed me that the idea of having more than one physical body or living multiple lifetimes on Earth was "anti-Christian." If so, then why was I being told differently? How did Christians come to believe that we only lived one physical lifetime on Earth when other religions seemed to believe otherwise? It seemed crucial to me to discover the truth since a lot of the lessons I was learning about our spiritual development were predicated on the basic assumption that we live multiple times in physical forms.

When discussing anything related to reincarnation, fundamentalist Christians point to the Scripture in *Hebrews* 9:27-28 that says, "Just as man is destined to die once and after that to face judgment, so Christ was sacrificed once to take away the sins of many people; and he will appear a second time, not to bear sin, but to bring salvation to those who are waiting for him."

Paul was correct when he stated that man is destined to die once — each body with its current lifetime's level of transformed versus untransformed soul does indeed only live and die one time. Each time we return to a unique physical body we do so with a different amount of perfected spirit; and therefore, we also have a totally unique soul.

The amount of perfection achieved in our souls depends on the lessons previously learned and the degree of loving we have obtained. Thus, the perfected aspect from our previous soul lives on and continues to be merged into new souls attached to new physical bodies until we have achieved perfection and become "all loving." We understand that with each incarnation, and each new level of spiritual school we complete, God's saving purpose remains unfinished — we have been saved and maybe even graduated into perfection, as did Jesus Christ. But our salvation as a race will not be complete until Christ returns a second time and we all move together into the Kingdom of God.

What do the orthodox believe happens to the spirit within our soul between our body's death and the "second coming" or final salvation? The Catholics believe in an intermittent state called "purgatory." In *The Occult Revolution*, Father Richard

Woods, O.P. says, "The doctrine of purgatory is itself a kind of reincarnationism, since it is basically a belief that the soul can still atone for sin (be purified) after death" (Woods, pg. 178).

Knowing that Paul wrote *Hebrews* is important for interpreting the philosophical thought surrounding the book. That must have been why I was introduced to Paul and told these basic, and seemingly, unrelated facts about a Book from the Bible of which I had no prior knowledge. Paul taught that believers are already in the kingdom of Christ (Col. 1:13) but await the coming of the kingdom of God (1Cor. 15:50). He has already experienced the new life (2 Cor 2:16) but he looks forward to the inheritance of eternal life (Gal. 6:8). He has already been saved (Eph. 2:5) but he is still awaiting his salvation (Rom. 13:11). He has been raised into newness of life (Rom. 6:4) yet he longs for the resurrection (2Cor 5:4).

Although Paul does not say what is the state of the dead between death on earth and the resurrection he knows there is a gap and that something exists but it has not been revealed to him. He does know that if he died before the second coming, "a new body awaits him which will be suited to the new eternal order of the age to come." (2Cor. 5:1 NEB).

What were some of the other things that Paul taught that had special significance to the Gnostics and now, apparently, would also to me? Paul explains in 1Corinthians, "There are also heavenly bodies and there are earthly bodies; but the splendor of the heavenly bodies is one kind, and the splendor of the earthly bodies is another. The sun has one kind of splendor, the moon another and the stars another; and star differs from star in splendor." (1Cor. 15:40-41) What were the "splendors" that Paul referred to? Were splendors the same thing we knew as human traits or characteristics? Was he insinuating that inanimate solar objects, like the sun, also contained some type of unique trait or characteristic?

Jesus explained to me that as the physical body "lives on" through reproduction, so does the spiritual body. Our spiritual parents are co-chosen by God and us the same as our physical parents. Our souls may be a combination of many spirits; thus, we can inherit traits, or "splendors," as Paul calls them, from these parents just as we do from our earth parents. When Jesus told me that, "Peter is Billy Graham" did he refer to part of Peter's spirit being in the body of Billy Graham? Just as part of Billy Graham's biological parents are in him as well?

Yet, still, as each body is as unique as a snowflake so is each soul a unique creation during any given lifetime. Since our fetal soul is more highly developed, or transformed, each time our spirit returns to a physical body on Earth, we truly are unique one-time only physical and spiritual beings. But the core spirit or "I being" returns many times until born, perfected, and matured.

He told me it was as simple as any paradox! We live only once in order that we may grow to live eternally. Accepting God's divine love, which nourishes our fetal soul, keeps it alive until it can become perfected or all loving. The opposite is true as well. Cutting off the soul from its spiritual nourishment kills the soul and, thus, destroys the "I being" which is of the same "blood" as its divine spiritual parent — God.

Most "miscarriages" or soul deaths occur, as in the physical human, during the first trimester or during "Stage One" as Peck calls it. Souls rejecting the opportunities of receiving the spiritual nourishment, and everyone is given these opportunities, will perish. Peck's "Stage Two" is the second trimester where more development takes place but not tremendous amounts of actual growth. "Stage Three" is the final trimester where growth is exponential and the fetus begins to be constricted by its limited surroundings. "Stage Four" is the birth event followed by growth and development in a new environment with ensuing maturation resulting in perfection. This is when the "new life" is recognized.

A completely transformed "I being" receives it's rightful place within the Tree of Life and begins to reproduce itself in its own spiritual progeny, thus, achieving one aspect of eternal life. The transformed, or perfected spirit, can also choose to reincarnate in whole, if necessary, to perform a given task for the goodness of God here on Earth. The sacrifice made by the one, in its return to the prison of a body, is done for the good of the All. As Paul explained, we all wait with Christ, either on Earth in a physical body or in Christ's domain in heaven, until his second coming. No spirit moves forward to join with God until every other, still thriving soul, has rejoined in the Light.

I began thinking about the unbelievable things I was hearing. We know that the human body lives on and passes down to successive generations many attributes, e.g., genetic predisposition in some diseases, physical characteristics, mental aptitudes, etc. These are in the measurable realm and documented by our science. A child receives 50% of its physical base from each parent through the miracle of DNA. In turn, the parents of that child have also received their physical being from each of their two parents.

If a person reproduces, then it is easy to see how part of that person can technically live forever through its progeny. But that is only in the flesh and blood world. I wondered if it was a coincidence that my work in the physical world to develop a treatment for the prevention of premature delivery or miscarriage of human babies had any correlation to these new understandings and preventing the miscarriage of souls? Was there such a thing as "spiritual DNA" and, if so, what scientific and spiritual documentation could I find to support this wild idea?

Chapter Eighteen

What is a soul mate?

Earlier, when I had asked John what a soul mate was I received the answer describing a friend as, "One soul dwelling in two bodies." But I wanted to know more about other people's roles in our lives. How do we all fit together and why do we need to love other people?

Jesus explained it best using the analogy of a tree. The tree is mankind with roots connected to the Creator (God). The branches represent "soul groups" or, more accurately, "spirit groups" of which each of us belongs. We are all related via the trunk but some more closely related than others, e.g., the smaller the twigs, the fewer the leaves (I beings) and the closer the relationship. We are all connected to the "collective conscience" but more closely tied to our soul group members' conscience. The "soul" represents the vessel containing the I being along with other perfected splendors from our spiritual parents that will be used for our life purposes in each incarnation.

The soul groups are ordered, similar to grade levels, both within the All and within each group with some members slated to be born into the "elect" in one given lifetime rotation while others are still maturing. "Many are called but few are chosen" (Mt. 22:14) during each lifetime.

Jesus already taught us that there is a hierarchy of some sort in heaven when he was describing how John the Baptist was the greatest man ever born on earth but still he is not as great as even "the least in the Kingdom of Heaven" (Mt. 11:11). The higher the order the more potential the soul group has for understanding the "truth" and, thus, being born, or graduating, sooner versus later.

Highest order soul groups perform the most challenging tasks and, if successful, receive even more tasks both in this life and in the next incarnation until they are "perfect" as Jesus refers to it (see Mt. 25:14-30 story of the Talents). What Jesus taught applied to both the physical body and spiritual body. This was true throughout the New Testament. We are physical beings to understand the workings of our spiritual selves. This is why examples and lessons in our physical world are geared to help us learn truths in the spiritual world.

Soul groups share memories and thoughts because they really are closely connected. That also explains why we meet people who we instantly recognize and feel as if we have known for years. It is not because our physical bodies, or even current souls, have met before but rather our spirits or, I beings, have lived and loved together previously. We have arranged these circumstances prior to our incarnation to assist our soul mate, who could also more correctly be called "spirit" mate; and, thus, also propel our own soul into further maturation.

Connections between human soul mates help to reawaken the spirit hidden in the subconscious part of the soul. This reawakening illuminates the truth within the soul and begins to transform the seed of faith into the tree of knowledge, which causes us to "re-member" with Christ, thus, creating the whole. It is only as "whole beings" that we awaken to the full understanding of our spiritual selves. Was this what Jesus had meant when he had said to me, *"Have faith until you have knowledge?"*

Just as in physical intercourse when two halves come together to make a whole so it is in soul mate connections as well — soul mates serve as the keys to unlock one another's spiritual door. We cannot rejoin with the spirit of Christ or enter the Kingdom of Heaven without the help of our soul mates. We truly need one another's assistance — we need each other's love.

Souls are literally expanded when they give or project spiritual love. This giving away of love attracts a double portion of divine love from the spiritual realm, thus, creating more love in our souls. This infusion of additional spirit stretches the soul beyond its previous capacity. In the same way, the soul grows by accepting divine, or unconditional love, from human beings, including the self!

The soul incorporates the additional spiritual love thus grows, expands, and literally <u>becomes</u> more spirit. The divine light of the spirit then illuminates the truth and radiates more warmth or love. Spiritual knowledge, in essence, is acquired through divine love. The more our soul loves, unconditionally, the more it is capable of loving and understanding the truth of the All.

In Paul's letter to the Romans, Paul reveals in 8:23 that the elect share both in the suffering and in the anticipation of the adoption of the called as sons of God. The elect cannot enter into the Kingdom of God until their psychic counterparts are "raised" to join in union with them so that all may receive access to God together.

The elect are to recognize that they are not their own; they have been redeemed (1Cor. 6:20) not for their own sake but for the sake of redeeming the called. In other words, the twelfth graders must become tutors, mentors, and friends to the younger students in order to assist them in progressing through "school" and, ultimately, to their own graduation.

Jesus made a very important point to me about our physical sex and how it related to our soul. He said that the spirit, and thus the soul, was androgynous or without a sex type of what we know to be male or female. What he explained to me is easier to understand by picturing the eastern, non-sexually significant symbols of Yin and Yang. These are depicted as two interlocking units that come together to form a complete circle. It gives a good visual display of two soul mates — of which the Gnostics would have called the pneumatic (Yang) or "elect" and the psychics (Yin) or "called."

Jesus chose both soon-to-be Yang and more underdeveloped Yin among his twelve Apostles. He needed teachers at every level for his spiritual "school." The fact that they were all physically male served the politics of the day and became an analogy representing spiritual type. His often cited exclusion of females as Apostles did not represent the fact that *biological* females were not to be found in both spiritual groups — they are and in equal numbers. The physical male became equated with the Yang for the same reason Jesus used other earth-based examples to represent corresponding spiritual truths: it was an analogy for those who "had ears to hear", to understand.

The analogy was of that between the physical male (Yang) who, during sexual intercourse, projected life giving sperm into the receptive female (psychic) to awaken the egg, join with it, and become whole. Neither, half-unit, by itself can form a new life — they need each other. The aggressive nature of the forcefully projected sperm, which sought out the awaiting egg, served to represent what happened in our spiritual lives as well: both in our progression through school with our soul mates' assistance and then at our graduation or our final union with Christ. Once we have obtained perfection through growth achieved from our marriage with Christ we begin spiritually reproducing by projecting our "splendors" into the souls of our own spiritual progeny.

Jesus said that we change our "type" depending on the soul mate we encounter. In other words, become either Yang or Yin: giver or receiver of divine spirit. Our soul recognizes and adapts itself in order to come into neutral alignment with this mate; thus, providing whatever component is missing for our growth. We all must become Yin, or receptive, when accepting the more divine power of Christ. This requires submission and giving up control, which so many humans are reluctant to do!

The concept is simple. We learn from those who are stronger and have mastered training techniques that we require and, in turn, we teach or contribute to those who are weaker. As in the physical world, it benefits us most when we train with those more advanced in the skills and knowledge we want to master.

By only loving and accepting those into our lives who are like us we are guilty of "homospirituality" which, like its earth-based counterpart homosexuality, does not produce offspring. Although it is important to love those who will love us back, in order to create new spirits, either our own or another's, we must learn to love, accept, and assist those who are different from us and may not love us in return.

Paul expends concerted effort in relaying this message that the "strong" are to help the "weak" in their soul's journey. "The 'strong' are to welcome the weak, to avoid arguing with them (Rom. 14:1) but to maintain their own liberty of conscience as those who 'know,' as Paul does, that nothing is, in itself, unclean (Rom. 14:14)." (Pagels, Gnostic Paul, page 45) Pagels also points out, "Paul warns, however, that those who are 'strong,' are not to despise the rest for their weakness (Rom. 14:3), nor are they to allow their own liberty to offend the psychics (Rom. 14:13-21)" (Pagels, Gnostic Paul, page 45). The strong, then, represent the elect or God's chosen.

The Gnostics also tried to explain this type of adaptability or alignment within the soul. The Valentinians described the same person as either male or female in the context of different relationships. In relation to the divine, the pneumatic, or elect, is female or receptive — receiving divine spirit. Yet in relation to the psychic, or called, the pneumatic takes the role of spiritual "projector," and is "male."

Jesus showed me a passage from *The Gospel of Thomas* that portrays how one's physical sex and spiritual type, elect or called, are not equated. "Simon Peter said to them, 'Let Mary leave us, because women are not worthy of life.' Jesus said, 'Behold, I shall guide her so as to make her male, that she too may become a living spirit like you men. For every woman who makes herself male will enter the kingdom of heaven." Clearly, human females can also be chosen or transformed as well as human males.

In fact, Mary Magdalene became symbolic of many of the teachings that Jesus tried to impart. In the *Gospel of Philip* it states ". . .the companion of the Savior is Mary Magdalene. But Christ loved her more than all the disciples and used to kiss her often on her mouth. The rest of the disciples were offended by it. . . They said to him, 'Why do you love her more than all of us?' The Savior answered and said to them, 'Why do I not love you as I love her?'"

Jesus himself was guiding Mary Magdalene into becoming "male," or part of the elect. Their physical intimacy represented their spiritual union, or marriage, and the resulting transformation of Magdalene from a Yin to a Yang, from a called to a chosen, from a female to a male.

Peter, who represented the orthodox views, the psychics, and the church, rejected Mary as "one of the guys." In the *Pistis Sophia*, Peter complains about Magdalene's role with the Apostles and questions her right to speak about spiritual issues. He asked Jesus to silence her but Jesus responds that ". . .whoever the Spirit inspires is divinely ordained to speak, whether man or woman." Notice Jesus uses the terms "man or woman" to represent biological sex type versus his usage in the *Gospel of Thomas* of "male or female" to denote spiritual "sex type."

I was starting to wonder — had I, as Jesus declared, actually been born, both physically and spiritually, for some purpose related to awakening others to these hidden truths, once common to early Christians, but buried for centuries? Did the fact that I had become the strongest woman in the world, despite numerous handicaps, somehow represent my spiritual conversion from weakness to strength, from Yin to Yang? Is this how Christ awakened us to the truth?

The answer came from Paul when I was shown a passage in *Romans* that explained, "For the Scripture says to Pharaoh: 'I raised you up for this very purpose, that I might display my power in you and that my name might be proclaimed in all the earth.'" (Rom. 9:17) I was beginning to see the connections between the physical and spiritual once again. We are here for a reason and predominate among those reasons is to learn how to love.

M. Sue Benford

Chapter Nineteen

"The answer is always Love"

My head had been spinning for days. I tried to tell Dan the things I was now learning but he refused to listen; or maybe, he just could not listen. His usual warm smile and loving gaze had turned cold, replaced with the coldness of a blank stare.

One day over lunch, he informed me that unless I stopped professing these crazy things about Christianity and Jesus he could no longer love and support me. If I did not conform to his same fundamentalist beliefs about the Scripture, he could no longer accept me. Apparently, several of his Christian friends had berated him for associating with me and suggested he leave me if I refused to come "confess my sins" to their church ministers. He feared their rejection and retribution.

He said that the fact that we had engaged in non-marital sex was a grievous sin of which I needed to repent. He claimed I was a naive and immature Christian who was totally out of line believing I was chosen to receive special instruction from Jesus himself. He claimed that anything but what he, and other "mature" Christians believed, was blasphemous. Because my beliefs were different, and beyond his comprehension, Dan was convinced that these "lessons" had to be from Satan and not from God. From his perspective, beliefs that were different from everyone else's had to be wrong and evil!

My face grew red with anger and rage. I could not believe what I was hearing. Was this the same man who refused to speak to his own parents because they had been "unloving" to him as a child? Was this what Christian love and forgiveness was all about? And now he was turning his back on the only person who had ever dared to love him. The only healthy, loving, intimate relationship he had in his life was being cast aside in the name of Christianity.

As I opened my mouth to heatedly confront his grievous accusations, something happened. In the midst of my rage I became calm. I could feel my rapidly beating heart slowing to a gentle pace. A peace and serenity overcame me. The words that flowed from my mouth were nothing like what I was planning to say.

Quietly I said, "Is that what Jesus has taught us? You, who profess to be wise and learned in the ways of our Lord, tell me the truth? Are we to love only those who are like us, think like us, and look as we do? Is it not our task to love in spite of our disagreements, weaknesses, and frailties? Are we not taught to cherish those among us who we perceive as weak and naive or, rather, to turn in wrath and walk away?"

"And I say to you, my friend, that the world is still flat. The one voice proclaiming the absurd news that it was round was an evil heretic in his day, too. But according to you, because his belief was different, it was wrong. God could have elevated the disbelievers in space ships to see that the world was actually round but, I tell you the truth, many still would not have believed and would have falsely accused God of deception."

"You say that I am evil because I do not believe as you do; I could say the same words to you. But I will not. You see I love you regardless of your beliefs and in spite of your weaknesses. I accept you as Jesus accepts you — wherever you are in your soul's journey. Have I ever approached you in a way that was unloving, unforgiving, or unjust? When I do, then tell me I am possessed by some evil but, until then, learn what you can from this love of ours."

"Know ours has been a spiritual marriage, created by God, to help us both. The physical intimacy you shun and curse as a weakness is wrongly accused for the body cannot sin apart from the soul. Our physical joining only served to celebrate and mimic our spiritual link as soul mates — soul mates joined together by God and for God's purposes."

"God does not denounce non-legalized sex, he denounces non-spiritualized sex. Any sex, rather commissioned by man's law or not, is righteous and just and forms a marriage in God's eyes when it awakens the soul further in its understanding of love and the splendors of the spirit. God is always present, but especially, when love is present."

"But sexual pleasures wrought in the world of lust, betrayal, dishonesty, manipulation or abuse are ungodly and immoral whether they occur in a legalized union or not. But it has not been the tail of lust that wags the soul of the dog in our relationship. If you take nothing from what we have shared take only that one understanding and know that I care, and will care for all eternity, about the growth of your soul. What God has joined together, truly, no man can put asunder."

Dan sat in stunned silence with his eyes cast down at the table. He was speechless — something I thought lawyers never were! In his heart he knew I was right, he wanted to believe I was right, but it was not developmentally possible for him to understand the truths I now spoke. I would have to go the rest of my spiritual journey alone — without a soul mate. Dan had helped me cross the threshold but I now realized that he could not continue on the rest of my journey.

I remembered something Scott Peck had written describing the inability of people at earlier stages of spiritual development to accept those at more advanced stages. Peck observed that, "The greatest problem of these different stages — and the biggest reason it is so important to understand them — is the sense of threat that exists between people at such different points on the spiritual journey. To some extent, we all may be threatened by the people still in the stage we have just left, because we may not yet be sure or secure in our new identity. But for the most part the threat goes the other way, and we particularly tend to be threatened by people in the stages ahead of us."

I now experienced, first hand, this fear by a person not yet ready to be transformed or born. A strict fundamentalist, Dan was in the second trimester, or Stage Two, of his fetal soul's development.

I found it interesting how Dan, and most other fundamentalist Christians like him, considered themselves already "born" when, in actuality, they had only truly just been "conceived." I wondered how they justified their unloving and unforgiving behaviors, towards themselves and towards others, if they really thought they were now born into the all-loving Christ. Who was right — Dan or me?

Jesus explained to me the cognitive differences between developing souls in terms of grade levels in school. He said that no grade was more worthy or loved by God than another but each did have its own set of rules and responsibilities to master along with its own level of understanding. He said that we would not expect a first grader to understand the same things that a twelfth grader did. Nor would we apply the same responsibilities and freedoms to the two different grades — tests would be different and privileges would be different.

He said that those in the higher grades, and the graduates, must always defer to the understanding of the lower grade levels. To do otherwise would be "unloving" and unacceptable behavior for the higher-grade student.

In other words, Dan was not wrong; in fact, quite the contrary. He was portraying his understanding of being a "good Christian" according to his elementary understanding. He would have to continue his attempt to become "perfect" through following the only rules and tests allotted for his grade. Eventually, most likely in another lifetime, he would progress to new challenges, rules, and understandings.

Jesus said that is why he and the disciples spoke in parables about things visible in the physical world. It was so every grade level would have something they could grasp onto and comprehend, regardless of the developmental capacity of "their eyes and ears" for seeing and hearing the invisible, or spiritual, truth represented by the physical world analogies.

He said that part of the difficulty and fear among the younger grade levels is that when they encounter information from the higher-grade levels they wrongly interpret that, if the information is true, they might be held responsible for knowing it. Subsequently, they fear being tested on material they have no possible way of comprehending and, thus, failing.

Jesus explained to me how it works by using the analogy of a two-year old child who wants to run into the middle of the street. The child's loving parent understands that if the child runs into the street there is a chance the child will be hit by a car and killed. But how does the parent control the child's dangerous behavior without altogether removing the child's freedom which the parent knows is crucial for the child's growth? The child is not yet mature enough to understand a detailed and rational explanation about the inherent dangers, the possible outcomes, and the possibility of his or her own death.

As a result, the loving parent tells the child that he or she may not run into the middle of the street under any circumstances. If the "law" is broken, then the child will be disciplined. At his or her level of understanding the child only perceives the law and the possibility of disciplinary repercussions — the reason why the parent is invoking the law is beyond the child's comprehension.

The first time the child disobeys the parent's rule and runs into the street, the child receives a ten-minute "time out" and is not permitted to play outside for two hours. Jesus told me this represents the concept of "an eye for an eye" or discipline designed equal to the transgression involved. But the loving parent does not disallow the child freedom to make the same erroneous choice a second time — she or he, in essence, "turns the other cheek" and permits the child, if he or she so chooses, to disobey the law again. If the child runs into the street a second time then the discipline is escalated to represent the repeat offense. Perhaps a fifteen-minute time out plus not playing outside for the rest of the day (which the child interprets as practically a lifetime of unjust and cruel punishment on the parent's part).

The child does not perceive the love behind the parent's action, only the law and the discipline can be understood. The child does not even understand the "why" to the rule but only the behavior that must be exacted to meet the letter of the parent's law. The street itself might even be viewed as evil and dangerous in and of itself because by going into the street one breaks the law and discipline is invoked.

For some time to come the young child obeys the parent's law simply out of faith that the parent is protecting them or out of fear that punishment will be invoked for disobedience. The focus from the child's perspective is totally on the law itself because he or she cannot understand the abstract concept of being killed by a car while playing in the street.

But as the child grows and begins to gain more awareness, the street, the law, the car, and the parent take on new perspectives in the child's eyes. The child learns that the street itself is not evil and may be crossed, at first, with the assistance of someone more mature and, then, by following other rules like "stop, look, and listen." Neither is the car, in and of itself, particularly evil but can cause trauma or death if encountered in the wrong way. The parent's original law is now obsolete, not wrong, just unnecessary because the child can, on his or her own accord, realize the dangers of the street and how to avoid being hit by cars.

The child also sees a very different side to the parental discipline. The child understands that had the discipline not been invoked he or she would never have learned right from wrong and may have been killed in the process of discovery. What once appeared as the cruel and mean actions of the all powerful parent now could be understood as the loving guidance of a parent trying to save its child.

Once the child has grown and matured even further he or she has gained enough knowledge and insight to fully understand the significance of danger when crossing the street, the reason the parent had to discipline him or her when the law was disobeyed, and that the law itself was not the important aspect after all but saving the child's life was really what it was all about.

Jesus told me to read the story about a high level "student" in the Bible named Job. He said that Job's tests were geared only for him and would not have been given to other lower level students. He also told me that Job, ultimately, passed the tests and was rewarded for his achievement. Jesus wants us to know that we will never be tested outside our need for understanding or capacity to learn.

He said that the task at hand for all spiritual grade levels is to accept and recognize the importance of each level in the school. Elementary students must realize that there are truths they cannot and will not be able to immediately comprehend but that they need higher-level students for guides, mentors, and friends. Also, their lack of comprehension does not diminish the validity of the truth. Just because early man did not know or believe that the world was round did not make it less true!

Secondary students must understand that their lessons are not meant to be taught directly and specifically to the younger students, but rather, translated into loving lessons that the younger students can comprehend. Higher-grade levels must also realize that, when they are in the "classroom" with lower level students, they must abide by the rules inherent to that classroom.

In other words, if Dan perceives physical intimacy outside the law of man as a "sin," then I must respect that as his truth and not foster other ideas or behaviors. Only when the thoughts and behaviors of the lower level students are going away from Love, either of God, self, or other souls, should higher level students provide direction, correction, and insight.

Jesus then told me to go get my Bible and turn to the verse in Matthew, which described God's paramount Law. He said that we need to understand the basic premise for how all grade level lessons and tests were determined and for what overriding purpose. The verses Jesus showed me said, "Hearing that Jesus had silenced the Sadducees, the Pharisees got together. One of them, an expert in the law, tested him with this question: 'Teacher, which is the greatest commandment in the Law?' Jesus replied: 'Love the Lord your God with all your heart and with all your soul and with all your mind.' This is the first and greatest commandment. And the second is like it: 'Love your neighbor as yourself.' All the Law and the Prophets hang on these two commandments.'" (Mt. 22:34-40)

Jesus wants us to understand the significance of his statement when he says, "<u>All</u> the Law" is geared to meet and support God's paramount Law. This means everything we encounter in life, everything we are taught, guided to do, given as gifts, or disciplined for is a result of only one goal — the creation of divine spirit within our souls.

The reason love is so important is because it is the only true nourishment for the growth of spirit within our soul and it is the only thing that, without it, can kill the soul. That is why love is God's paramount Law — not to bolster God's ego, because He does not have one; but rather, to save our spirits to live until they are perfected, or all loving, and returned to their true home — the Kingdom of God.

With my own love cast aside, my beliefs persecuted, Jesus' words reverberated in my head, "All men will hate you because of me, but he who stands firm to the end will be saved." (Mt. 10:22) I had learned that our soul mates propel and assist us to a certain point then we join with Christ for the remainder of the journey. Would I have to walk the rest of my spiritual journey alone? I continued to pray for the ultimate spiritual partner for the remainder of my long journey.

When I asked Jesus how I should respond to fear and persecution in the future he replied, "The answer is always Love." It was a lesson I was still learning.

Chapter Twenty

Read Thomas!

One night in meditation, I was a little disappointed when Jesus revisited the issue of Thomas. He told me plainly and simply, *"Read Thomas."* With all the flurry of new and exciting information I was being told I had almost forgotten about any prior instructions regarding Thomas. I thought I had "closed the book" on the *Book of Thomas*. But not surprising, I was wrong again.

Jesus told me that I needed to revisit the *Book of Thomas* and that I would find additional information. Initially I thought he meant for my documentation on Matthew and Thomas' relationship but this was not what he meant after all. Although I had previously skimmed the Book, I had not read it for content other than documentation about Matthew and Thomas' relationship. When I finally sat down and thoroughly read the Book I found some startling revelations and teachings by Jesus related to the topic of hidden truths about creation of souls and reincarnation.

In addition, Jesus further explained to me the significance of Thomas' transformation and how the Bible illustrated Thomas prior to his "birth" and how the Book, attributed to Thomas, portrayed Thomas after his "birth" or transformation. The missing link to my story was now in place. I could now understand all the focus on Thomas and his Book.

Both Matthew and Thomas realized something crucial had taken place when Christ descended upon Thomas. Thomas had been transformed at this point by the Holy Spirit just as Saul was instantaneously transformed into Paul on the road to Damascus. This transformation was the final step, or the birthing event, which initiated Thomas into the elect group and prepared him to undertake the mysteries of the all-knowing or Gnostic Christian.

As a skeptic and doubter, Thomas had been like an eight-month old fetus that appeared to be behind all the others in spiritual understanding and faith because he did not move as well or as frequently in the spiritual womb as did the younger fetuses.

What everyone failed to realize, up until the time of Thomas' birth or awakening, was that Thomas was well advanced of many of the other Apostles and spiritual leaders of the time. His birth at the time of the Holy Spirit's descent signaled a major step in Thomas' spiritual development. Even Jesus recognized Thomas had joined him as his "twin" and "true friend," or soul mate, at this point. Later, John, seeing the transformation in Thomas, continued to refer to Thomas as "the twin" but now with a significantly different meaning.

With this new knowledge, the writings attributed to Thomas took on a more significant meaning. Thomas clearly had the ears to hear and the eyes to see that propelled him into the realm of the all knowing. He joined John, Paul, Mary Magdalene and several others in becoming privy to Jesus' secret teachings.

In the *Book of Thomas*, Jesus is talking to Thomas about understanding "who you are, how you exist and how you will come to be." Jesus goes on to explain to Thomas that, "For he who has not known himself has known nothing. But he who has known himself has also already obtained knowledge about the depth of the All. So, therefore, you alone my brother Thomas have beheld what is hidden from men, that is, that on which they stumble if they do not recognize it." What was being told to Thomas was a first time revelation that had previously been hidden from others and it had to do with understanding our basic make-up.

When Thomas explains the difficulty in preaching about the invisible truths, Jesus responds with, "If the things that are visible to you are hidden before you, how, then, will you be able to hear about the things that are not visible?" Jesus says the same thing in John 3:11, "I have spoken to you of earthly things and you do not believe; how then will you believe if I speak of heavenly things?"

Jesus goes on to say, "You are beginners!" And: "You have not yet attained the measure of perfection." Perfection, in God's eyes, is being incapable of choosing deeds that are not based solely in love for oneself or another human being.

Thomas goes on to ask Jesus to explain "the things which you say are not visible, but are hidden from us!" Jesus teaches, "All bodies have come into being in the same way that the beasts are begotten — that is without reason. Therefore, they are in this way visible as well, that is as a creature stretching out after another creature. Because of this, however, those who are above do not exist in the same way as the ones who are visible, but they live from their own root. And it is their fruits that nourish them."

Jesus refers to those above having their "fruits" that nourish them. Fruits can refer to the increase and obtainment of spiritual understands such as love, joy, peace, patience, kindness, goodness, faithfulness, gentleness, and self-control (Gal.

5:22) But if the beings above have already obtained perfection they would not need to obtain, for their I being, the characteristics described in Gal. 5:22.

Their fruits are provided when "one of the lost sheep is reunited with the flock." As Jesus taught in Mt. 18:13, "And if he finds it, I tell you the truth, he is happier about that one sheep than about the ninety-nine that did not wander off." The sheep are the spiritual progeny who, after wandering away from the spiritual teachings (by becoming seekers and doubters), become enlightened souls rejoining with the Light and learning the truth.

This same story is told in *The Gospel of Thomas* except here Jesus clarifies that "the biggest" sheep is the one to wander away from the flock. This, once again, represents a larger, more developed fetal soul that has begun to outgrow its current environment and is preparing to be born.

We also know that the Bible refers to being fruitful and multiplying (Ge. 1:22) as a form of reproduction. Would it not be nourishing to the perfected spirits to see transformation in their offspring, especially, if it is not possible for them to join in God's Kingdom until everyone is perfected anyway?

Jesus goes on to say, "But that which changes will perish and disappear, and has then no more hope of life. For this body is bestial." He then ends this thought with, "Because of this, then, you are minors! How long will it take until you become perfect?" Once again, Jesus refers to our on-going developmental process to become all-loving creatures incapable of choosing behaviors other than those driven by love for ourselves and our fellow humans.

Thomas asked Jesus, "O, Lord, the visible light here, which shines for the sake of men, why does it not only rise, but set as well?" Jesus responds, "O, blessed Thomas, only for your sakes does this visible light shine, not in order that you may stay in this place, but rather, that you may come back out of it. But when all the elect have abandoned bestiality, then this light will also withdraw up to its own home. And its own home will receive it again because it was a good servant."

We know that "bestiality" is the physical reproduction of bodies. We also know that the elect are God's chosen and predestined souls given the task of tutoring and loving other souls towards perfection. Thus, when the chosen souls have stopped reproducing themselves in human form, in an effort to assist other souls who are incarnate, and both called and elect are perfect, then God will pull the light from earth, take all of those who have been transformed, and join with Him in their rightful home. The light will stay here on Earth until we have learned what we need to be perfect or all loving and rejoin with God. When the light departed, what would be remaining on the Earth?

Something from my long ago childhood poem resonated in my mind as I read the words Jesus spoke to Thomas:

> "When all are gone who have built the earth,
> And the graves have vanished from within the ground,
> And with time now sleeping idly without a cause,
> Darkness moves in without a sound."

Did this removal of God's light and the abandonment of bestiality by the elect who "built the earth," have any connection to my poem? The overlaps seemed eerily similar.

Jesus further explains about the idea of "the perfect." He tells Thomas, "Therefore we have to speak to you. For this is the doctrine for the perfect. If, then, you wish to be perfect, you must observe these words. If you do not observe them, your name is 'Ignorant', since it is not possible that a wise man dwell together with a fool. For the wise man is filled with every wisdom. To the fool, the good and the bad are the same. For the wise man will be nourished by the truth and he will become like the tree growing by the torrent stream." Here Jesus was equating becoming an all-loving, or perfect, soul with being wise and being wise as those who observe these words. He also points out that the wise person will be nourished by the truth using the same word "nourish" that he described for those up above.

The interesting point of this passage is that it confirms that the ignorant man cannot dwell with the perfect or wise man. Darkness cannot exist in the light. Until we approach God, life, ourselves, and other souls with only the divine light of truth and love, we fall into the ignorant category and must return to Earth until we are perfected. That is when our souls will cease their "bestiality." According to Jesus this is a time to celebrate.

Perhaps the most telling of Jesus' teachings to Thomas comes in this next passage when Jesus explains, "For the vessel of their flesh will dissolve. And even when it disintegrates it will be part of the visible world, of that which can be seen. And then the visible fire will give them pain. Because of the love of faith which they had previously they will be brought back into the visible world. Those, however, who can see are not parts of the visible world. Without the first love they will perish."

Jesus explained to me that those who have accepted God's love, or spiritual nourishment, will thrive and be "brought back into the physical world" to develop their fetal soul further through life's challenges and experiences and, eventually, become all loving beings. Those "who can see" are those who have perfected their souls through a transformation and need not return to a physical body.

He said it is our choice to make: God does not ever reject us only we can reject God or, as he told me before, unconditional love to grow our souls. That is the only true sin, or mortal sin, which kills our soul. In essence, we choose death over life — a spiritual suicide. Everything else human's classify as "sin" is actually only forgivable transgression, which was taken away or absolved by Christ.

It was apparent to me that the early Christians did, indeed, believe in the idea of reincarnation. I began to wonder what the other Gnostic texts contained. Did they support or reject the things I had been learning? Did anyone else "know" the things I knew?

M. Sue Benford

Chapter Twenty One

John's secrets

Unbeknownst to me, the writings attributed to the Apostle John were controversial to early Orthodox Church leaders. I was surprised to learn, as the New Testament was becoming stabilized in the late second, or early third century, that the *Gospel of John* was still being disputed. Only by a narrow margin was it accepted into the canon of the New Testament mostly because of the famous verses 14:5-6 which say, ". . .Thomas said to him, 'Lord, we do not know where you are going; how can we know the way?' Jesus said to him, 'I am the way, the truth, and the life; no one comes to the Father, but by me.'" Early church leaders claimed that this passage meant followers must come through the church as the only means to gain entry into the Kingdom of Heaven. It was clearly political, which explains the exclusion of other texts such as the *Gospel of Thomas* and many other early Christian writings.

The Book of *Revelations*, also attributed to John, was hotly disputed for even longer. Many early church leaders refused to accept it for centuries. But why was there so much debate and concern about the writings of Jesus' most beloved disciple? The reason was that many of the orthodox accused John's writings as being heretical. His "truths" appeared remarkably similar to and undeniably supportive of teachings linked to Gnosticism especially his writings about "finding the light of God within."

The followers of Valentinus themselves demonstrated that many sayings and stories in John supported many of the basic concepts of Gnostic teachings. But the Orthodox Church leaders decided that the *Gospel of John* could serve the needs of the emerging institution. Ironically, John was quite possibly, the most "all knowing" or Gnostic of Christ's followers.

History shows that as the early church gained power in the third and fourth centuries, being different, as the Gnostics were, was accepted as long as the basic institutional balances of the church were not disrupted. Hundreds, and possibly thousands, of Gnostic Christians literally abandoned their prior social lives among the community and adopted the lifestyle of the solitary or "monk." They literally stopped interacting with and contributing to society at large.

The early Gnostics had the right idea but the wrong approach by eliminating all worldly contact. Their enhanced relationship to God through solitude, visions, and meditation was desirable but not practical for the masses. They had, in essence, cut off the tail of the dog (worldly temptations and life lessons) to avoid letting it wag the dog (the soul). They had taken away the darkness that needed to exist in order to contrast the light.

Jesus taught us that the bigger gain is made when we learn to control the wagging tail through the strength developed within the dog. We gain strength through experiencing life's challenges, realizing God's strength in us, and loving each other. None of this could be accomplished, long term, through the approach used by the Gnostic monks. Refusing to play the game never resulted in the making of a champion.

Included among the early monk's literature were the documents found in 1945 at Nag Hammadi. Most likely, these documents were buried in 367 CE when Athanasius, the Archbishop of Alexandria, ordered the destruction of all apocryphal books that contained "anti-orthodox" sentiments. Such sentiments included the acknowledgment of women in religious and spiritual proceedings, divergent perspectives on martyrdom, the role of the church as the only conduit in linking humans with Christ, and reincarnation among other philosophical differences between the sects. The monks buried their precious documents to preserve them for the time when Christ would unearth them to be used again.

If Gnostics were truly enlightened then why did they lose out to the orthodox? The answer is quite simple. Christ himself orchestrated the downfall of the early Gnostic movement. He permitted it to thrive just long enough for the many Books to be written by those who had been initiated, or born, and who now communicated with the Holy Spirit directly in meditation and through dreams. These were some of the writings now revealed to us through the findings at Nag Hammadi that help explain many of the things we are now learning.

The time was not yet right for the powerful Gnostic teachings to be widespread. Christianity needed to take root and expand, fetal souls were still very young and needed to be nourished and strengthened in an elementary way before they could progress to secondary or more advanced education. In addition, science had to take its own course for centuries uninhibited by the "truth of the invisible powers" described by Jesus at the temple in Jerusalem when he was twelve.

John, along with several of the other Gnostic apostles, knew this all too well. His, and the others' teachings, took on a two prong meaning — one meant for the "all knowing" and one for the still developing fetal soul. Both versions provided interpretations and representations that would contribute to a soul's growth no matter what its level of development. Both would prove crucial to the future of Christianity — one sooner and one later.

One writing, attributed to John, that was excluded from the canon because, unlike his others, it could not be used to support any of the early church doctrine, was *The Secret Book of John*. In this Book, John asks Jesus "where did we come from?" The book describes Jesus' response to this question. Using images, words, and symbols that John and his contemporaries could relate to, Jesus gives a remarkable account of our spiritual family ancestry. He, in essence, puts the names on our spiritual family tree.

In addition, Jesus reveals what the spiritual "splendors" are that Paul described. He virtually tells us what we inherit from our spiritual parents and how that occurs. Jesus also illustrates how angels are involved in our creation and on-going lives.

Many of the passages from this secret book reflected what Jesus and John had been telling me about our creation, about the role of soul mates in our lives, and about how we developed into enlightened beings. As I read the text I had to stop multiple times because I was in shock and in awe at how similar John's portrayal of these issues matched what I had been told and had come to understand. Just as with Pagels' books, I was able to see beyond the mere words and into their true meaning.

Passage by passage I read the text and was guided by John and Jesus in understanding its meaning. The following are some of the highlights, along with my understandings, from John's secret book.

Chapter 3:3-6 "Its Thought became active, and she who appeared in the presence of the Father in shining light came forth. She is the first power: she preceded everything, and came forth from the Father's mind as the Forethought of all. Her light resembles the Father's light; as the perfect power, she is the image of the perfect and invisible Spirit. . ."

Chapter 3:8 "She is the first Thought, the image of the Spirit. She became the universal womb, for she precedes everything . . ." Here we see the creation of the spiritual womb that will ultimately conceive, nurture, and give birth to the human souls to come.

This idea of a spiritual womb was revealed elsewhere in Gnostic texts. The work attributed to the Gnostic teacher Simon Maus suggests a mystical meaning for Paradise, the place where human life began: 'Grant Paradise to be the womb; for Scripture teaches us that this is a true assumption when it says, 'I am He that formed thee in thy mother's womb' (Isaiah 44:2) Even Moses, using allegory, had declared Paradise to be the womb and Eden, the placenta.

Chapter 3:9-10 "Barbelo asked the invisible virgin Spirit to give her Foreknowledge, and the Spirit agreed. . .Foreknowledge comes from the Thought of the invisible virgin Spirit. . ." These are the splendors that Paul spoke about: spiritual characteristics are being created and delineated.

Chapter 4:1-3 "The Father entered Barbelo with a gaze, with the pure, shining light surrounding the invisible Spirit. Barbelo conceived, and the Father produced a ray of light that was similar to the blessed light but not as bright. This ray of light was the only Child of the common Parent that had come forth, and the only offspring and the only Child of the Father, the pure light."

This represents spiritual reproduction. It also demonstrates that we were not produced directly or concomitantly with Christ but came afterwards as the progeny of other generations. This is similar to how our physical bodies were produced generations after Adam and Eve — none of us would claim Adam and Eve were our immediate parents. Once again, the physical represents the spiritual.

Chapter 5:15-16 "In the third eternal realm was stationed the family of Seth, with the third star, Daveithai. The souls of the saints were stationed there." This demonstrates that the elect or saints get positioned differently from those still trying to reach that level. This also indicates that humans are assigned to orders similar to the angels.

"In the fourth eternal realm were stationed the souls of those who were ignorant of the divine Fullness. They did not repent immediately, but continued to be ignorant for a while and then repented later. . ."

In this passage, John is attempting to show that we develop, over a period of time, into perfect or repenting souls that are no longer ignorant. This is the "holding area," so to speak, until I beings are returned to Earth in new souls and bodies to attempt further spiritual growth through the assistance of life lessons and soul mates.

Chapter 9:6-7 "The throng of angels stood by and received these seven psychical substances from the authorities. Then they could create a network of limbs and trunk, with all the parts properly arranged. The first angel began by creating the head: . . ."

This passage eludes to, what I later would learn were, the use of atomic (visible) and subatomic (invisible) materials that were available from cosmic substances to create the human being which would contain both a physical and spiritual body. The physical body was created first but was temporarily left without a divine-spirit-containing soul to evolve on Earth until it reached a certain intellectual capacity.

During this period of evolution, humans remained without the choice for good or evil identical to the other creations of God. This is represented by the story of Adam and Eve in the Garden of Eden who were free of sin and evil. When humans had evolved to the necessary degree required, God introduced the spirit into the once divinely compelled biologically-based soul.

The subatomic particles used to create the soul were matched to those of the particular angel who had created the body/soul part. By doing this, the basic structure, power, and force of the corresponding angel was kept in tact. Thus, various solar and cosmic forces, represented by angels, are felt in accordance to the rhythms and forces of the subatomic, or etheric, angelic creator of that particular body part.

In this manner, guidance is possible from the angelic realm as our guardian angels "read" ahead what our life mission is and direct, or compel, us in the most appropriate path. Imprinting, at the time of birth, which is the point the spirit completes its descension upon the body, provides the life "road map" for the individual based upon the stars formations, alignments, etc. We each receive our own individual "soul print," which is as unique as our fingerprint.

This knowledge of our soul's link to the cosmos gave rise to Astrology and helps explain the compelling feelings we have related to certain celestial movements and positions. By studying our road maps ahead of time it is possible to gain insight into the direction predestined for our lives — a destiny that has been co-created by our soul with God. Interestingly, just as two people might take a vacation trip to Florida by driving down the same highway, each person will have his or her own unique experiences. The road map, in other words, does not dictate the trip!

That is why Paul explains that the sun and moon have their own "splendors." He knew of this crucial connection between us and the materials we were (both physically and spiritual) created with — these seven psychical substances.

With the infusion of divine spirit into the soul, humans were given the freedom to deny or disobey God's paramount Law (sin) and to choose between actions of good and evil, loving and unloving. Prior to this, humans were like the other animals and angels who cannot sin or act contrary to what was prescribed by God. It is only through this exclusive capacity to choose loving actions or not, to accept or refuse God and our divine selves, that humans can eventually rise above all other creations and take their rightful place with Christ in the Kingdom of God.

Chapter 11:21-23 "I said to the Savior, 'What is this forgetfulness?' The Savior said, "It is not as Moses wrote and you heard. For he said in his first book, 'He caused Adam to fall asleep.' Rather, this forgetfulness made Adam lose all sense. Thus the first ruler said through the prophet, 'I shall make their minds sluggish, that they may neither understand nor discern.'

Chapter 12: 1-8 Then enlightened Afterthought hid herself within Adam. The first ruler wanted to take her from Adam's side, but enlightened Afterthought cannot be apprehended. While darkness pursued her, it did not apprehend her. The first ruler took out part of Adam's power, and created another figure in the form of a female, like the Afterthought that had appeared . . . Adam saw the woman beside him. At once enlightened Afterthought appeared, and removed the veil that covered his mind. The drunkenness of darkness left him. He recognized this being that was like him, and said, 'This is now bone from my bones and flesh from my flesh!' For this reason a man will leave his father and his mother, and will join himself to his wife, and the two of them will become one flesh. For he will be sent a lover, and he will leave his father and his mother."

This demonstrates how soul mates unite to spiritually awaken one another. One is enlightened, seeks out the other, joins with him or her and reawakens enlightened Afterthought. It also describes what John had earlier told me that soul mates were *"one soul dwelling in two bodies."*

The story of Adam and Eve describes this pulling apart of the whole and creating two halves that, on their own effort, could never create a new being — similar, once again, to the sperm and the egg. However, when united in love, or physically through love making, the two become one and create a newborn both physically and spiritually. The "lover" that John says we will be sent is our soul mate. Or, was that, soul mates?

I asked John whether or not we should choose only one soul mate in a lifetime to love and mate with in a permanent marriage. He said that there was no such thing as a "permanent" marriage while we are in physical bodies. He said the concept of permanency in our relationships is an illusion.

The strength and power of the loving bond between soul mates has nothing to do with length of time together as perceived by our calendars. Sometimes loving relationships of only a few weeks can propel a soul forward with more force than those that last fifty earth years can. Nor does it matter what man's law has to say about the soul mates' bond.

But I was confused. Why, then, did the Catholic Church denounce divorce and remarriage? John said that, whereas, God brings together souls in marriage for spiritual birth, man joins the flesh for biological birth. The church understands the law on the elementary level with the paramount focus on the joining of the flesh. He said man can only join man but only God can join spirits.

True joinings by God for spiritual birth are everlasting. Unconditional love, the premise of the spiritual marriage or mating of souls, never ceases because it is just that — unconditional — regardless of physical proximity, living arrangements, legal protocol, time, physical death, or any other condition found in the World.

Therefore, the church is correct in one respect, divorce really does not exist in God's eyes. That is why Jesus said, "So they are no longer two, but one. Therefore what God has joined together let man not separate." (Mt. 19:6) John told me to read what Paul had written in the context of spiritual marriage or soul mate union.

He showed me the following passages: "For the unbelieving husband has been sanctified through his wife, and the unbelieving wife has been sanctified through her believing husband. Otherwise your children would be unclean, but as it is they are holy. But if the unbeliever leaves, let him do so. A believing man or woman is not bound in such circumstances; God has called us to live in peace. How do you know, wife, whether you will save your husband? Or, how do you know, husband, whether you will save your wife?" (1Cor. 7:14-16)

John told me that Paul was trying to explain that, overriding the laws of man or legalized marriage, if a soul mate chooses, or is called to a new path for his or her own spiritual growth, then the transformed, or believer, must let him or her go. No human can determine which relationship will propel the soul and transform the disbeliever — only God can determine that.

That is why it is so critical that we love one another, unconditionally, no matter who they appear to be on the surface or whatever their level of spiritual development — it is for the ultimate birth of our souls. "Lover" does not necessarily represent that a soul mate is a potential sexual partner or even a person of the opposite sex. A more accurate description of "lover," is really a friend. Our "lover" is one who desires to give of him or herself to help enhance our spiritual development. This is a part of a soul mate's calling. We are all many others' soul mate.

Chapter 12:12-14 "I did this to teach the human beings, and to awaken them from deep sleep. For the two of them were fallen, and realized that they were naked..."

Once Adam and Eve had been given spiritualizable souls, they realized who they were and became ashamed and frightened of their physical and spiritual vulnerability. They now knew sin because they had been granted the freedom, which permitted them to deny God if they so chose, to choose good from evil, to choose love or fear. The lessons of our life exist to awaken us to who we truly are and where we came from so that we may gain the knowledge which, in and of itself, abolishes sin and chooses perfection, or rather, love in every option.

Chapter 13:15-18 "When Adam came to know what his own foreknowledge was like, he produced a son like the Child of Humanity. He called him Seth, after the child in the eternal realms. Similarly, the Mother sent down her Spirit, which is like her and is a copy of what is in the realm of Fullness, for she was about to prepare a dwelling place for the members of the eternal realms who would come down. The human beings were made to drink water of forgetfulness by the first ruler so that they would not know from where they had come." This demonstrates that spiritual beings reproduce and send to Earth progeny with splendors that are "a copy" of their spirits.

The first ruler, or Worldly ruler, had to make humans forget their relationship to divinity because it would only be through this feeling of detachment and thus, inferiority, that humans would choose worldly splendors over divine splendors meant for the children of God. This inferiority complex comes from human's ignorance of their true heritage and divine rights. Today it masquerades as low self-esteem, feelings of inadequacy, depression, guilt, alienation, and the like.

Chapter 14:8-11 "...'If the Spirit descends upon them, they most certainly will be saved, and transformed. Power must descend upon every person, for without it no one could stand. After birth (physical birth on the Earth), if the Spirit of Life grows (continued fetal soul development through spiritual nourishment), and power comes and strengthens the soul (progressive resistance spiritual exercises that awaken and grow the spirit), no one will be able to lead this soul astray with evil actions (the God-strength is far stronger than the opposing forces in the World thus perfection is achieved). But people upon whom the contrary spirit descends are misled by this spirit, and lose their way."

Once again, through spiritual strength that is produced by the soul selecting difficult life challenges, the soul learns about its relationship to and dependence on the continual infusion of "blood" or divine love. Thus, the I being within the vessel of the soul is ultimately grown to such proportions that it is "born" or transformed into a fully spiritual being that can not choose unloving actions of any kind — it is pure light which is pure love.

Chapter 14:15-17 "He said to me, 'The contemptible spirit grows stronger in such people as they lose their way. This spirit lays a heavy burden on the soul, leads her into evil actions, and hurls her down into forgetfulness. After the soul leaves the body, she is handed over to the authorities who have come into being through the first ruler. They bind her with chains, throw her into prison (another human body), and abuse her (life obstacles, temptations), until finally she emerges from forgetfulness and acquires knowledge. This is how she attains perfection and is saved.'"

Interestingly, John uses the feminine or receptive "she" to describe a soul that is not yet perfected. This is because, from the divine perspective, we remain receptive "Yins" until we are transformed into the projectors of life or "Yangs" that correspond to the male. Once we are completely full of the spirit, accomplished through spiritual strength obtained in life lessons, we no longer have to be receptive but rather have become "male" and thus capable of projecting our own perfected spirit into other souls.

Chapter 14:18-20 "I said, 'Lord, how can the soul become youthful again, and return into her Mother's womb, or into Humanity?' He was glad when I asked about this, and he said to me, 'Truly blessed are you, for you understand. This soul needs to follow another soul in whom the Spirit of Life dwells, because she is saved through the Spirit. Then she will never be thrust into flesh again.'"

This represents two important concepts. First, that through spiritual reproduction, or passing along splendors of the elect into each of our souls, we are assisted on our developmental journey. It also represents following the loving guidance of a soul mate who has already achieved a higher spiritual level and can assist the still sleeping soul to become awakened. Our "lover" projects unconditional love, or divine spirit, into our soul thus increasing the amount of spirit or light within our soul. Increased light illuminates more thus more knowledge and understanding is achieved about the spiritual realm. In addition, increased light provides more warmth, or love, within our souls that we, in turn, can shine upon ourselves and others.

Chapter 16:1 "Now I am the perfect Forethought of all. I transformed myself into my offspring: I came into being first, and went down all the paths of life."

Here Jesus is explaining that before he came to Earth incarnate he reproduced his spiritual splendors in his offspring who worked in all the various roles of life here on Earth. Numerous teachers tried to explain to humans who they were and the knowledge that was required to grow their souls. Unfortunately, the mission to awaken souls and link them to God was largely not accomplished at this time.

Chapter 16: 3-4 "I went into the realm of great darkness, and continued until I entered the middle of the prison. The foundations of chaos shook, and I hid from the inhabitants of chaos, for they are evil. So they did not recognize me."

This represents the existence of the seed of Christ present in Jesus at the time of his birth. The seed grew, for the most part, unaware or "in the dark" until the time of Jesus' baptism which was in the middle years of a typical physical life. He caused a lot of upheaval but mostly remained incognito as a peasant and not a King.

It was necessary for Christ to come to Earth incarnate to provide the crucial umbilical cord, which linked the fetal souls to their source of nourishment provided by the Holy Spirit. Christ literally was the savior for all people because up until that time all the other efforts to accomplish the task of linking humans to God had been, with few exceptions, unsuccessful. His appearance incarnate also was to demonstrate our own divinity and relationship to God.

Humankind's capacity for controlling the wagging tail of evil had been sorely lacking. Our self-esteems were so low that very few could relate to a distant divine source; thus, we were almost unilaterally selecting worldly sources to try to fill the dark void within our hearts.

Chapter 16: 5-8 "A second time I returned, and went on. I had come from the inhabitants of light . . .(this represents Christ's spiritual descent for 40 days following his resurrection from death on the cross). I entered the middle of darkness and the center of the underworld, and turned to the task before me. The foundations of chaos shook, and were about to fall upon those who dwell in chaos, and destroy them. I hurried back to the root of my light, (the Tree of Life in heaven) that the inhabitants of chaos might not be prematurely destroyed."

This is a very telling and interesting passage. Here Jesus is confirming that we must have chaos in our lives in order to live and grow to perfection. Without this chaos we would perish because we would be without the challenges and spiritual progressive resistance exercises that make our soul spiritually strong.

It also demonstrates that if the World forces perished before fetal souls have been fully perfected with the help of life challenges they would be born unperfected and thus incapable of rejoining with the Light of God because darkness cannot exist in the light. In other words, human souls, and the accompanying I beings of spirit, would die.

Chapter 16:10-11 ". . .I brightened my face with light from the consummation of this world, and entered the middle of this prison, the prison of the body. I said, 'Let whoever hears arise from deep sleep."

The prison is once again identified as being the human body and the Holy Spirit's descent into the mature and fully grown soul of Jesus in the middle years of life. Here Jesus is also demonstrating that not everyone can hear what he has to say and, thus, only those who can will be able to awaken to who they really are.

Chapter 16:12 "A sleeper wept and shed bitter tears. Wiping them away, the sleeper said, 'Who is calling my name? What is the source of this hope that has come to me, dwelling in the bondage of prison?"

Christ, being the ultimate Yang or projector of divine spirit, awakened many I beings housed within the souls of the Yins. The newly awakened soul has a dramatic emotional experience and cries like a baby just being born into a room of bright lights, strange noises and people. Full of questions but also full of hope the newborn recognizes a kind of freedom that has just occurred that released him or her from the tight and restrictive confines of the physical body and spiritual womb. The newborn also recognizes its "change of venue" from the once dark spiritual womb to the light spiritual world. The transformation provides a completely different perspective for the newborn.

Chapter 16:14 "Arise, remember what you have heard, and trace your root. . ." Jesus is advising the aware person to not only get up and out of the spiritual womb where he or she has been sleeping but to also examine where we came from and learn what our spiritual family tree consists of in the way of splendors and spirits.

After reading *The Secret Book of John* and thinking about the controversy surrounding this apostle, I began to question John's relationship to Christ and now to me. I had never quite understood where I fit in the spiritual family tree. I had met many of the spirits that rightfully belonged there like Paul, Jesus' mother Mary, Mary Magdalene, Thomas, and, most recently, the Gnostic leader Valentinus who appeared to me as a big, stocky man with a Julius Caesar type haircut.

But John was more than any of these others — he seemed to be the one orchestrating my dreams and visions, introducing me to Christ, and leading me to Scripture and other historical documents. He had been the first to appear to me in meditation when I was seeking an angel but, disappointingly, discovered a regular "person." But was it rational to suppose that the Apostle John was truly guiding my spiritual transformation in some way?

I remembered what some Christian friends had told me. They said that it was impossible that John, or any other dead person, could actually be "alive and communicating" in any manner. They claimed that the Bible never mentioned anything about Jesus' apostles returning or otherwise continuing to influence the development of humans. I was confused.

One night as I was getting into bed, I had an unusual inclination to read the Bible. I was not in the habit of reading anything before I fell to sleep including the Bible. I had learned that these unexplained feelings often meant that I should follow a specific direction so I retrieved my Bible and climbed into bed.

I had no idea what I should read so I asked John to guide me to the page he wanted me to see. I closed my eyes and turned to the last chapter of his Gospel where Jesus was reinstating Peter and directing him to "take care of my sheep." But the verses my eyes fell upon came after these instructions to Peter. There was something in these last few passages that I had never seen before.

"Peter turned and saw that the disciple whom Jesus loved was following them. (This was the one who had leaned back against Jesus at the supper and had said, 'Lord, who is going to betray you?') When Peter saw him, he asked, 'Lord, what about him?' Jesus answered, 'If I want him to remain alive until I return, what is that to you? You must follow me'. Because of this, the rumor spread among the brothers that this disciple would not die. But Jesus did not say that he would not die; he only said, 'If I want him to remain alive until I return, what is that to you?'" (John 21:20-23)

The apostles' "job descriptions" had been written: Peter, and his spiritual offspring, would dutifully _follow_ in Jesus' footsteps by nourishing the developing fetal souls (elementary students) through the church; and John, and his spiritual offspring, would lead the mature fetal souls (secondary students) through the birth or transformation process. John would indeed remain "alive" until Jesus returned. His splendors would be projected into many souls and his guidance would provide comfort and direction to those newly transformed. John was Jesus' most beloved disciple for this very reason he represented God's ultimate goal, birth of souls into the spiritual realm.

John knew the ultimate truth about soul mates and how our love for each other would propel our souls forward. He, too, knew what Jesus had meant when he told me, "The answer is always Love."

A famous tradition concerning John that was handed down by St. Jerome in the 4th century, tells about the apostle in his final days living in Ephesus. Frail and invalid, John had to be carried to church meetings by his disciples. At these meetings he would proclaim only one thing, "Little children, love one another!" After a while, the disciples grew weary of hearing this one phrase repeated over and over so they asked, "Master, why do you always say only this one thing?" John replied, "It is the Lord's command and if this alone be done, it is enough!" I finally knew why John was my guide.

M. Sue Benford

Chapter Twenty Two

Why do bad things happen to good people?

One of the most pressing questions I had for Jesus was about the evil in the world and why God allowed "bad things to happen to good people?" This had been a question that had plagued and perplexed me throughout my life. My life was a perfect example of the terrible things that happen to the innocent and undeserving. Cancer at the age of five, permanent physical handicaps, an alcoholic and suicidal mother, loss of my only brother, two painful and disastrous marriages, and a profession that lead me to know, love, and lose hundreds of little children.

I had asked God the question "why" when I was only seven. Why did He allow these terrible things to happen in the world? After all, if He was so loving of a parent why let us fall, get hurt, cry, and hurt others in the process? One night in meditation, Jesus explained it all to me. It never dawned on me until Jesus showed me the hierarchy controlling all spiritual beings by using a corporate model that I would understand. He showed me that God was undeniably the CEO (Chief Executive Officer) who ruled the company with total authority. He, the Christ, was the President who answered only to the CEO. Beneath him were the departmental vice-presidents who, themselves, had large staffs and a variety of tasks predetermined by God's "Business Plan."

The vice-presidents were the archangels, including the fallen one, Satan. I was shocked at first by what I heard. It was the antithesis of everything I had believed. What was Satan doing in God's corporate structure? I did not know much about the stories in the Bible but I did know that Satan had been cast down to the underworld to battle <u>against</u> God and the good angels.

Jesus explained that God had "ordered" Satan and his followers to wreak havoc on the Earth. Satan, also known as the Evil One, did not act apart from God's will. He said that without bad there can be no good, without wrong there can be no right, without darkness there can be no light. There would be no lessons to learn, no challenges to face, no faith to muster, no differentiation between one soul and the next. Ignorance could not be discerned from wisdom, nor love from fear. In essence, no progressive resistance training for the soul and, thus, no spiritual strength development could be gained.

As with the physical body, without gravity and resistance our muscles cannot grow strong. It is only by challenging these "forces of the World" that we develop and become strong enough to be born. Satan is only permitted to act within the "Business Plan" established by God and for God's ultimate goal, which is to reunite humans in the light of their origin as perfect or all loving beings.

Jesus said that once our souls are transformed and thus "born into the spiritual realm" we understand Satan's limited control over us because we recognize the truth in what John told us, "...the one who is in you is greater than the one who is in the world." (1John 4:4) Once transformed, or born, our souls join Christ in the presidential office and continue working, with spiritual guidance, to become mature in their perfection (similar to how a newborn infant grows into a mature human adult).

Steiner offered poignant insights into the role of Satan in our lives. He described certain angels as being "countermanded" by God. Instead of acting as progressive influences, they were placed in the course of development to cause obstacles. Steiner's belief was that if the path were smooth, what was intended to come into existence could never arise. Spiritual strength could never be achieved without overcoming resistance.

One of the ways in which the "adversely commanded forces" operate is by using our own physical predisposition to challenge us. Humans are actually two complete but interconnected creatures: physical, or biological beings, and ethereal or spiritual beings. As the blood is to the physical body, the divine spirit is to the ethereal body.

The Secret Book of John explained that our physical bodies were created first but left to evolve prior to receiving the divine spirit within the soul. In essence, early humans functioned the same as God's other earthly creatures by being absolutely true to their biological instincts and inclinations. Early humans could not deviate from God's will; therefore, they could never truly sin by acting contrary to God's paramount Law.

This non-spiritualized human creature had many strong impulses built into its nature. Two of the strongest were the instinct for survival and the instinct to reproduce, which are the same with other animals. Along with these was the instinctual selection of pleasure over pain.

When the human soul became spiritualized, other factors came into play beyond just those of biological instincts. Humans became aware, on a subconscious level, of greater or higher purposes beyond the mere physical. This once unerring early human was now no longer simply responsible for following innate biological programming but now had to look beyond its physical existence into the realm of God's greater purpose for humankind.

Temptations to pull the human creature back to its predominate focus on early biological instincts was key to the resistance training human's required. Satan, and the countermanded forces, often used these strong urges within the physical body of humans to detract them from their greater, albeit less obvious, higher goals which unconsciously drove them to seek the spiritual realm. That is why early Christians attempted to completely block out the world, or lower body (biological) forces, in their search of higher spiritual levels.

Early on in this developmental process Satan got a strong hold over humans. The hidden splendors of the invisible world could not be seen amidst the plainly visible splendors in the physical realm. Humans wandered far away from God's course, floating dangerously close to oblivion. Instead of choosing spiritual over physical, the opposite was happening.

Christ sent many of his own perfected splendors into and among the human creatures but nobody was successful enough to turn the raging tide. Early religions sprung up and many of God's truths were revealed but they were not sufficient. The powers of the World, physical temptations and biological compulsions, were overwhelming the new, immature light of God within human souls. The connection had grown very dim between the Creator and His human children.

That is why Christ came to Earth incarnate. He literally came as the savior of the human race whose souls had not thrived under the opposing forces of the World. Jesus attached the life line between man and God; he created, and then became, the umbilical cord delivering the much-needed spiritual nourishment to grow the human fetal soul. Unlike any other human being to walk the planet before him, Jesus Christ was the only one of his kind.

Jesus' death saved humans and reconnected us to God; however, we still have to choose to receive the spiritual nourishment through the connection. As Paul had tried to explain, we were saved but still awaited salvation. Christ became the saving life line — our spiritual umbilical cords — but we have to still learn to accept and use the spiritual nourishment that God provides through this cord.

After Jesus' death, the spiritual light within human souls began to slowly flourish. As Christ had commanded, the institutional church was established and grew in power and strength supporting the development of many young fetal souls. Along side this movement, John guided the mature fetal souls through the birth or transformation process and on their journey to mature spiritual perfection. Once transformed the human could more handily control the "wagging tail of the dog" so that the world forces were no longer in control. Becoming perfect in God's eyes, for His human children, is to become an all-loving soul by choice and not by His command.

Perhaps that is what Jesus had meant when he told me that, *"Evil can not touch you now."* I originally thought it was because Michael and his angels protected me but now I saw another explanation. With the advent of my transformation or birth, I began to use the resources of the World but they no longer used me. I no longer was inclined toward an unloving thought and, now when one entered my mind like it had during my discussions with the fundamentalist Christians, I was quickly parlayed into a loving response. Like my biological parents used to do, now my spiritual parents were helping to correct my behavior while I was still too newborn to fully do it myself! I was beginning to travel the road of perfection.

Once I understood that all of my life's experiences had been set up as lessons, to help me become perfect or all loving, it started to make sense. At those low times in my life, especially in the recent past, I became more aware of heavenly interventions. In each case, I grew in one way or another and, by accepting that these interventions were the positive influence of God, I benefited from the situation and obtained a new level of spiritual growth. Without the adversity, or the forces of the World, the strength would never have materialized — the strength to expand my soul and know God's unconditional love.

Chapter Twenty Three

Who was Jesus Christ?

Of the numerous revelations I had been given by John, Jesus and my angelic guides, none disturbed me more than the discussion about who Jesus really was. I had always felt safe in believing that Jesus Christ was a perfect human being who never committed a transgression. I believed that he was born perfect, lived perfectly, and died perfectly as a God would have done. I wanted to see Jesus in this light because then I could allow myself the luxury of imperfection — after all, I was not like Jesus. I was a frail and broken human being who could never be sinless, or perfect, like Jesus who was more of a God than a mortal. I used this separateness as an excuse.

Like I had done with my powerlifting predecessors, I saw Jesus as superior to me. When I compared myself to him I was so far beneath him that I could not possibly aspire to gain his level of strength.

I shied away from picking up the spiritual "weights" and getting into the game. I sat on the sidelines ignoring any inclinations to participate in God's mysterious sport. Jesus was a world champion that I knew I could not emulate.

The only hints I had garnered from Christianity reinforced my beliefs that he was much more than I, or than any other human being, was. I was told that he never sinned, never lied, never did anything "bad," never acted otherwise than a God — he was born perfect, lived perfect, and died perfect.

I was no fool. Yes, I could possibly attain physical goals that I had set but never in this world could I achieve what Jesus did. And if I even so much as tried to be like Jesus I knew that I would be persecuted and mocked by the "real" Christians who accepted a lower position in God's Kingdom.

In the course of my research, I had borrowed many books from the public library. Some proved more helpful in my quest for the truth than others did. One book that I initially put aside as not useful was a book called <u>The Lost Books of the Bible</u> that was originally compiled in 1926 and published by Bell Publishing Company, New York. Since my path was leading to the more recently discovered texts at Nag Hammadi I did not pay close attention to the references in this book. At least, not until I was told to look closer.

I was diligent about returning all the books I borrowed to the library by their due date; therefore, I was surprised when I received a notice in the mail one day that I was overdue in returning one of the books. The book was <u>The Lost Books of the Bible</u> and I only vaguely remembered having checked it out.

As I was calling the library to ascertain whether or not there was some error on the library's part; I got a strange feeling that I still had the book somewhere in my house. Sure enough, when I looked through my personal stack of books I found that I must have accidentally included this library book with my own collection.

As I prepared to return the book to the library I heard a voice say, *"Read Thomas."* I thought this was odd; I did not see how the works I had read pertaining to Thomas in any way related to this book. Although I had never read this particular book, I did not imagine there was any link.

When I opened the book and started to flip through the pages I came to one entry entitled *Thomas's Gospel of the Infancy of Jesus Christ*. I was stunned to see something by Thomas in this text. The editor indicated that it is attributed to Thomas, and conjectured to have been originally connected with the *Gospel of Mary*. I would soon learn that it was also connected with the *Gospel of Matthew*.

The document begins, "I Thomas, an Israelite, judged it necessary to make known to our brethren among the Gentiles, the actions and miracles of Christ in his childhood, which our Lord and God Jesus Christ wrought after his birth in Bethlehem in our country, at which I myself was astonished; the beginning of which was as followeth." What was Thomas so astonished by? What had Jesus done as a child that was so amazing and how did that relate to what Jesus wanted me to know?

This account by Thomas reveals a Jesus who was born with all of his extraordinary gifts already in place. The seed had come to Earth with everything it would need to grow into the tall tree of Christ. But the story teaches that Jesus, like us, had to learn to control his biological self and use his gifts for good and not evil. Even Jesus Christ himself did not avoid the challenges of the World and the body when he came to Earth incarnate!

But why was Thomas telling this story and why to the "Gentiles" and not to the Jews? Why was this account left out of the accepted Gospels of the New Testament? Jesus told me that Thomas told the story in support of his father Matthew's teachings but left it separate to avoid retribution from the Jewish

Pharisees. Put together, the two Gospels support the prophecy of Isaiah and other crucial concepts we need to understand.

At the time of his discipleship, Matthew was under attack by the Jewish community to which he felt deeply connected. This was devastating to the apostle who wanted, more than anything, respect and admiration from his own people. In her book, <u>The Origin of Satan</u>, Pagels eludes to the fact that Matthew saw the Pharisees as the chief rivals to his own teachings about Jesus. As a result he decided to present Jesus and his message in palatable terms acceptable to the Pharisees and their large following.

In order to gain credence with the oppositional Pharisees, Matthew revises Mark's story by saying that the spirit descended upon Jesus not at his baptism but at the moment of his conception. So, Matthew says, Jesus' mother 'was discovered to have a child in her womb through the holy spirit' (Mt. 1:18). In other words, Jesus' birth was no scandal but a miracle — one that precisely fulfills Isaiah's ancient prophecy.

How did Thomas' account of Jesus' childhood help support Matthew's attempts to prove Jesus was the promised Messiah? One major thing that Matthew intentionally left out of his story was Jesus' early wrongdoings or transgressions. Matthew was concerned to refute damaging rumors about Jesus such that he neglected or even violated observance of Sabbath and kosher laws.

But herein lay the catch — Isaiah had prophesied that the Messiah would have to learn good from evil: "He will eat curds and honey when he knows enough to reject the wrong and choose the right. But before the boy knows enough to reject the wrong and choose the right, the land of the two kings you dread will be laid waste." (Isa. 7:15-16) These passages left Jesus' disciples in a quandary: tell about Jesus' early transgressions and "humanness" and risk losing credibility or attempt to prove the prophecy without including such damaging evidence.

Matthew and Thomas came up with the solution: tell the accounts in two separate types of stories to either share together or apart depending on the audience present — Jewish or Gentile. Unfortunately, Thomas' infancy gospel became rejected as an individually significant document and, apart from his father's gospel, it could be interpreted by some as damaging to Jesus' credibility. But understanding its origin and purpose helps prove that Jesus was, indeed, the true Messiah promised by God through Isaiah's prophecy.

Thomas wrote, "Another time Jesus went forth into the street, and a boy running by, rushed upon his shoulder; at which Jesus being angry, said to him, thou shalt go no farther. And he instantly fell down dead: which when some persons saw, they said, 'Where was this boy born, that everything which he says presently cometh to pass? . . Either teach him that he bless and not curse, or else depart hence with him, for he kills our children.'"

Unlike us, Thomas was not astonished by the fact that Jesus had to grow and develop into perfection as did other human beings; he was amazed, and wanted us to be amazed, by the fact that his gifts were already present at his birth — he was the Messiah at birth just as Isaiah had prophesied.

Thomas, having been transformed himself by the Holy Spirit, already knew and understood how transformation occurred. Therefore, Thomas' account of Jesus' early years focuses more on Jesus' extraordinary gifts than on his transgressions or lack of "goodness."

Jesus had to grow, awaken, strengthen, and await the Holy Spirit to become perfect but not to become who he would ultimately be. The exact same way we do. Jesus was not exclusively a God — he was also a human being just like us. He avoided <u>nothing</u> here on earth: he committed wrongful acts, he pleaded for God's help, he accepted the Holy Spirit into his life and he was transformed — that is the lesson.

"But we see Jesus, who was made a little lower than the angels, now crowned with glory and honor because he suffered death, so that by the grace of God he might taste death for everyone...For this reason he had to be made like his brothers in every way, in order that he might become a merciful and faithful high priest in service to God...Because he himself suffered when he was tempted, he is able to help those who are being tempted." (Heb. 2:9,17-18)

Another text included in <u>The Lost Books of the Bible</u> also describes the same Jesus in his early years. Entitled *The first Gospel of the Infancy of Jesus Christ*, this text, according to the editor, was accepted by the Gnostics. In this account of Jesus' early years many of the same reports are given as those in Thomas' gospel, only more detail is focused on Jesus' early imperfections.

This Gospel also depicts the transition point in Jesus' life when he was twelve and remained behind in a temple in Jerusalem to talk with doctors, elders, and learned men in Israel. At this point, Jesus now realized "who he truly was" and what his role was to be in the world. He queries those in the temple by saying, "Whose son is the Messiah? They answered, the son of David: Why then, said he, does he in the spirit call him Lord when he saith, The Lord said to my Lord, sit thou at my right hand, till I have made thine enemies thy footstool?"

Jesus also reveals certain facts of unknown origin, which the elders cannot begin to understand. Things, which were not known at the time in any book that Jesus, could have read. One such higher understanding was portrayed in Jesus' knowledge about the cosmos. "When a certain astronomer...asked Jesus whether he had studied astronomy? The Lord Jesus replied, and told him the number of the spheres and heavenly bodies, also their triangular, square, and sextile aspect; their progressive and retrograde motion; their size and several prognostications; and other things which the reason of man had never discovered."

Jesus also had a great knowledge of both physics and metaphysics. "There was also among them a philosopher, well skilled in physics and natural philosophy, who asked the Lord Jesus whether he had studied physics? He replied, and explained to him physics and metaphysics. Also those things which were above and below the power of nature."

Jesus' twelfth year, and this occurrence at the temple, was a turning point for Christ. He awakened to his calling. After his parents found him at the temple, "Then he returned with them to Nazareth, and obeyed them in all things . . . And the Lord Jesus grew in stature and wisdom, and favour with God and man."

"Now from this time Jesus began to conceal his miracles and secret works, And he gave himself to the study of law, till he arrived at the end of his thirtieth year; At which time the Father publicly owned him at Jordan, sending down this voice from heaven, 'This is my beloved son in whom I am well pleased;' The Holy Ghost being also present in the form of a dove. This is he whom we worship with all reverence, because he gave us our life and being, and brought us from our mother's womb. Who for our sakes, took a human body, and hath redeemed us, so that he might so embrace us with everlasting mercy, and show his face, large, bountiful grace and goodness to us."

Jesus' baptism by the Holy Spirit represented his transformation from a Yin to a Yang, from a called to a chosen, from the ignorant to the wise. It was his "birth" into the spiritual realm. His role and his gifts were different from ours but the process was and is the same. Jesus demonstrated his ability to overcome the devil, or the World, when he was challenged in the desert <u>after</u> his baptism. This shows us how, as I had been told by him previously, once a soul is transformed, *"Evil can not touch you now."* It is the same for us as it was for him. This is what he wanted me to know.

Jesus wants us to relate to him not as a god but as a big brother: once a fellow biological being who is also a child of God. "As Jesus started on his way; a man ran up to him and fell on his knees before him. 'Good teacher,' he asked, 'what must I do to inherit eternal life?' 'Why do you call me good?' Jesus answered. 'No one is good — except God alone.'" (Mark 10:17-18) Jesus did not say, "Only God and I are good and you are bad." In this context, "good" refers to actions antithetical to the contrived laws or beliefs of man <u>not</u> to sin, which involves thoughts and actions denying God's paramount Law, refusing to accept God's divine love, which kills our soul. This is an extremely important concept to grasp because it is so often misunderstood and, thus, the cause for our defeatist attitudes in striving for perfection, or all lovingness to each other, which is the second part to God's paramount Law.

"For we do not have a high priest who is unable to sympathize with our weaknesses, but we have one who has been tempted in every way, just as we are — yet was without sin." (Heb. 4:15) Jesus did "bad" things in the eyes of other humans

— just ask the Pharisees or the people in his home town! But he never sinned — that is, he never rebuked God's love, denounced his mission in God's service, denied God's existence, or put himself above God.

Jesus alone was born with the special gift of knowing; therefore, he was not able to disbelieve the existence of his Father or the divine spirit dwelling within his soul. He never broke the first issuance of God's paramount Law and, thus, ultimately, grew into perfection and achievement of the second part of God's paramount Law within a single lifetime on Earth.

That is why we are born sinners — not because we stole a candy bar from the store when we were five, which broke a law of man, but because we deny, ignore, or refuse God's unconditional love as spiritual nourishment for our souls! We are born incarnate in our early lifetimes with spirits so small and dim that they barely are noticeable in comparison to the World.

Some spirits stay small and immature throughout many lifetimes and others are extinguished altogether through refusal of the spiritual nourishment they desperately need. In biological infants this refusal to grow and develop is called "Failure To Thrive." By killing our divinely-related souls we are, in essence, killing a part of God.

Paul taught us that, ". . .if righteousness could be gained through law, Christ died for nothing!" (Gal. 2:21) He goes on to explain that, "Now that faith has come, we are no longer under the supervision of the law." (Gal. 3:25). And finally, "For in Christ Jesus neither circumcision nor uncircumcision (a part of Jewish law) has any value. The only thing that counts is faith expressing itself through love." (Gal. 5:6)

God does not discriminate between the good and the bad on earth, ". . .He causes his sun to rise on the evil and the good, and sends rain on the righteous and the unrighteous." (Mt. 5:45) Our faith, and subsequently, knowledge and acceptance of God's love must come first before we can become sinless and then, ultimately, perfect.

Through nurturing our first spiritual seed from God, through faith, and progressing our souls through love, we no longer <u>can</u> sin. Our faith, which by its very definition is susceptible to doubts, becomes transformed into actual <u>knowledge</u>. Knowledge does not permit the denial of God's existence, unconditional love, or our heritage as a divine spiritual being.

It is as if you are physically blind and someone tells you that the color of grass is green. You must rely on faith that the person is telling the truth and that the grass is really green. But if your eyesight is restored and you can see for yourself that grass is green, then you no longer have to rely on faith because it has been replaced by knowledge.

Once we have obtained this first faith in the divine we can proceed to becoming perfect or all loving. Jesus was ". . .made perfect through his suffering"

(Heb. 2:10) not, as many might believe, as a result of his birth upon the Earth. "During the days of Jesus' life on earth, he offered up prayers and petitions with loud cries and tears to the one who could save him from death, and he was heard because of his reverent submission. Although he was a son, he learned obedience from what he suffered and, once made perfect, he became the source of eternal salvation for all who obey him." (Heb. 5:7-9)

Jesus began working <u>towards</u> perfection at the time of his birth upon the Earth — because he always had knowledge of God and his divine spirit as his special gift. But he did not begin working <u>from</u> perfection until his baptism when the Holy Spirit descended upon him. Working from perfection is the opposite of working towards perfection.

While we are still working towards perfection, which occurs when we acknowledge the existence of the divine spirit in our lives, our frame of reference is that of a physical being attempting to achieve spiritual goals. We struggle against the World's "tests" and are rewarded when we "defeat" one of the forces and accomplish something loving for others or us. We find ourselves living as physical beings whom have to constantly be "encouraged" by the forces of the World to be true to God's paramount Law and make spiritual love a part of our daily lives.

Once we have been transformed we begin working <u>from</u> perfection. At this point, our perspective has changed from that of a physical being trying to do spiritual tasks to a spiritual being doing spiritual tasks while still operating in the physical world. Now, instead of being rewarded for occasional loving thoughts and behaviors brought on by forces of the World, we are corrected by our spiritual parents if we deviate from this new norm of "all lovingness" or perfection. We operate, at this point, as the true beings that we are. We know we are eagles or, rather, beings of the Light. The light of knowledge has replaced the darkness of the womb.

Our focus has changed from having to make time for God and spiritual love in our lives to having to make time for the World. Once we have achieved a full measure of perfection in a given lifetime we no longer return to Earth for additional life lessons but only, perhaps occasionally, as teachers for a higher purpose. At this point, the newborn eaglet has learned to fly.

Another analogy is comparing those working towards perfection with first graders just entering school. Prior to school they were not subject to any types of formal lessons but only confined to following their parent's most rudimentary "laws" until they were mature enough for formal training.

Once admitted to school the child learns specific lessons required to pass each grade (they are now working towards the goal of perfection). If the child remains in school and completes each grade satisfactorily, he or she finally progresses to graduation. Once graduation occurs the student begins working from a completely different perspective (from perfection). The graduate is now challenged with new and different tasks to succeed in the "real world" whether it be the physical world for biological students or the spiritual world for souls.

But as Jesus taught, as humans, we can expect to become sinless and perfect but we can never, and should never, be completely good. It is impossible for any of us, at least while still incarnate, to always be "good." That is reserved for God alone. But how often is the actual progression from sinlessness (accepting God's omnipotence and unconditional love) to perfection (becoming all loving to ourselves and our fellow humans) to goodness (not doing anything perceived by others as wrong or evil) reversed to be goodness to perfection to sinlessness? By reversing the true progression we doom ourselves to lives of guilt and fear taking us ever further from God's paramount Law of Love — for Him, others, and ourselves.

However, when we become sinless and working from perfection, this transformation in and of itself controls our selection of good over evil actions. But why can we not, or should we not, ever be totally good? The answer is because being good is, in some cases, antithetical to God's paramount Law of accepting God's spiritual nourishment and being an all loving or perfect being. Many times we sacrifice our very souls by being good and relinquishing our spiritual development to those other than God. By attempting to always be good, was I, in essence, sacrificing my very soul as my dying brother had suggested? Did my spiritual steel door keep, not only other people's love out, but also the spiritual nourishment of God's unconditional love at bay? I realized that, if I had chosen to believe only what others told me was "good," ironically, I never would have become a Christian! More importantly, had Jesus always done the "good" thing as perceived by his contemporaries, Christianity would never exist.

Jesus' message was clear. He was one of us in every way and did not consider himself above his fellow human beings in the eyes of God or man. Nor did he consider his gifts and talents exclusively his alone — we would be made as strong as him, thus elevating us to his level as President. We would then be over the vice presidents and others, including Satan.

M. Scott Peck in his book, <u>Further Along the Road Less Traveled</u>, gives an example of why Jesus wants us to know who he really was and how that relates to us. During a seminar consisting of Christian therapists and counselors, a story was told about Jesus being called to resuscitate the daughter of a wealthy Roman. After telling the story, the audience of six hundred were asked whom they related to in the story. Only six of six hundred Christian professionals related to Jesus himself.

Peck noted a definite problem in that only one out of a hundred identified with Jesus. After all, is that not exactly what we are supposed to do — act like and try to emulate the actions of Jesus?

Peck was on target. Jesus wants us to see his transgressions, or humanness, and how he was transformed with the descent and his acceptance of the Holy Spirit. He wants us to truly know the man he was and not only the God that he was before and after his lifetime incarnate. If we do not learn the truth about Jesus, his trials and tribulations, his challenges and frailties, then we can never truly accept the truth of our own potential and accept ourselves for not always being good.

We will always think of ourselves as chickens even when the truth is that we are eagles. We will focus only on our weakness and not on the strength we can gain with spiritual assistance. As long as we persist in seeing Jesus as superior to us, and never having struggled with the World to gain his own identity and perfection, we are doomed to accepting our lesser selves.

Jesus is our version of a spiritual world champion. A record breaker in every category! But as with the records set in the physical world, spiritual records are also meant to be surpassed even if we cannot fathom the possibility of having the potential to accomplish such a grandiose feat. "I tell you the truth, anyone who has faith in me will do what I have been doing. He will do even greater things than these, because I am going to the Father. And I will do whatever you ask in my name, so that the Son may bring glory to the Father." (John 14:12-13)

What are the "greater things than these" we are expected to accomplish? The answer, once again, is always Love. The greater things are found in our individual efforts and contributions to the distribution of God's love throughout the world. "And this is his command: to believe in the name of his Son, Jesus Christ, and to love one another as he commanded us. Those who obey his commands live in him, and he in them. And this is how we know that he lives in us: We know it by the Spirit he gave us." (1John 3:23-24)

As I wrote this chapter I dared to think about how my own life mirrored that of Jesus'. It dawned on me — had I, like Jesus, been awakened when I was twelve? Did my poetry reflect a certain unconscious attempt to reveal what lay ahead in the seed sown into my soul before my birth? Would we all find similar hints of our destiny somewhere in our pasts or maybe it was written in the stars? And how would we ever truly be able to detect or discern "the Spirit" that God had given us? I had many more questions that needed to be answered.

Chapter Twenty Four

The invisible truths

After months of receiving these thoughts and understandings from John, Jesus, and the others, I started to become skeptical and scientific about the whole ordeal. Trained in the hard sciences as a nurse, I focused on viable theories and facts. I accepted only the highest rigors in research from others and myself, quickly dismissing any untestable hypotheses. In order for me to consider these "revelations" as potentially valid I would need to see some scientific proof supporting these occurrences.

One morning I awoke to a very interesting vision. I saw myself walking down a road that came to a fork. Down one side there were flashing lights, direction arrows, sirens and other enticing noises that made it look like the Las Vegas strip. Down the other path the road was dark and there was nothing compelling about it.

Next to me, and gently guiding me by each of my arms were two angels. They kept encouraging me to take the Vegas" route. Clearly, it was the one I felt more comfortable in choosing but, if I wanted, there was nothing stopping me from choosing the dark path either. The angelic guidance was extremely subtle at first but became more compelling the more I showed interest in heading in the wrong direction.

Then a voice said to me, *"The stars are the road map for the soul."* Could this be true? Did we come to Earth with our own version of a Triple A "Trip Tik" outlining the paths for our most productive route in life? If so, how did it all connect — what did modern science have to say about this wild idea?

I had never understood or believed in Astrology, so I was not familiar with how people looked at the stars to provide guidance for their lives. I was reluctant to begin pursuing a study of Astrology because, to me, it was in the opposite direction from the scientific approach I was seeking. But as with everything else that I was supposed to learn, I was compelled to begin learning about this connection between the cosmos and us.

I researched many books on the subject and had my own Natal Chart compiled by a local astrologer. I used the various guide books available to help interpret my own chart to see if I found any similarities between what the stars said and what I knew about myself, my past, and my present course.

The books claimed that professional astrologers do not believe that the objects in the sky influence activities on Earth, as many lay people believed. "The great cosmic or celestial events happening around and beyond Earth . . .are not seen as causing events to occur on Earth, but as great signatures of events also happening here on Earth. In other words, there is no cause in the heavens followed by an effect here on Earth. Instead, both planetary and earthly events happen simultaneously and are mutually reflective. Neither is the cause of the other; both are the product of the moment, one acted out in the heavens above, the other here on the Earth below . . .there is only one grand 'play.' The great drama enacted in the sky is also acted out (in exact detail) here on Earth in the same instant."

The crux, then, of Astrology is to assist a person in seeing the influences that would be playing out in his or her life, where the focus would be, and where lessons would be highlighted, in order to illuminate the proper path. A path that, I was told, was well known and followed by our personal angels.

I was guided to a particular astrologer/psychic who lived in Cleveland, Ohio named Rosanna. I found her to be an extremely interesting and fascinating person who had received much acclaim for her astrological prowess and psychic abilities. I scheduled both a phone and personal appointment with her.

Rosanna had studied Astrology for over forty years and was considered one of the world's experts on the subject. She had developed her own set of tarot cards as tools to receive and interpret spiritual guidance. She gave me an introductory lesson about the cards and their significance.

I began studying my own chart with a renewed interest. It did seem to describe many of my well-known strengths, weaknesses, challenges, and talents. But those traits, I surmised, could possibly be ascribed to a great many people. But then I came upon something extremely telling that either had to be the biggest freak coincidence or something that leant significant credibility to the practice of Astrology.

On the date Feb. 27, 1995 the following unique narrative was given: "The above date marks the end of a number of years of hard work on your part, sort of an apprenticeship. Now you will begin to come into your own. Opportunities will present themselves. Now is the time to make that outward push and ride the crest of the wave into fame and fortune . . .This is also a time when you may . . .take on a new role in the community or with other people . . . These next 6 - 7 years will find circumstances working to help you and raise you up, push you forward . . . These are good years to grow up . . ."

I was astonished. My divorce from Jake had occurred on March 1, 1995 only two days after this earmarked date. I remembered feeling almost giddy at the idea of the divorce, certain that better things were going to occur but with no earthly reason to believe that to be true. It was only two months prior to that date when the voices had begun directing me down this path — a path I had stubbornly refused for years. I had indeed learned many lessons in this apprenticeship and now was beginning to grow up — not in body, but in soul.

But how was it possible that we were in some way connected to things happening in the distant heavens? Had not modern science, especially physics, proven that these types of distant invisible connections did not exist? I relished the idea of proving, scientifically, that the ideas of Astrology and psychic phenomena were absurd and impossible. I was led to an area within physics called quantum mechanics.

What I found in quantum physics astounded me. It had been quite a while since I had studied physics and even then we only learned the basics. Since that time other truths had been discovered about the invisible world around us. One of the things I was drawn to was the understanding we now had about subatomic particles and their actions. In his book, <u>The Tao of Physics</u>, physicist Fritof Capra, notes that the notion of a basic 'quantum interconnectedness' received renewed attention during the last two decades, when physicists came to realize that the universe, in fact, may be interconnected in much subtler ways than one had thought before.

Were these the same truths that Jesus had spoken about at the temple in Jerusalem when he was only twelve? Did this new understanding that invisible particles acted, not from local causes as Einstein and his colleagues had once surmised, but through some unknown invisible connection have anything to do with Astrology and the telepathic voices I was hearing?

Many contemporary physicists have alluded to the possibility that some type of superluminal quantum connectedness seems to be an explanation for some types of psychic phenomena such as telepathy. Ironically, physicists have held psychic phenomena in disdain since the days of Newton; in fact, most physicists do not even believe that they exist.

In the 1960's a physicist by the name of John Bell developed a theorem, which is a mathematical proof. What it 'proves' is that if the statistical predictions of quantum theory are correct, then some of our commonsense ideas about the world are profoundly mistaken. As Henry Stapp wrote: 'The important thing about Bell's theorem is that it puts the dilemma posed by quantum phenomena clearly into the realm of macroscopic phenomena . . . [it] shows that our ordinary ideas about the world are somehow profoundly deficient even on the macroscopic level.'" (Zukav, page 290)

Bell performed a series of experiments that proved that no matter where in the universe two identical particles were located they would simultaneously respond to one another. He discovered that no matter what the settings of the polarizers, the clicks in area A are correlated too strongly to the number of clicks in area B to be explained by random chance. They have to be connected somehow. However, if they are connected, then the principle of local causes (which says that what happens in one area does not depend upon variables subject to the control of an experimenter in a distant space-like area) is an illusion!

Was it possible that actions occurring in the solar system were somehow representative of how our own ethereal bodies, or souls, would respond? Could these actions be mapped out to indicate some type of universal human response to specific cosmic forces and activities?

Jesus explained it very simply to me. He said that we are all connected to every aspect of the universe by these subatomic energy particles. He showed me how the connection ranged from one thin line of particles extending between us and someone or something else very distant to us, in either time or space, and how that line grew and thickened as our interactions became more intense or connected to that particular soul or event. What he showed me looked like fluctuating radio waves of some kind.

He said everything that has occurred or will occur is already written in God's Book; we are connected to the past, the present and to the future in the same way. Time, in essence, is an illusion perceived only from the physical realm to assist us, while incarnate, in learning lessons and progressing our souls in a sequential manner.

This "subatomic connection" is why we can sense when someone will enter our lives after we may not have heard from them in a long time — we are recalling their unique frequency and sensing its increased power, thus, indicating a closing of distance. This is also how we "call" souls to us at certain times and for specific lessons. A certain chemistry may exist between bodies but it is a physics that attracts and connects souls!

Jesus also told me that our souls were uniquely imprinted with the road map of our destiny. We are the tree we will become at the time of our births. We choose it with God as co-creators of our own destiny: our families, our unique life experiences, challenges, talents, opportunities, everything that we will do or become. We draw up the plans and bring them with us when we are born — in the form of spiritual DNA.

But the irony is that we can ruin or destroy that direction by continuing to choose the wrong path throughout our life. Our developing fetal soul is compromised by denying spiritual nourishment from God, which, in essence, stymies our attempts at receiving and giving love to each other.

As John told me one night, *"You can not loan it if you do not own it!"* It is through our true spiritual, or loving, connections both with God and with others that we transform our own souls and complete the full circle back into the realm of God's Kingdom from where we originated. It is through our capacity to receive and give love that our true spiritual achievement is tested.

John said, in reality, we only loan our divine love because, eventually, it will come back to us when we are reunited with our soul mates in the All. But if our soul mate chooses death over eternal life in the All then we have made the ultimate sacrifice for our friend by extending, without return, that part of our own divine spirit.

Jesus explained that angels were made up of these same subatomic particles and did consist of their own "splendors" as Paul had described. They each have their own unique particle charge, or frequency, that elicits specific responses from our souls. Thus, we can communicate with angels if we take the time to tune in and "learn their frequency."

Is there any relationship between angels and the subatomic wave/particles called "photons?" In the book, Physics of Angels by Matthew Fox and biologist Rupert Sheldrake explain that science provides us with important metaphors or parallels to the idea of angels as immaterial and disembodied but capable of containing bodies and being present through their action — similar to the actions of photons. In fact, that is what quantum theory is all about.

"The wave aspect of the photon has to do with nonlocalized nature and its movement. The particle aspect has to do with its localized action. Insofar as angels act in particular places, they are like particles; insofar as they are disembodied and mobile, they are like waves, vibrations in fields." (Fox and Sheldrake, page 109)

Many people do not realize that most of the electromagnetic spectrum is invisible to our eyes. All forms of electromagnetic radiation involve photons or light. If angels are transmitters of light, visible and invisible, they may be generating various types of radiation which we can not visibly see including ultraviolet and infrared light, cosmic and gamma rays, radio waves, microwaves, and X-rays.

One night in meditation Jesus told me that the seven psychical substances mentioned in *The Secret Book of John* used to create our bodies and souls would soon be discovered. These substances combine to form the spiritual DNA we inherit from our spiritual parents — like that transferred from Elijah to Elisha. Encoded in these substances are matching codes to our soul mates, angelic and planetary splendors. He said that science would prove the existence of the Spirit and, ultimately, the existence of God!

He went on to explain that we would find specific patterns in the subatomic particles that form unique electromagnetic frequencies within the surrounding "aura" of energy around our bodies — some patterns will attract particular frequencies and some will repel. He said that we would be able to measure and identify the patterns of each individual aura, which is our soul, and demonstrate matches in frequencies among soul mates. The matches will be stronger when the paths are to be intertwined for life lessons and weaker when the mates are to separate. We will also, eventually, demonstrate that a definite subatomic, quantum link connects us all.

He said that we would learn that the electromagnetic aura composition is different between animals and humans because of the spiritualized soul of humans. Lower body, or instinctual, biological forces, although containing the divine spirit, compel the souls of animals. Animals cannot deviate from God's will created in their souls. Recent studies have demonstrated that the one unique separation between chimpanzees and humans is that the chimps do not understand "intention." In other words, they do not have the capacity to appreciate, or select, an alternative course of action aside from that which compels them biologically.

Angels, who also cannot do other than God's will, are on the opposite end of the spectrum. They are all-spirit, devoid of biological forces. While animals remain "ignorant" of deviating from the divine spirit, angels remain "all knowing" or one with the spirit. Thus, neither animal nor angel has the freedom to sin against God by choosing other than God's will for them.

Humans, however, are a combination of both animal and angel — an "anigel" if you will. We are physical beings drawn to specific biologically derived urges and instincts; yet, we have been given the seed of transformation within our souls. The seed, which is God's divine light and our heritage, can grow if the receptacle of the soul becomes receptive to allow for additional spiritual infusion. The previously dark spots within the soul then become charged with the divine light and eventually all darkness is replaced with the light. The soul becomes all loving and we become "gods."

Jesus explained to me that, when we are first born into human bodies, we begin with practically no discernible feeling or knowledge of the Holy Spirit (light) dwelling in our soul. As we become more receptive, and thus more transformation occurs, we begin recognizing that there is something beyond our mere physical compulsions making up our essence. This belief or "faith" that something divine actually exists grows stronger as we continue throughout our numerous lifetimes. We develop eyes that see and ears that hear. The lighted parts of our soul increase with each spiritual infusion and actually expand in illumination and divine love.

As we reach transformation, and our vantage point changes from the physical world to the spiritual world, we recognize that our former seed of faith (blindness due to darkness) has now grown into the tree of knowledge (clear vision within the light). Once transformation has occurred, we understand our true heritage and place in the spiritual hierarchy, thus we are no longer controlled by the forces of the World that lead us away from spiritual nourishment. In essence, we become stronger than the forces of the World.

But how do we grow our soul such that the spirit can grow in us? Jesus told me that when we love another human being we draw near to that person, either in thought or action and, thus, merge our soul with their soul — the "flesh" of the two lovers becomes one. The soul is the spiritual "flesh" containing the life-giving "blood" or spirit.

Initially, I was having a hard time picturing exactly how this transference occurred, so Jesus explained the connection between the soul and the spirit to me by using the analogy of a sponge and water. The soul is like a dry sponge capable of expanding, growing, and becoming more pliable and "sponge-like" when it receives water, which is like the spirit. The sponge collects water in two ways: either through infusion directly by a water source or through direct contact with another sponge that contains more water, which seeps into the drier sponge in order to cause an equalizing effect.

The sponge "learns" through trial and error that some water is not the same as other water. Some water only reaches the surface layers of the sponge and still other types evaporate rapidly leaving the sponge even drier and harder, or less "sponge-like," than before. Only a very specific and drenching type of water can penetrate the many layers of the sponge and remain for the duration of the sponge's existence.

The sponge also discovers, however, that if it cuts itself off from this specific type of penetrating water, eventually, its life within the world of air will dry it out completely and it will no longer possess the true qualities of a sponge — it will be more like a rock.

Once the sponge has accepted enough water deep within its numerous layers, it realizes that it has many different characteristics than it once possessed as a dry sponge or barely damp sponge. It is almost totally transformed from what it once was.

Now the sponge realizes that it no longer can gain water from being next to other sponges because it has the most water — it can only give water to other sponges at this point. But it soon finds that there is a source still with more water than that contained in its sponge layers. This source is pure water itself — water unencumbered by a sponge-like body.

The sponge is drawn to this new environment of water instead of air because it knows that what truly makes it a sponge, and not a rock, is the water within. It understands now that it can only become complete by changing its realm of existence. It is guided or "pulled" into the water source providing it with a completely different perspective of the world it once inhabited.

For a time the sponge floats upon the surface slowly absorbing the pure water deep within its layers. When it has obtained a full measure, and can no longer absorb any more water, the sponge is "rung out" and cast aside for it has served its purpose. The water once contained inside the sponge is released into the pool to join with the pure water it had once floated upon, been filled with, been created by. Now as pure water, the former sponge realizes that its sponge-body had only been a receptacle, for the purpose of gathering water, and not, as once believed, the essence of which it really was.

From a scientific perspective, projecting unconditional love, which is divinely granted to us, triggers a certain subatomic response in the I being particles of the soul that helps awaken the soul to the existence of the spirit. The awakened spirit expands and strengthens the soul and helps open the spiritual door, allowing even more light, or divine love, to shine through.

This infusion of divine spiritual love into the receptor soul is, then, nourishment or "fruits" for the soul. Love to the fetal soul is comparable to blood to a biological fetus. The growth of the soul allows for the infusion of more divine spirit. The more spirit one has the more loving, or closer to perfection, one becomes and the more faith and, ultimately knowledge, one obtains as a result.

The cycle continues, if permitted by the human soul, until transformation is reached. God assists us by demonstrating how the World can only fail in providing us with the love that we need to grow our souls. Each of our life lessons demonstrates that the World cannot provide divine love to nourish the soul — only God can. When we have finally exhausted the resources of the World, God demonstrates how we always, and only, have the first divine love.

Souls "mate" to produce growth within the soul, which will eventually lead to a full transformation. The essential key to recognize is that only God's unconditional love will propel and fuel the human soul. Love disguised as need, manipulation, lust, sex, infatuation, or anything less than totally unconditional as that from God, will not substitute for the real thing.

We can fake many things in our physical lives but the soul cannot be tricked into recognizing patterns and frequencies that do not provide genuine love. We can grow our soul by accepting love offered from God, loving ourselves, and then other humans. We, in turn, assist others by sharing that love we have received.

Jesus said that is why we are not supposed to hide our light, which signifies a soul recognized as containing spiritual love, but rather, shine it widely on others so that they can grow in spirit, too. Once souls have obtained an adequate level of spirit and are ready for transformation, then only the Holy Spirit itself can provide the required amount of "water" to guide the last stages of the soul's conversion into pure spirit.

In other words, Christ himself is the final "soul mate" we encounter on our journey. No matter which spiritual path of moral "goodness" and love we have taken up until this point, in order to take the final transformational step, we ultimately must unite in marriage with Christ.

This is why Jesus alone was able to guide or transform Mary Magdalene, Thomas, John, and Paul. Mary Magdalene was made "male," Thomas became recognized as Jesus' "twin," John was known as Jesus' "most beloved disciple," and Paul carried "the mark of Jesus" on his body. All representations of the final stage in their souls' transformational journey, their graduation, their souls' birth.

John recognized that humans would have to love each other to grow their souls prior to having faith or knowledge in a divine being. By the end of his lifetime he had deduced that there was one fundamental way to ignite the divine sparks of light within our soul. John wisely instructed the little children, who were still ignorant of the divine Being, "Love one another and if that alone be done it is enough!"

He knew that we are all born ignorant of God's and Christ's existence; therefore, we cannot be faithful to something we do not yet know exists. That is impossible. But we have all been given the capacity to love, unconditionally, as God first loved us — in the divine seed planted within our souls.

I was stunned at these overlapping spiritual and scientific revelations. Was it possible that we would actually detect and be able to monitor our souls and spirits? Would we be able to "type" spiritual essences like we currently type blood and determine degrees of spirit contained within our souls? Would we identify spiritual relatives like we identify biological relatives?

I was more than a little amazed. All these scientists, theologians, and philosophers seemed to be providing matching pieces to the puzzle I was trying to put together. The scary thing was that it made an incredible amount of sense and the more I learned the more my guides told me. Not only was I completing the puzzle I had begun, but also the puzzle was getting larger and I was finding new pieces all the time. As they informed me, the larger you make your own receptacle of knowledge the more we can fill it!

Intertwined with the cosmic mysteries I was being taught, and reading about, lurked a small voice from deep within. Our missions on Earth were twofold: the service of God and the service of our soul. I felt like I was making headway in the former with my studies and revelations but there was still something dark and unsettled within my own soul. Something I needed to resolve from long, long ago that kept me tied and bound to anxious feelings. What it was I did not know but I sensed I would soon find out one way or another. School was still in session and my next lesson was about to unfold.

Chapter Twenty Five

Graduation day

On November 19, 1996 I was scheduled to attend yet another workshop conducted by Lillian. The focus of this workshop was on learning about our past lives. Initially I did not feel that I needed to attend this workshop but something compelled me to register for it anyway. I felt that I had garnered enough from the past life reading I had received when I learned that Jeff and I had previously been married and lived in Ireland. To be honest, I had always felt that it was detrimental for people to focus on the past whether it was from this lifetime or some other. I would have to be convinced otherwise.

The night before the workshop, as I was starting to drift off to sleep I had a very strange vision. I was sitting on what looked to be high school bleachers along with hundreds of other students. In front of the large crowd was Jesus, standing at a podium giving us what could be described as a graduation speech. He said, "By your coming here today you have made us very proud. You will go off tomorrow on new paths and in new directions, that today you might not understand. All are lessons that will be revealed to you."

I turned to the girl sitting next to me and asked her if she knew what her lesson was going to be. She said no but she seemed eager and excited. I did not have a clue what my lesson was going to be either but I felt more anxiety about it than the other "graduate" seemed to be feeling.

The next morning as I awoke, I heard a strange yet vaguely familiar voice projecting loudly into my mind, *"Strong Woman, we are here for you."* Still half asleep I inquired, "Who are you?" To which the deep, masculine voice replied, *"I am the angel Michael and I want you to know we are here for you."* I was startled at first; but then, I remembered what Jesus had told us the night before about something happening tomorrow, which was now today.

I remembered Michael. He was the angel Jesus had called to several months ago and commanded to protect my soul mates and me. He was intimidating with his muscular build and arrows strapped across his back. Why did he come to me now? And why did he call me "Strong Woman?" No one had ever called me that before. Was he referring to my physical strength or to something else — something that related to this supposed graduation that was taking place today?

And then I remembered something else from the distant past. My mind flashed back to the winter's day when I walked up to the large glistening white statue standing guard in front of the Catholic Church — the church called St. Michael. I had marveled at the magnificence of this unknown winged being and I recalled what I had said. In my childish ignorance I had asked the statue, "Who are you?"

The words I had just spoken now rung in my ears, as did the answer I received, *"I am the angel Michael and I want you to know we are here for you."* Had he answered long ago to deaf ears?

The day was proving uneventful. The last thing I had scheduled on my agenda was the workshop. At the beginning of the session, Lillian explained that we were to ask our angels to take us back to a time, to a life, where we still had unresolved issues — lessons to learn. She said we would be guided to the appropriate time period and circumstance that we needed most.

Using the techniques we learned, I asked my angels to guide me to a life that would prove enlightening. The first life I revisited was when I looked like some kind of ancient man dressed in animal skins and furs. My "house" was dome shaped and made of the same animal skins. I felt a deep depression, anger, and confusion. My beloved wife had died a short time before, following a quarrel we had about something insignificant. In my ignorance, I thought she had purposely abandoned me because of my seemingly mild transgression. I was left alone in the world only to die years later, unbeknownst to anyone, in the woods while I was hunting.

My angels said that this was "where it all began." My fright at being left alone, abandoned, and unloved for something I erroneously thought I had caused through my "bad" behavior. My repeated life quest to "save souls" stemmed from my own deep-seeded fear that I would be alone in the world if everyone I loved was physically gone.

I knew of no God and I felt no kind of spiritual presence in that early lifetime. The divine spark within me was very small but I had chosen to shine what little I had on one other person. She, in turn, had projected her own divine light on me.

But this one love of my lifetime had "abandoned" me. Knowing no God or divine power, I thought it was completely dependent on me — it was my task to "save" the people I loved so that they would not take the love away from me. If I were always "good," then they would not choose to leave me. My desperate need to unilaterally secure love, which I thought came from the World, had taken root in that long-ago lifetime.

Almost immediately upon leaving that life I was transported to Ireland and to my life with Kevin. I saw myself, at the age of forty-five, dying of tuberculosis. Kevin stayed by my side until the end. Kneeling beside my deathbed, he cried as he held my hand, begging for my forgiveness for the humble life that he had provided me.

But I could not talk. I was too weak and lacked the air in my lungs to tell him the truth. I would never be able to tell him how much our life together had elevated me spiritually and emotionally.

I left that life never letting him know how much he really meant to me. As I was destined to learn, one of my soul's tasks was to be able to tell and demonstrate to others how much they meant to me before it was too late. But more importantly, I had left with a terrible guilt — a guilt that burdened my soul for not having "saved" him.

He never saw the light of truth in that lifetime — the very truth that, ironically, his love had illuminated for me. The truth, which told me that, more important than the World and its possessions, was the love from God and the Spirit. He had enriched me beyond the World and propelled my soul toward its ultimate "graduation" day.

As I left that lifetime, I heard Jesus say, *"You must understand, you can not save his soul, you merely show the way. Only he and God can save his soul."* All this time I had lived with tremendous guilt about not completing a task that was not mine to begin with. We cannot save each other, only love one another and let God do the rest. And we are never alone. God truly does provide the love that we seek. These lessons finally sunk in.

I now could let go. Finally, I could release Kevin, who was now Jeff, and graduate to the next lesson I needed to learn. As fate would have it, within four days I read in our local newspaper that Jeff was getting married. I knew his fiancé from before, too. She had been in Ireland and had known Kevin before he met me. She was a path he did not choose in that lifetime but needed in this lifetime. I felt sure that he would now learn the difference between splendors of the World and splendors of the Spirit.

When I called Jeff to wish him well he said that he was expecting to hear from me. He somehow knew that I would contact him, understand, and be happy for him. He had received my letter and realized, not so much its implications for him, but its profound meaning for my spiritual growth. I remembered him telling me that, "this is the path I must be on now." Finally, the words sunk in and I knew what I had never understood before. I told him what he already intuitively sensed — that I would always be there for him. He would be my soul mate for all of eternity and, I knew that, one day, he would join me in the Light.

M. Sue Benford

PART THREE

"It is entirely possible that behind the perception of our senses, worlds are hidden of which we are unaware."

Albert Einstein

"But in the days when the seventh angel is about to sound his trumpet, the mystery of God will be accomplished, just as he announced to his servants the prophets."

Rev. 10:7

Chapter Twenty Six

It's not Margaret!

"It's not Margaret." The words rang in my head like clanging cymbals jarring loose a distant recollection. I flashed back to myself as a young child in a hospital bed, weakened by the ravages of cancer and chemotherapy. Nurses repeatedly walked into my room greeting me by my given name, "Hello, Margaret, and how are you today?" Regardless of my physical condition, I always managed to whisper the same indignant reply, "It's not Margaret. My name's not Margaret!" Puzzled, the nurses would look at the name tag on my bed and raise a confused eyebrow. The name tag, indeed, did reveal that my first name was Margaret.

Now, nearly thirty-five years later those same acrimonious words again reverberated in my head. Only this time there was no hospital bed or confused nurse. Sitting alone in my living room watching a mindless television game show, I no longer had to defend the usage of my nickname, Susie, to an unassuming populace. So why was this message all of a sudden being brought to the forefront of my conscious thoughts?

Like so many of the other ethereal voices I had become so accustomed to hearing in the recent past, I somehow "knew" that this message also held some special significance. But what was it? What was I supposed to discover about my first name, the name which proudly was given to me in honor of my paternal grandmother?

My grandmother was an Italian immigrant who came to this country from a small village near Rome. A devout Catholic who had eight children (five surviving) by the time she was thirty-one, she lost her husband when her last child, my father, was barely three months old. "Maggie," as the Americans liked to call her, was a pillar of strength and determination. Working two jobs, she managed to keep her large family together through the great Depression. She never remarried, fearing a new husband might be cruel to her first husband's children. Certainly an interesting and heroic story but not at all mysterious in any way. Or at least, so it appeared on the surface.

I decided that the person who might be able to shed some much needed light on this subject was my mother. After all, she had named me. What I learned from my mother was profound and a bit disturbing. When I asked her about the origins of my first name she confirmed that it was an *attempt* to name me after my grandmother.

The word "attempt" seemed out of place. What did she mean? She went on to explain that, because all of my grandmother's friends called her "Maggie," my Anglo-Saxon mother assumed that it was short for "Margaret." It was not until after I was born, and officially named, that my grandmother asked a startling question, "Who did you name her after?" My parents were perplexed when they replied, "You of course, Ma." Grandma, equally confused, responded in her broken English, "But my name's not Margaret. My name is Magdalena!"

My jaw dropped in disbelief. Mother revealed that had she known my grandmother's true name, it would have been my name as well. But instead, Maggie became Margaret and, up until now, my grandmother's, and subsequently my name, lay undisclosed.

Knowing what I knew about the insights provided by my spiritual guides, I realized that there was, most likely, something deeper and more spiritual about this revelation. But how could that be true in this case? So what if my grandmother's name was in actuality the same as the prostitute in the Bible, Mary Magdalene? What did that have to do with me or with spiritual truth of any kind?

Up until this revelation I had paid only a cursory amount of attention to the scarcely-acknowledged woman in the New Testament who appeared to be some kind of "special" friend of Jesus'. It seemed unlikely that any connection would be revealed between this rarely mentioned woman and anything I was uncovering in my research. Just in case, I decided to dig a little deeper.

As so often in the recent past, I was amazed to actually find something significant about my insights. According to many religious scholars, Mary Magdalene held a high-level position in the ranks of the Gnostic Christians and was favored with visions and insight that far surpassed Peter's. In fact, one of the Gnostic texts called *The Dialogue of the Savior,* praises her not only as a visionary, but as the apostle "who knew the All."

It is not surprising considering the patriarchy of the early Christian era why Magdalene was little more than a bone of contention to many of her male colleagues. The *Gospel of Philip* tells of jealousy between the male disciples and Mary Magdalene, who is identified as Jesus' most intimate companion, "the companion of the Savior is Mary Magdalene. But Christ loved her more than all the disciples and used to kiss her often on her mouth. The rest of the disciples were offended by it...They said to him, 'Why do you love her more than all of us?' The Savior answered and said to them, 'Why do I not love you as I love her?'" Furthermore, in *The Dialogue of the Savior,* the author not only included Mary Magdalene as one of three disciples chosen to receive special teaching but also elevates her above the apostles Thomas and Matthew.

The symbolism of the early rivalry between Magdalene and the disciples is not lost on us today. Of all the disciples most opposed to her inclusion in the respected inner circle of early Christianity, Peter, the widely accepted "rock" of the orthodox church, stood out as Magdalene's number-one enemy. In the *Gospel of Mary* the story is told that when the disciples, depressed and frightened after Jesus' death, asked Mary to encourage them by telling what the Lord had told her secretly, she agrees, and teaches them until Peter, furious, asks, "Did he really speak privately with a woman, (and) not openly to us? Are we to turn about and all listen to her? Did he prefer her to us?" Distressed at his rage, Mary replies, "My brother Peter, what do you think? Do you think that I thought this up myself in my heart, or that I am lying about the Savior?" Matthew breaks in at this point to mediate the dispute: "Peter, you have always been hot-tempered. Now I see you contending against the woman like the adversaries. But if the Savior made her worthy, who are you, indeed, to reject her?" At that point the other disciples agree to accept her teaching.

Months before any of these thoughts or visions about my name, or Mary Magdalene, I experienced a sequence of visions that I never quite understood. In one vision I saw myself as a young woman with long, dark brown hair wearing a brown linen dress tied at the waist. It was night time and I was in a large, make-shift tent dimly lit by some unseen source, perhaps a candle. Several other people were in the tent, all men, talking in hushed whispers. I could not make out exactly what they were saying because my focus was more on my own feelings of distress and apprehension, a fear approaching panic. I did not know who I was, exactly when this event occurred or why I was frightened and feeling "misplaced." As I read these passages about Mary Magdalene, the images began to make more sense.

Another vision I had experienced, also many months prior to this revelation, was equally as difficult for me to explain or understand. I was in this same type of tent as a part of a circle of men who were holding hands around a small fire at night time. We were praying during some type of ritual. This vision came eerily alive when I read the book entitled, <u>Jung and the Lost Gospels</u>, by Stephan A. Hoeller. In it, Hoeller writes, "Then he (Jesus) said to the disciples, 'Before I am delivered up let us sing a hymn to the Father and then we shall go forth to whatever awaits us.' Then he stood in the middle of the room, asked the disciples to form a circle around him, holding each other's hands, and after the recitation of each verse to answer with the word 'Amen.'" (Hoeller, page 125). Could my vision be the reenactment subsequently requested by Christ of his disciples to commune with him following his departure from Earth?

Another aspect from my vision also proved strangely prophetic. The only person I remember, by name, was the last person to enter the tent and join in our circle: the others greeted him as "Thomas." Unlike Jesus, he had dark, short hair almost like a contemporary hair cut and no facial hair (I wondered if he was too young to grow a significant beard). I remember feeling safer at this point and reassured that Thomas had arrived. Although he was younger and more reserved than the others, he gave me a sense of calm and a feeling of shared kinship that I lacked from the others.

In an eerie affirmation, I came across a painted image of Thomas. Identical to the one in my vision, the apostle had brown, short hair and no facial hair. I was both startled and amazed.

But why the focus on, and feelings about, Thomas? Hoeller helped to explain this aspect of my vision as well. "Contained within *Acts of Thomas*, as apocryphal scripture long known in Christendom, this poem is poetically attributed to Thomas, *the apostle of Jesus, most highly regarded by the Gnostics*." (Hoeller, page 154) I had grown to realize that there was a certain significance to Thomas; apparently the early Gnostics agreed.

Mary Magdalene played another key role in the Christ story as well. It was she who first saw the resurrected Christ. "Then the disciples went back to their homes, but Mary stood outside the tomb crying. As she wept, she bent over to look into the tomb and saw two angels in white, seated where Jesus' body had been, one at the head and the other at the foot. They asked her, 'Woman, why are you crying?' 'They have taken my Lord away,' she said, 'and I do not know where they have put him.' At this, she turned around and saw Jesus standing there, but she did not realize that it was Jesus. Jesus said to her, 'Mary.' She turned toward him and cried out in Aramaic, '*Rabboni*!' Jesus said, "Do not hold on to me, for I have not yet returned to the Father. Go instead to my brothers and tell them, 'I am returning to my Father and your Father, to my God and your God.' Mary Magdalene went to the disciples with the news: 'I have seen the Lord!' And she told them that he had said these things to her." (John 20:10-18)

Was it a mere coincidence that my true birth name was supposed to have been "Magdalena?" Or that now I was practically reliving the events that occurred surrounding Jesus' death and resurrection, complete with detailed images and understandings far beyond my surface capacity to comprehend?

As I had been accustomed to doing for the past year, I took my questions to the only one who would know — Christ himself. In his ever cool, calm, and collected way, which seemed especially notable in comparison to my state of shock and disarray, he volunteered all the answers. He told me that my insights were correct and that I was seeing through the eyes of my spiritual ancestor, Mary

Magdalene. Her splendors were in me just as Elijahs' had been passed on to Elisha. As he had explained to me before, while the body passes down splendors, or characteristics, of the physical self; the spirit passes down splendors of the mind. These were lessons that Paul had once taught, too.

He allowed me to relive the moments of his death and resurrection. The images chilled me as I not only watched them but experienced them deep within my soul. I looked on, halfway becoming and halfway observing, as a despondent Magdalene walked into the tomb behind several men who carried Jesus' lifeless body. She fought back tears, albeit unsuccessfully at times, as the man they called Joseph of Arimathea recited instructions on where and how to lay Jesus' body.

A long piece of cloth covered a stone slab elevated about three or four feet high in the center of the tomb. One of the ends of the cloth dangled loosely over one end of the slab. Jesus' body was laid on the cloth. Several others walked into the tomb, including Jesus' mother. They touched his body and sobbed.

Joseph, a short stocky man with a long white beard and white hair, seemed concerned that everyone not tarry too long. At one point, he peers out of the tomb and looks up at the sky mumbling something about sundown. Magdalene and the others do not want to go yet, something is left undone related to the body. Joseph assures them it can be done later. Magdalene is not immediately convinced but the others slowly move toward the tomb's exit.

He touches her arm trying to coax her to the door. She hesitates and arranges Jesus' body in a "proper" fashion on the cloth. Joseph grabs the end of the cloth and begins to cover Jesus. Magdalene stops him, bends over and kisses Jesus on the right cheek. By this time, all the others had left the tomb; they stand just outside whispering something inaudible. Joseph covers the body with the cloth and the two depart.

Sometime later, Mary Magdalene approaches the tomb carrying a large wooden bowl filled with a concoction of some sort. She is alone but expecting others to soon follow to assist her with doing something to Jesus' body. The big, circular stone that had been positioned at the door of the tomb has been rolled away. She is shocked and scared. Had someone taken Jesus' body to further desecrate his memory? The Romans, and Jews, both knew they had not completed final preparations.

She peers into the tomb fully expecting it to be empty. Her eyes cloud with tears as her expectations prove to be correct. Through the haze, she notices something strange about the stone slab — it's glowing with an unusual light illuminating the darkened tomb. She wipes her eyes thinking the illusion is caused by her tears and backs away from the tomb.

She hears a voice behind her questioning her distress. She turns around and sees a blurry image distorted again by the swelling tears. She does not immediately recognize the man but hopes he may know something about Jesus' body. She asks him.

The man calls her by name and she recognizes him as Jesus. She moves toward him but he puts his arm out as if to stop her from nearing. In her mind, she sees the image of the Spirit influxing the top of his crown region via the soul surrounding his body. Jesus' physical body disappears. She was to go tell the other disciples what she had seen and heard.

She is very afraid by this idea of relaying information to them — only a few of the disciples are sympathetic to her involvement with Jesus. Several, Peter especially, hold to the traditional Jewish laws which exclude woman from spiritual practices. What will they say? Two she knows she can trust, Thomas and John. They have always stood up for her and supported her intimate relationship with Jesus accepting that if, "she's good enough for him, she's good enough for us."

Her mission is tenuous, her position still unknown. She asks herself, "Why did he do this to me? Why me and not one of them? What was the Lord trying to prove revealing these mysteries to me, a woman?" He said all of her questions would eventually be answered. She needed to have faith. She did, of course, but she still trembled at the thoughts of what the world would say and do to her.

At this point, I was left with more questions than answers. What did history have to say about Mary Magdalene and the role she played in Christianity? Did she have a special connection to the resurrection of Jesus and, if so, what was the symbolism of this now?

M. Sue Benford

Chapter Twenty Seven

In His image

By this time, my head was swimming with information, revelations, understandings and many questions. I had spent the better part of two years trying to come to grips with this new life, which had fully seized and adopted me. While documenting my most recent insights on the computer late one night, I heard a voice command, *"Go watch TV."* My first thought was how odd this seemed for "the guys," the nickname I affectionately came to call my spiritual advisers, who had never before given such a seemingly trite statement or command. Perhaps I was just overly tired and needed a break from the heavy-duty work that had consumed my free time.

I sauntered into my living room and grabbed the remote. Plopping on the couch, I began to channel surf. It had been so long since I had been actively involved in any television programs that I had no idea what was on or what I was looking for. That is, of course, until I came upon an older man pointing out physical wounds on what appeared to be the image of a man on a piece of cloth. My heart lurched into my throat and my bottom jaw dropped. I could not believe my eyes — it was him! The man on that cloth was Jesus. No doubt about it, it was the same person who I had been conversing with all these many months. What was this cloth and how did it come to bear Jesus' image?

I watched the remainder of the show barely able to breathe. My hands quickly scribbled notes, names, references, and questions. I learned that the cloth was known as the "Shroud of Turin" and that, in fact, it was believed by many to be the actual burial cloth of Christ. But how did that ethereal image of him get on the linen cloth? And, more importantly, why had he left the image in the first place?

The show ended and I raced to the telephone to call Lillian, the psychic who had once taught me to "talk with angels." I reasoned that she was raised as a Catholic so would probably have heard of this relic, unlike me, who was discovering it for the first time. Sure enough she had heard of the Shroud. She confidently informed me that it was a fake — a forgery made sometime during the medieval period in Europe. She told me that it had been "carbon dated," to determine its true age. This test showed that the cloth came from the Middle Ages. She warned me not to pursue this area of interest any further as it was a field wrought with controversial and heated debate. But I knew there was something wrong in this explanation — and with the carbon dating test. I knew it would not be so simple for me to discount this image, which was exactly the same as the man I had come to know and love.

That night in meditation, I asked Jesus specifically about this cloth. Not only did he confirm its authenticity as his actual burial cloth but he said, *"You will tell the world how the image was created and what it means."* At this I was appalled. I had absolutely no interest in throwing myself to the wolves of either orthodox religion or scientific skepticism. From the little I learned about the Shroud of Turin from the documentary, it was the most studied artifact in human history with well over 250,000 hours spent trying to unravel its mysterious origins — and still there were no definitive answers. I explained to him that I was definitely the wrong person for this job as I would not accept any nebulous or etheric "mumbo jumbo" he might give me to explain tangible evidence. There was no way I was going to subject myself to the inherent persecution that would accompany any unsubstantiated claims of the "truth" about this revered Catholic relic.

In what I considered to be a stroke of brilliance, I offered Jesus a "deal." I told him that I would agree to tell the world about the mysteries of his burial cloth on one condition — that he provide me with tangible proof that I could literally hold in my hand to show others. This "proof" had to be scientifically-testable and the image formation process replicable using existing tools and methodologies. I figured he would back down under all these conditions. But he did not. His only response was, *"All right."* Even with this response, I breathed an overt sigh of relief, never dreaming in my wildest thoughts that there actually was some physical and scientifically-testable proof for this 2,000-year-old relic and its etheric image.

M. Sue Benford

The reverse image, as it appears on a photographic negative, has a more realistic quality. (Courtesy Vernon Miller, © 1978)

Actual Shroud of Turin face as it appears to the unaided eye. Note the image appears as a photographic "negative." (Courtesy Vernon Miller, © 1978)

Strong Woman - *Unshrouding the Secrets of the Soul*

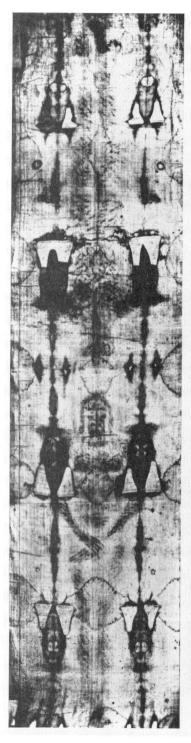
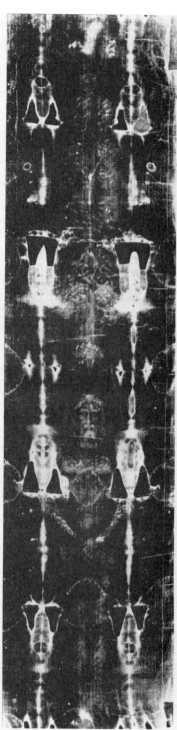

Full dorsal (back) image of the Shroud of Turin (Courtesy Vernon Miller, © 1978)

Full frontal image of the Shroud of Turin (Courtesy Vernon Miller, © 1978)

M. Sue Benford

Chapter Twenty Eight

The Shroud, the Grail and Magdalene

I began to wonder — what happened to Magdalene after Jesus' crucifixion? The Gospels, as well as Paul's letters, are void of any references to her following the resurrection. While researching this question I stumbled across some Old French folklore that told the story of how Mary Magdalene had fled Jerusalem under the watchful eye of Joseph of Arimathea. Along with her brother (believed to be Lazarus) and sister (believed to be Martha), she landed on the southern shore of France in Provénce carrying the "*sangraal*." Was that the same thing as the "Holy Grail?"

Some scholars believe that it is one and the same. When "*sangraal*" is broken into parts - san and graal - it means "blood royal." Legend has it that Magdalene arrived in France with the royal blood of Jesus — some of whom believed this was Jesus' biological daughter named "Sarah." But how was it possible for a child of Jesus' to be born when he was never married? Apparently, there is a very old tradition identifying Mary of Bethany with Mary Magdalene. In medieval art an unidentified woman is also identified with the Sister-Bride of the ancient mythologies. She was her Bridegroom-deity's mirror image or 'other half,' a feminine alter-ego so to speak. The relationship of these two was much more than a sexual union; it was a deep spiritual intimacy and relationship most accurately described as "sister-like." The Sacred Marriage of the Bridegroom with the Sister-Bride was based on much more than a physical passion; it was a marriage of deepest spiritual and emotional connection — a linking of soul mates!

It is interesting to note that there are seven lists in the four Gospels that name women linked to Jesus. In six of the seven, the name of Mary Magdalene is listed first, even before Jesus' mother. In all likelihood, the Gospel writers are indicating the status of Magdalene in the Christian community as that of Jesus' wife. This would be a reasonable assumption as early Jewish tradition forbid Rabbi's from teaching children unless they were married. Then why would the gospel writers not just come out and say that Jesus was married? Why cover up such an important fact? Perhaps it is because Jesus did not follow the traditional orthodox procedures for marriage; thus, technically, he was not considered legally married by the community. A later sect of Christians, deemed to be heretics by the Roman church, called the "Cathars," demonstrate this same objection to orthodox laws and procedures. Scholars suggest that it is likely that these spiritually-focused and devoted followers of Christ refused to be wed in orthodox wedding ceremonies on the grounds that they did not consider those ceremonies necessary. Likewise, Jesus refused to participate in standard Jewish rituals that supposedly "married" two individuals to demonstrate what he had already taught me: man can only join bodies; whereas, God alone can unite souls.

Another group of heretical Christians also believed very strongly in a married Jesus. The authors of <u>The Holy Blood and the Holy Grail</u> concluded that the Order of the Knights Templar believed that Jesus was fully human and married, that his royal blood still flowed in the veins of the noble families of Provénce, and that the messianic promises of the Hebrew Scriptures would someday be fulfilled in a descendant of Jesus.

But was this descendant the flesh and blood person or the spiritual inheritor of his splendors? Jesus proclaimed that his kingdom was "not of this world;" therefore, his true heirs would rightfully descend from his spiritual splendors not his physical splendors.

One relevant Jewish myth of Yahweh and Matronit (his soul mate) reflects the theme of the Grail legends: the king is powerless and incomplete without his "Eve." In this legend, it is never stated that the lost Grail is the Bride. But the identity of the <u>Fisher King</u> of the Parsifal legend of Wolfram von Eschenbach is much more apparent — the wounded king is called Anfortas, a corruption of "in fortis," which means "in strength." Not so ironically, this is also the Latin name for the left pillar of the Temple of Jerusalem, called "Boaz" in Hebrew.

The name of this pillar is also the name of the ancestor of King David and is an unmistakable reference to the promise made to the Davidic bloodline, the line of the princes of Judah, that the dominion of its princes would be established forever "in strength," since Judah was the strongest of the twelve sons of Israel's patriarch Jacob.

I started wondering how all this related to me until I stumbled on one of the hidden symbols disguised in watermarks by medieval paper-makers. As a result of extreme rebuke by the orthodox church, the alternative church (also called the

Church of Love (*Amor*), which is Rome, or Roma, spelled backwards) was forced to spread its message covertly via coded symbols.

One of the most frequently depicted symbols was the bear. The bear was highly significant because it was the animal that represented the Merovingians (or heirs from the vine of Mary Magdalene). He was known as the "strong one" who had been asleep for a very long time and who would awaken soon. Many times the bear is shown with a trumpet or horn, which was the symbol for heretical preaching. According to legend, its blast has the power to shatter rock. With respect to Christianity, the 'rock' that the heretical preaching splits is "Peter's rock," the concretized and rigid doctrines of the institutional church.

I was amazed not only to see the reference to the bear as the "strong one," but one of the pictures showed a bear with a Tau, or capital T, cross extending down from its belly. I stopped cold realizing that was the exact location and description of the cross on my stomach! Perhaps this odd rendition of the bear, or "strong one," and cross was just a coincidence of extreme proportions, but perhaps not.

Another somewhat chilling overlap between the Cathars "alternative" Church of Love and the things I had been learning, was their attachment to the apostle John. Some of the artwork portrayed both John the Baptist and John the Evangelist along with the Madonna and Child. It is not too difficult to understand the relationship connection between the Baptist and Mary, as he was Jesus' cousin and Mary's nephew, but what is less obvious is that John the Evangelist was equally honored by the hidden church. In fact, the Cathari wore a copy of his Gospel concealed under their clothes! As a part of their rituals, each grand master takes the name Jean (John) upon election to the most high office. John was intimately connected with the progression to enlightenment and spiritual transformation — just as I had been told.

One of the things still confusing me was the connection between Jesus' burial cloth, the Holy Grail and Mary Magdalene. Was it merely a coincidence that the ultimate demise and massacre of the Cathars in 1244 occurred only three years prior to Emperor Baldwin II's request to exchange pieces of Christ's burial shroud for the body of Mary Magdalene? Did the Emperor perhaps know the connection between Magdalene first seeing the risen Christ and his etheric image on the burial shroud? Was it possible that the Holy Grail is the burial Shroud of Christ that caught Jesus' blood after his death? And, most importantly, what mystery was concealed in the cloth/Grail that, apparently, Magdalene knew?

In the work entitled "Enshrouded in Silence" by Fr. Maurus Green, it states that "Peter ran with John to the tomb and saw the recent imprints (*"vestigia"*) of the dead and risen man on the linens." The translation of *vestigia* is akin to footstep, footprint, trace or marks and has remained unchanged since the seventh century. As a result, it is easy to interpret this passage as meaning that what Magdalene and the disciples saw was a mark or imprint on the burial shroud.

But the object that many believed to be the actual burial cloth of Jesus' was deemed heretical and kept "off limits" in Constantinople from 944 to 1204. Its history prior to this time is unclear and not well documented. Only a select few within the orthodox hierarchy were privy to the true nature of the mysterious cloth and its faint markings.

Another possible connecting point between the Shroud and the Grail is in the Latin word "*gradalis*" meaning "by degrees." One of the legends surrounding the Grail in King Arthur's court was that the worthy knights would uncover the mystery of the Grail by degrees until fully realized. In similar fashion, some early Edessan and Constantinopolitan rituals, involved revealing the image on the burial shroud to congregations gradually, by raising it section by section to also denote a gradual developmental process in uncovering the mysteries portrayed in the Shroud. Considering these links and the information I had gathered, it was not hard to surmise that Joseph of Arimathea's linen cloth was the vessel that captured Jesus' blood following the crucifixion. It is interesting to note that at the time the burial Shroud of Constantinople disappeared, during the Crusade of 1204, the legends of the Grail began to spread.

But what did it all mean: the Shroud, the Grail, descendants of Magdalene and Jesus? What meaning was I supposed to get from learning all of this? To those who believe Magdalene has something to offer to Christianity, they point to the fact that the new age of Aquarius is now dawning. Perhaps it is more than a little ironic that the Roman numerals for the year 2000 are MM. Is it time for new "Magdalenian" insights into the meaning of Jesus' life, resurrection, and the faint Shroud markings he left as a final lesson?

Although I was certain I would never have to publicly disclose my understandings about the Shroud as a result of Jesus' certain default on our "deal," I continued to receive profound insights about the cloth and its image. He told me that we have been left this remnant to have a guide, leading to our discovery of the spirit in all humans. The Shroud is a kind of "picture" of Jesus' soul and when modern technology can reproduce it, we will also be able to record other soul images. Thus, we will have concrete proof of the existence of the soul and life beyond our mortal existence. This type of irrefutable evidence would also be vital to prove that what Jesus and John had been telling me about human souls was true all along. Jesus also explained to me that the Shroud was akin to a spiritual "crutch" for us. Soon, maybe very soon, he would take away this crutch so that we would be forced to walk on our own. In otherwords, the Shroud image will ultimately disappear!

And as for the mysteries of the Shroud/Grail, like a book slowly revealing its plot and characters, I was beginning to discover some fascinating aspects about our Creator and His creations. Perhaps now was the time the slumbering bear of heretical folklore would finally awaken and reveal the secrets of the Holy Grail. From what I was learning, this would occur not a moment too soon.

M. Sue Benford

Chapter Twenty Nine

Spiritual soul mate

Soon after my discussions with Jesus about the Shroud, I was told that I needed to get access to the Internet. I had opposed this obvious high-tech approach to information gathering but the guys seemed adamant that it was time for me to advance into the information age. So for my birthday present in 1997, I signed up for Internet access, thus opening a whole new world. Little did I know that only a click away would be my ultimate spiritual soul mate.

Throughout my numerous discourses with my spiritual sources, I repeatedly requested (more like begged) for another soul mate to share the remainder of my spiritual journey. I wanted him to be a spiritual person in line with my own understandings and path. One night in a conversation with John, I became frustrated that my answers to these personal questions and requests had gone seemingly unanswered. Although they had assured me months earlier that, indeed, my ultimate spiritual partner would soon arrive, I had not received any more information. I badgered John to tell me more about this soul mate. Finally, after a great deal of badgering, John provided a birthday — August 15th. It was not a lot to go on, but at least it was something.

In the following days, I began to use my newfound Internet search capabilities to attempt to locate more information about the Shroud of Turin. I came across the name and phone number of one the leading physicists involved with the Shroud, Dr. John Jackson, and gave him a call. Dr. Jackson's wife, who answered the phone, assured me that he did not have time for me as he was quite busy. However, she did say that I might want to try a particular Benedictine monk and Catholic priest, Fr. Joseph Marino, who for over twenty years had diligently studied and collected all related Shroud research. He might have more time to talk with me.

Call a monk/priest? I had never had any dealings before with the Catholic clergy with the exception of sitting next to a few at the Josephinum library. What would I tell this "Father" when I called him — "Hey, I've got some insider information about Jesus and his burial cloth, want to know more?" My recent polite expulsion, as a result of my "unusual" experiences, from the conservative Protestant church I had been attending, had left me more than a little gun-shy at telling my story to the clergy, let alone such a devout Catholic!

I was not even sure how to make the connection. Mrs. Jackson had said that the monks were not permitted to make long-distance phone calls as a result of their vows of poverty, so I would have to leave my number and hope for a collect call in return. I hesitated for a while but then on the afternoon of July 23, 1997, I got up the courage to make the call and leave as mundane a message as possible on the Abbey's phone system.

In a few hours my phone rang and I heard the operator say, "Collect call from Fr. Joseph Marino, will you accept the charges?" My heart started pounding as I answered, "yes." The next voice rang in my ears as if it were accompanied by cymbals, "This is Fr. Marino, is this Sue Benford?" Although normal in tone and intonation, there was something profoundly different in this man's voice. Was it how all monk/priests sounded? Was I simply paranoid and insecure in what I was about to tell him? Or perhaps was I in awe of him as I had been with the female powerlifters from my past? And, did the Catholic church still burn heretics at the stake? The questions raced through my mind in no particular order.

For some odd unexplainable reason, I felt extremely comfortable with this voice on the other end of the phone. I told him about my "visions" and insights, both in general, and as they related to the Shroud of Turin. I could tell he was cautious but intrigued by the things I was saying. He had never before heard such wild stories, either in the church or in the scientific Shroud community. Nevertheless, he kept talking to me.

A nagging feeling overcame me after we hung up from that first phone call. What was it I was sensing? There was something different about this soul — something significant. My intuition told me he was to be someone important in the unfolding spiritual equation of my life, but who? Could it be that he was the "one?" The soul mate that John had predicted and promised would assist me along the rest of my life's journey? Surely that idea was ridiculous to even contemplate. After all, he was a monk and a priest, sworn to celibacy and fidelity to the Catholic Church. Yes, it was true I had asked to be sent a "spiritual" man but this was impossible!

I buried these feelings and my intuition for another week or so while my newfound friend and I continued to communicate almost daily via the phone and Internet. But soon the flood gates were once again fully opened. During one of our conversations, Fr. Joseph mentioned an upcoming celebration at his mother's house to honor his birthday. Innocently, I inquired exactly when his birthday was. His answer stopped me cold — August 15th. My chest tightened and I could not breath as I recalled my insight from John about my soul mate's birthday. What would I do with this information? Certainly I could not tell this to Fr. Joseph. Was this the guys' idea of some cosmic joke —"Have you heard the one about the priest and the heretic?"

That night in my meditation I confronted Jesus and John with my dilemma. They verified that, yes, Fr. Joseph was indeed my soul mate and would be my partner in uncovering the spiritual mysteries at hand. If this was true, I asked, then why he was not getting divine signs and signals about the new spiritual direction of his life? Jesus said that he was receiving numerous signs but that I should tell him that he needed to, *"Put the umbrella down. Truth is raining all around you like raindrops."* This was insane and totally out of the question. How could I possibly relay such a "message" to this priest/monk who I had never met and had just begun to know? Not to mention that, although I knew his birthday was the same as my future soul mate's, he had no such knowledge and at that point our relationship merely consisted of long phone conversations, mostly about the Shroud of Turin. I reasoned that there were only two ways to pull off a bandaide; slow or fast. Either way — they both hurt. I opted for the slow route first.

In our next phone conversation I approached the whole subject of "miraculous signs" quite gingerly at first, but to no avail. He just was not getting it. The best I was accomplishing was to garner a lecture on the Pope's beliefs and the "church's stance" on such things. Men! Clueless, no matter what collar they're wearing!

I decided to take the plunge so I just blurted it out, "Jesus said for you to take the umbrella down and you'll start seeing signs that you and I are soul mates and your mission is with me. Do you have any idea what he's talking about? Have you perhaps been missing some unusual happenings and passing them off as coincidences?" My heart nearly stopped during what seemed like an eternal pause after my last question. The answer was devastating, "No, I do not have any idea what you're talking about. I do not think I've been missing anything and I do not even understand what he means by 'put the umbrella down.'"

I could not believe his naiveté and lack of mystical understandings. This would certainly be some miracle for Jesus and John to pull off if they intended for this sweet, charming, and completely-sheltered monk to join in the spiritual fray for which I was headed. I decided to simply exit the conversation as gracefully as possible by saying, "Well, just do me a favor and pay attention to possible signs they might be sending. Do not stretch to interpret anything but, if something gives you that 'Ah ha!' feeling then do not discard it as a mere coincidence — think about it." Then I thought to myself, "Okay, guys, it's up to you! I really want to see you pull this one off."

That night in meditation it was me who was doing all the laughing instead of John. It was now my turn to sit back and let them do all the work. Could they possibly provide enough tangible, miraculous signs for this innocent and devout monk to understand he had a new life's mission that would mean rebuking his solemn priestly vows and leaving his beloved monastery and church? After all, I had failed miserably with my job of relaying Jesus' message. Now it was entirely up to them. I asked them and they seemed quite confident that, indeed, they would succeed. It was meant to be. I inquired of Jesus exactly how long he thought this miraculous feat would take and he confidently proclaimed, "One year." I marked my calendar for July 23, 1998 — exactly one year from when Fr. Joseph and I first made contact. What a year it would turn out to be!

The next night after our "umbrella" discussion, I received a somewhat panicked phone call from Fr. Joseph. Apparently, he had toiled the night before, distressed over the thought that I might be right and he may have to leave his secure, comfortable life and beliefs. He could not seem to shake the obsessive thoughts that lasted well into his morning routine. As he stated, his main concern was, "What would other people think?" He feared disdain and retribution from family, friends, and the church.

The next morning, during the monks' usual contemplative reading, the book chosen was one by the famous American Trappist monk, Thomas Merton. A particular passage rang out from the solemn silence that encompassed the proceedings, "Too often in the spiritual life we are too concerned about what other people will think about us and not about what God's will actually is for us." A chill ran down his spine as he took note of the very first "raindrop" to sink in now that the proverbial umbrella was down, "It's almost like they knew exactly what I was thinking and feeling and that passage was specifically to answer my nagging fears. We've never read anything from that particular book before!"

Knowing what I already knew about the impact of miraculous signs, all I could do was smile to myself and reassure him that this was just the beginning. I recommended that he document everything that he believed was a sign and record its particular significance to him. Every "sign" should be put in writing and evaluated for its own merit. Over the course of the next several weeks, Fr. Joseph's journal became heavy laden with sign after sign, spiritual message after message, irony after irony. The guys were busy at work and it was becoming impossible to deny their influence any longer. Fr. Joseph and I decided it was time to meet.

It had been only six short weeks since our "introduction," when I scheduled my first weekend trip to St. Louis. Although the plane flight was a mere one hour in duration, it seemed to last an eternity. The butterflies in my stomach had grown to mutant proportions as they danced around threatening to expel my tuna salad lunch.

After the plane landed, I let the other passengers off first so that, hopefully, few would be remaining in the boarding area. I figured I might have difficulty recognizing him from the fuzzy picture on the Abbey's website. But a more real concern was that I would faint, embarrassing both of us so much that he would instantly book me on a return trip to Columbus.

Neither of these two worries came to past. Fr. Joseph stood in the background awaiting my arrival. I knew instantly who he was at first glance. Not just who he was in the flesh, but also who he was as a spirit. Although he had foregone his usual monastic black "dress," his life in the monastery was subtly revealed in his half-bang hair cut and plain, black attire. He grinned sheepishly and his dark eyes twinkled. The attraction was immediate and lasting on all levels — physical, emotional and spiritual. If I had ever had any doubts about our joint mission, they were all swept away at that very moment.

After this first meeting, our relationship and its implications escalated to the point that Fr. Joseph felt it was time for an objective third-party validation of what was happening. For him, that third-party would be his longtime spiritual director, counselor, and fellow priest, Fr. Tom, a biblical scholar and devout enthusiast of the Church's long and successful history. His massive physique was well matched by his loud and boisterous nature. Fr. Tom's mere presence commanded attention, and his voice reverberated as he spoke. Needless to say, the two priests' counseling sessions, which once comfortably focused on petty irritations like Fr. Joseph's annoying kitchen duty, now took on a completely new perspective and importance. To say that Fr. Tom was not happy by the recent turn of events in Fr. Joseph's life is one of life's gross understatements. In Fr. Tom's mind, the inquisition was now reopened and I was being called to the witness stand. In response, I booked another flight to St. Louis, which included a meeting at Fr. Tom's parish.

Now, would be the real test. Was, as Fr. Tom suspected, all of this a demonic charade or twisted plot by an insane woman aiming to undermine the righteous and all-powerful Catholic Church? The odds were so incredibly stacked against me ever being acknowledged or accepted as "legit" by him or his conservative institution. After all, look at who I was, a spiritual nobody, a non-Catholic, twice-divorced mother of two, a female "strong woman," and a heretic. Not exactly the ideal spiritual soul mate for one of the church's chosen few!

Fr. Tom's parish was in the old part of the Italian section of St. Louis. Small family pizzerias lined the streets beckoning to passersby. The smell of freshly-baked bread and slow-cooked pasta sauce reminiscent of my grandma's kitchen, filled the air. I felt torn between the comfortable quaintness of the surroundings and the foreboding shadow cast over my visit. We climbed the steps of the parish rectory and knocked on the door. A short, elderly Italian woman answered the door and in broken English said solemnly, "Fr. Tom is waiting for you upstairs." Although

I was with Fr. Joseph, who came dutifully armed with bulging folders recounting his many documented signs, I knew that the only thing I had on my side to protect me was the truth. Nothing more, nothing less, just the story of my life and my experiences was all I had to offer. Would it be enough to fend off what I knew would be an onslaught of accusations and insinuations? Would the guys intercede on my behalf and convince this skeptical keeper of the 2000 year old Catholic Church of my sincerity, mission, and the veracity of my statements?

The door was partially open to Fr. Tom's study. He sat authoritatively in his arm chair intensely scanning a well-worn Bible, which rested on his lap. Most likely, gathering evidence against me.

"Fr. Tom?" Fr. Joe quietly announced our arrival. The Bible shut with a thud as if he feared its contents might fall into the wrong hands and he quickly parlayed it to the nearby end table next to his chair. The air in the room gently whirled as Fr. Tom sprang from his easy chair. He reached out both hands to clasp Fr. Joe's hand and immediately followed it with a brotherly hug. "Fr. Tom, I would like you to meet Susie, the woman I've told you so much about." For the first time, the big man turned to look at me. He forced a smile to his face as he motioned to the couch, "Please, be seated." Dutifully, we took a seat on his couch — me on one end, Fr. Joe on the other. "So, Susie, Fr. Joe tells me you've been hearing voices — seeing things, too, right? How long has this been going on?" Although it was crystal clear the direction this inquisition was about to take — hearing voices, seeing imaginary things, needing to be institutionalized — for some unexplainable reason, a calm engulfed me. What had been butterflies the size of pigeons in my overturned stomach, all completely disappeared. Words started coming from my mouth so full of peace, assurance, and love that I knew their origin was not from within my own consciousness but from the guys.

The two priests sat and listened as I spoke of Jesus and John, my experiences, and new found understandings. I could see and feel Fr. Tom begin to relax into his chair as I spoke. Every now and then he inserted a "trick" question to challenge the nature of my calling, the quality and integrity of my spiritual guides. But never once did I falter. Always prepared with the answer superior to what he had expected or imagined possible. Clearly, our first "session" was not decisive. He could not overtly condemn me or, God forbid, condone my mission and the involvement of the Pope's priest. The jury was still out.

The visits to St. Louis continued for a number of months. During each visit, we met with Fr. Tom and, like at the first visit, the words spoken were of truth and spiritual understanding, leaving no doubt of their origin. Ultimately, the unspeakable came to pass — Fr. Tom blessed the new mission of the monk and our new found spiritual and physical alliance. Although he was rebuked and scolded by the "powers that be" at the Abbey and in the Catholic church, Fr. Tom stood by his own guidance. He could not renounce the truth of either my nor Fr. Joseph's experiences, nor could he deny the presence of the spirit when we spoke. On July 23, 1998, exactly one year after our first conversation, a U-Haul truck pulled up in my driveway, and my final soul mate stepped into his new life as my partner in what was still to become the greatest spiritual undertaking of our existence.

Chapter Thirty

A plate in the hand

It had been nearly a year since Joe came to live with my family. During that time of acclimation, I continued my research trying to verify the mysteries I was being told. My work produced nearly a dozen peer-reviewed scientific articles in only a year — each supporting a little more of the hidden truths.

Through a long series of what, at the time, appeared to be a series of "coincidences," I made contact with a gentleman named Peter, who claimed to own a camera that had once produced thousands of images of the undetectable "bioenergy field." Would this be akin to taking a picture of the soul? I was curious. I had shared my early writings with Peter's colleague, Jon, the world's leading authority on channeling and mediumship. Clearly, Jon had knowledge of the "real thing" when it came to gathering information from spiritual sources; thus, he wanted to introduce me to Peter.

A longtime paranormal researcher and President of the United States Psychotronics Association, Peter was both open-minded and skeptical. He had heard every story involving "spiritual name dropping" that one person could possibly desire to hear — most he passed off as nonsense or insanity. But Jon was his friend and business partner, so he agreed to listen, although hesitantly. Jon had told him my "story" and of my claims of speaking directly with Jesus and the others. This, however, did not impress Peter, a Jew from Ireland who had been ridiculed and taunted by the predominantly Catholic community in which he was raised. "Another born-again Christian!" I could almost hear his thoughts as we first spoke.

But just as with Fr. Tom, something happened during our first conversation, and Peter took note. I was not like the "holy rollers" he so frequently encountered in Kentucky, where he now lived and worked. Through his subdued Irish brogue I could hear a certain confidence and suppressed enthusiasm — almost as if he had found me and not the other way around.

He proceeded to tell me the story about the remote-imaging camera he had come to acquire several years earlier. For some unknown reason, he had been inwardly compelled to use his mother's inheritance in order to scrape together enough money to save this aging piece of equipment from oblivion. It had belonged to one of the world's foremost subtle energy researchers, British engineer George DelaWarr. DelaWarr, a former WWII officer in the British military, had been given the assignment of exploring the "mind control" claims being reported about the Russians. The allies were desperate to know if the intelligence about this new potential weapon was true and if it posed a threat to Britain. This started DelaWarr's several-decade research project into the field of radionics, homeopathy, and subtle energies. Beyond his initial mission, DelaWarr discovered and built many subtle energy detectors and, ultimately, a camera capable of recording images of distant objects based solely on a sample obtained from that object.

I found the story fascinating but somewhat implausible. After all, if such a device existed then why did the general population not know about it? Why was science not testing and using it? If DelaWarr had, indeed, produced thousands of these remote images, then certainly Peter could send me one to scientifically examine? Without this proof, my skepticism would never be squelched. At this point, I had many more questions than answers.

Peter had never before sent one of DelaWarr's original photos to a researcher, and with good cause. Back in the 1950s, when the plethora of images were created, 4 x 5 inch glass plates were used to collect the subtle energies. The plates were old and very fragile. With a limited supply of his unique treasure remaining, risking shipment to a total stranger was out of the question. Peter and his colleagues, Jon and Andrew, whose names were not lost on me in their similarity to Jesus' disciples, had already examined the plates and were satisfied with their authenticity as legitimate remotely-collected images. But something in him clicked, and he agreed to send me one of the fifty-year-old original glass plates that had been used to collect an image under controlled scientific conditions at a London hospital in 1951. I doubted that I would be impressed.

Several days after my initial conversation with Peter, I had nearly forgotten about DelaWarr and his glass plates. Joe and I were busy planning and preparing for our upcoming trip to Richmond, Virginia where I would attend my first Shroud of Turin conference. I could hardly wait to meet all the well-known Shroud researchers that would attend from all over the world. My thoughts were preoccupied, anticipating what new reports would be presented, when I was startled by the ringing doorbell. I peered out the window and saw the big, brown UPS truck in front of my house. At the door a man in a color-coordinated brown worker's suit extended a package and asked me to "Sign here please." Obediently, I complied, trying to guess what I had just received.

The return address on the small box indicated the package had arrived from Kentucky. My mind flashed back to a few days before and the conversation Peter and I had in which he promised to send me an original glass plate from the DelaWarr labs in England. I eagerly unwrapped the well-secured and heavily padded shipping materials and carefully removed a single 4 x 5 inch glass plate. On one corner was a small green piece of masking tape with some scribbled numbers followed by the date "1/10/51." The sides of the glass had been slightly chipped and worn from the ensuing years. In the center of the plate was an intricately-detailed shades-of-gray image that appeared to curve and swirl around like intestines from a human body. I held the fragile little plate in my hands, tilting it this way and that, attempting to discern exactly how such a fascinating and unique image, with all of its precision, could have gotten onto the glass. As I did, a voice rang out, *"Evidence you can hold in your hand."* My heart nearly stopped — and time, I am sure, did. No, it could not be. This could not be happening. Certainly this did not have anything to do with the "deal" I had made years ago with Jesus demanding empirical evidence that I could literally "hold in my hand" if he wanted me to tell the story about his Shroud. After all, he never before had so conveniently provided concrete physical evidence to support any of his teachings or my insights. I thought I was safe in making this deal. Jesus continued, *"It has the same spatial encoding as the Shroud. Have it tested."* I had recently learned that it was this singular "spatial-encoding" feature, first discovered in 1978, that was responsible for giving the Shroud its three-dimensional (3-D) appearance when the light and dark relief patterns were analyzed using the "VP-8 Image Analyzer" device. The VP-8 is an analog device that converts image density (lights and darks) into vertical relief (shadows and highlights). When using either the VP-8 or commercially-available 3-D software systems, a normal photograph does not result in a three-dimensional image but in a rather distorted jumble of "shapes." X-ray images, although spatially superior to routine photographs, are also characteristically distorted (see **Figure 1**). No other known image had this spatial-encoding characteristic; thus, elevating the Shroud to its position as a singular enigma.

I understood what Jesus was telling me but how would I be able to get the DelaWarr image checked? I certainly did not have access to a VP-8 analyzer to "test" this small image or any of the other DelaWarr images for that matter. From what I knew, only two of these devices still existed in the world — both owned by Shroud researchers.

As fate would have it, both of the VP-8 owners attended the Richmond conference and one agreed to test my images for spatial-encoding characteristics. On my birthday in 1999, one month after receiving the glass plate, the reports were in, the images indeed had spatial encoding that was superior to any other possible images, except one — the Shroud of Turin. For better or worse, I was now committed to pursue this mystery to its ultimate resolution. After all, I had made a deal and Jesus had kept his part of the bargain. The evidence was in hand and our work had taken on a brand new focus.

Figure 1

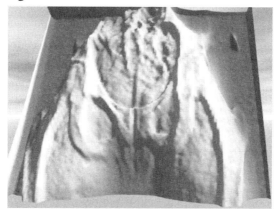

As illustrated in this pelvic X-ray, unlike the spatially-encoded DelaWarr images, major distortions occur in the resultant image. Noticeable distortions include: bone flattening, angle and curvature distortion, and lack of accurate soft tissue reproduction. Normal photographs, both black and white and color, produce even more severe distortions.

M. Sue Benford

Chapter Thirty One

But it's medieval!

Not only was the Shroud of Turin wrought with controversy about the creation of the etheric, subtle image of what appeared to be a crucified man in the center of the cloth, but it had suffered a traumatic blow after the Carbon-14 (C-14) dating test of 1988. This test, conducted by three independent and well-respected laboratories, indicated that the Shroud cloth was created sometime between 1260 - 1390 AD. In other words, it was medieval. The interest and attention given to the Shroud ground to a near halt following this announcement. Only the most obsessed and ardent believers continued on in their efforts to prove that the Shroud is the authentic burial cloth of Jesus. But even the strength of will and purpose by these few had not satisfied the scientific community or the general population. The vast majority remained unconvinced that any of the proponents' numerous "theories," for why the carbon dating was so askew, had any merit. Without a general belief that this cloth could possibly be the burial cloth of Jesus, what purpose would be served in demonstrating how the image was made? After all, if it were only a medieval hoax then who cared whether or not we could replicate the image or whether or not the Shroud had implications for us as humans?

One night in meditation I took my questions and concerns to the guys. They agreed that it was necessary for us to first explain why the carbon dating had resulted in a medieval date before we could successfully explain the image-formation process and its implications. There was only one big problem — some of the best scientists in the world had been struggling with this dilemma for twelve years and were unable to come up with an answer—how would we?

Typically, Jesus and John did not simply hand over direct answers to my questions. As good teachers, they made me work for the answers via my own efforts and initiatives. Often it was only after I had really gotten off track that they would intercede and steer me back in the right direction. The carbon dating question was no exception.

I initially pursued the theory that when Jesus' body was resurrected, there had been a biological nuclear reaction that released neutrons. These neutrons are known to cause a rejuvenation of cloth such that it appears much younger than it actually is. This explanation seemed neat and tidy in that it killed two mysteries with one stone — how the body disappeared and how the cloth ended up dating to the Middle Ages. At this point, I figured my work here was done. But, as with all my revelations in the past, my conclusions were premature.

One day while busy patting myself on the back for resolving this confounding dilemma, out of the blue, they said, *"You're wrong."* Me, wrong? Okay, maybe it was some other nuclear particle that I had overlooked — perhaps muons or pions or. . . *"You're wrong. The cloth was repaired."* What were they trying to tell me? I had worked very hard on my nuclear theory and, as such, I deserved to be right! I was devastated. How was this possible — did they mean that the small sample of the Shroud used to determine its age actually contained newer cloth used for repairs? Where was the evidence for such a claim? Certainly someone would have seen such an obvious flaw in the sample? After all, the repairs were not "invisible" were they? Then they said, *"Look and we'll show you."*

I ran to find Joe to tell him about this insight and to get his help in finding a picture of the actual Carbon-14 (C-14) sample used in 1988. Sure enough, he found one and there it was. The threads and the opposite sides of the separating "seam" that ran down the middle of the sample were noticeably different. The differences were subtle, and if you did not know what you were looking for, you certainly would not see it. We found a clear picture of one of the subsamples and sent it to several textile experts for blinded reviews. Sure enough, they all saw discernible differences in each of the two sides of the weave pattern. One of the most dramatic affirmations came in a blinded review by a "French tailor" who readily pointed out and described the "invisible" mending techniques that his European ancestors used to mend damaged linens. Nowadays the process is known as "inweaving," and it involves a skilled weaver using a patch of identical fabric and placing it over the damaged area, matching the fabric's pattern. The frayed edges are then hand woven into the material. Both the patch and the repair are invisible to the eye. In the Shroud's case, the interweave involved about 1/2 inch next to the original raw edge; exactly the amount of aberrant material noted in the C-14 sample. There was no doubt in the tailor's mind that, indeed, exactly this technique had been used on the linen sample I was showing him.

But how, why, did this type of repair occur in the first place? The story began to unfold and documentation miraculously appeared each day to support our theory that a major portion of the sample used to date the Shroud had come from

16th century material. What we learned was that the reinforcement with 16th century material occurred following the removal of the 5 1/2 inch x 3 1/2 inch section of cloth adjacent to the C-14 sample. This may have occurred as a result of the will and testament bequeath, drawn up on February 20th, 1508, by the Duchess of Savoy, Margaret of Austria, who wanted to leave a portion of the Shroud to her church (Wilson, 1998:67, 287). Margaret died around the beginning of 1531 (BSTS Newsletter, no. 51, June 2000, pg. 43), at which time her last will and testament was executed. It is likely that it included the excision of the 5 1/2 inch x 3 1/2 inch section. Supporting this timeline of events is empirical testing by the late chemist Dr. Alan Adler, which compelled him to conclude that the "missing panels were already missing at the time of the 1532 fire" (Adler, 1997:104). Since this would have been prior to the addition of the backing cloth in 1534, a more sophisticated patch-type repair would have been necessary to prevent unraveling of the raw edges. This type of detail to repairs would be consistent with the wealth and devotion of the Savoy family, who owned the Shroud at the time. All the pieces to the puzzle fit perfectly and in August 2000, Joe and I presented our findings at the "Sindone 2000," an international Shroud conference held in Orvieto, Italy.

Although our paper received rave reviews, little happened initially to forward our hypothesis into a bona fide theory. Then in the waning days of summer 2001, almost coincident with the world's thirst for spiritual affirmation following the horrific events of September 11th, a near miracle took place. Through a series of odd connections and seeming "coincidences" I found myself in contact with one of the most renowned members of the former 1978 STURP team. Ray Rogers, a retired chemist from Los Alamos Labs, was interested in reading our Orvieto paper. Soon after, he became singularly focused on testing our hypothesis. For a gentleman in his late-seventies, his energy and constant pursuit of this endpoint was amazing. On several occasions, I would receive numerous e-mail reports of his findings, which included key factors such as, that there was significant cotton in the adjacent Raes sample, some threads were literally "spliced" together as we had argued, the Raes threads were typical of the medieval backing cloth on the Shroud and not like the main Shroud threads. In a landmark report that was printed in the British Society of the Turin Shroud (BSTS) newsletter, Rogers concluded, "I believe it is quite clear that the material of the Shroud is significantly different from both the Holland [backing] cloth and the Raes sample from 1973. The samples used for the 'dating' of 1988 were cut from immediately above the Raes sample. It is very unfortunate that the 14C samples were not better characterized, because the evidence shows that it is highly probable that the samples were not characteristic of the Shroud and were spurious"(BSTS, Nov. 2001). Had we found the answer and, as such, did this now open the door for our work on the image formation process and the newfound DelaWarr connections?

M. Sue Benford

Chapter Thirty Two

Finding the soul

By July of 1999, I was working almost exclusively on investigating the DelaWarr images and linking them to the Shroud. I had read both of the books by Langston Day, who was assisted by George DelaWarr, and was astounded by their revelations and insights. What George and Marjorie DelaWarr discovered after 30 years of relentless scientific experimentation, was no less than to redefine reality, physical matter, and the workings of creation. A contemporary wrote, "their discoveries have penetrated beyond the atom to the origin of matter and are undoubtedly the beginning of a new chapter of science."

In essence, the DelaWarrs discovered what Eastern cultures have held true for thousands of years, but what I had only recently learned. That all living and non-living objects have a soul, an essence or "fingerprint" as Jesus had told me, which is interconnected with the observable matter. That thoughts are more than mere imaginings — they are "consciousness tools" available for accessing etheric energies and recording these subtle emanations with tangible and well-tuned instruments. That matter can be materialized and dematerialized using only our thoughts. And that the *"elan vital,"* or cosmic energy, which the Chinese call *"Chi,"* the Hindus call *"Prana,"* and the Japanese call *"Ki"* not only exists, but can actually be measured and quantified scientifically. It is this cosmic energy that makes up the soul, spirit and mind. Not a new idea to most of the world's cultures, but one that remains staunchly at odds with contemporary Western materialistic science.

If the DelaWarrs were right, understanding vital energy and learning to use it to benefit humankind could prove to be our ultimate salvation. I learned that the DelaWarrs spent most of their lives trying to do just that — apply their new knowledge in the service of humankind. In the end their ideas were ridiculed, and their lives ended in frustrated despair. Was it now time to revitalize the long-ago abandoned and ostracized DelaWarr ideas and equipment? Would a definitive and all-important link to the Holy Shroud and Jesus himself somehow serve to awaken the slumbering masses into realizing what I had been learning all along — we are, in essence, like Jesus — gods in the making? Beings capable of not only building the instruments and equipment that detect our subtle spiritual being, but realizing that our conscious thoughts are essential to make it all come to fruition. Had I been led to the evidence for what Jesus had told me years before, that science will prove the existence of the Spirit and, ultimately, the existence of God?

The DelaWarr's crowning achievement came with the invention and construction of their remote-imaging camera that could, literally, provide a visual image of any part of any object without the object being present in the laboratory. The results they obtained were nothing short of miraculous or "black magic," depending on your viewpoint.

The outraged scientific community called for intensive scrutiny of DelaWarr's seemingly impossible claims. Thus, in 1951, one of DelaWarr's infamous cameras was transported to St. Bartholomew's hospital in London for more in-depth testing. A young doctor and a few of his associates were trained in the operation of the camera and began using it with great success. The team produced more than 400 images under controlled conditions in which the doctor and other operators were "blinded" to the patients' condition. As reported by DelaWarr in the book, <u>New Worlds Beyond the Atom</u>,

"Case after case in the hospital was photographed from the patient's blood specimen and the results were checked by X-ray photography, biopsy or autopsy. . .Among the first batch of cases chosen from one of the hospital wards was one of tuberculosis of the lungs (see **Figure 2**), and one of gastric ulcer (see **Figure 3**). . . .In these photographs, which are prints from the plates and therefore 'negatives,' the disease radiations from the affected organs appear as large white patches. Notice that this is unlike X-ray photography in which the bones and more solid parts of the anatomy stand out clearly. What is being photographed is distant radiation, so that accuracy and clearness in anatomical detail is not to be expected at this early stage of the Camera's development." (Day/DelaWarr, 1956; 95-96).

The simple 3-D renderings I made of these two images, using a commercially-available software program, were quite compelling (see **Figures 4 & 5**). However, without the actual diseased organs in front of me, no definitive comparison was possible.

When the hospital administrators found out about this "unorthodox practice" and the impressive results, the young doctor was reprimanded, DelaWarr's work stopped, and the camera abruptly removed from the hospital, with all word of its existence and accomplishments suppressed.

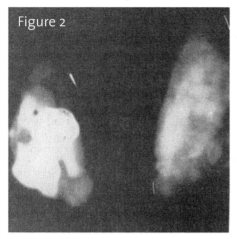

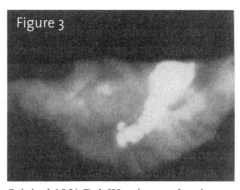

Original 1951 DelaWarr image showing confirmed tuberculosis of the lungs. (Reprinted from Day/DelaWarr <u>New World's Beyond the Atom</u>, Figure 41.)

Original 1951 DelaWarr image showing confirmed ulceration of the stomach (Reprinted from Day/DelaWarr <u>New World's Beyond the Atom</u>, Figure 42.)

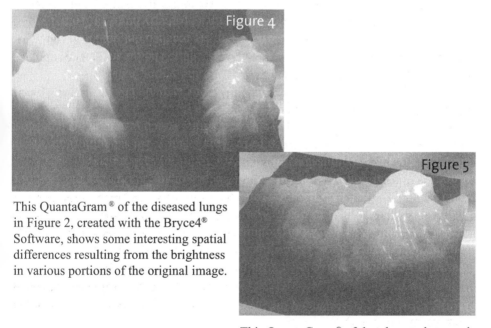

This QuantaGram® of the diseased lungs in Figure 2, created with the Bryce4® Software, shows some interesting spatial differences resulting from the brightness in various portions of the original image.

This QuantaGram® of the ulcerated stomach, created with the Bryce4® Software, seems to indicate an inflammation in a portion of the stomach. Confirmation of this is not possible without access to the actual organ imaged in 1951.

One of the camera's most remarkable feats happened when a local farmer had a sick cow that appeared to be having digestive problems. The cow refused to eat and was growing weaker as all standard veterinary practices proved futile. The cow's veterinarian had heard about the DelaWarrs' work and asked for their help. A small drop of blood was taken from the cow and placed in the DelaWarr camera. DelaWarr called these physical samples from subjects "witnesses," which I thought especially ironic knowing that the Shroud was called the "silent witness." Marjorie, who was operating the camera at the time, focused her attention on the cow's symptoms and its ailing stomach. What the camera recorded was the image of a cow's stomach with a round lump, and a long, thin highlighted line in the tail. The veterinarian operated on the cow and removed a round rock and a long, thin wire with two distinct "bumps" from one of the cow's stomachs. The two bumps in the wire had not been discernible in DelaWarr's original image. Once removed, the cow's symptoms disappeared (see **Figures 6 & 7**).

Questions abounded both in the 1950s, and now in my own head, about the legitimacy of DelaWarr's claims. Nearly a decade after his first book was published, DelaWarr was summoned to court to address charges of fraud leveled against him by a disgruntled patient. The prosecution asserted that DelaWarr and his cronies had manufactured each of the "miraculous" images using some sort of laser-like technology coupled with undisclosed stage magician slight-of-hand tricks. Although DelaWarr prevailed in the hearing, the fact remained, at that stage in history, there was no way DelaWarr could definitively prove that he had not fraudulently created his unique images. It was not until my discovery of the spatial encoding in the DelaWarr images, based upon the insights I had received from Jesus, that DelaWarr was fully vindicated of any wrong doing or deception. In one simple picture, we had the proof. The wire in DelaWarr's original cow's stomach photo was the exact same wire removed by the vet. A 3-D rendering of the original photograph clearly shows the wire's two distinctive bumps, an aspect that was not discernible in the original DelaWarr image (see **Figure 8**). This crucial discovery proved beyond a shadow of a doubt that there was no way the DelaWarr images could have been faked in the 1950s as the device needed to decode them, the VP-8 analyzer, was not invented until 1976.

With a renewed vigor, I began intensely studying some of the other DelaWarr images as well. In another remarkable case, a young woman believed she was pregnant and wanted to find out when her baby was due. She sent a sample of her blood to the DelaWarr labs in England from her home in Ireland. As with the cow's blood, the DelaWarrs put the blood sample in the camera. This time, however, they were not exactly sure how to set the camera and focus their thoughts; thus, they tried numerous settings for one month, three months and six months gestation. The images that resulted were quite blurry for one and six months, but crystal clear for three months — the obvious, recognizable form of a human fetus

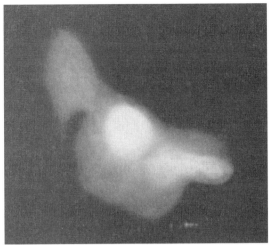

This image was used to detect the cause of disorder in a cow. The QuantaGraph® reveals a long thin (white) object in the mouth of one of the cow's stomachs as well as a light "gray" object (surrounded by a white circular area). (Reprinted from Day/DelaWarr New World's Beyond the Atom, Figure 45.)

Figure 6

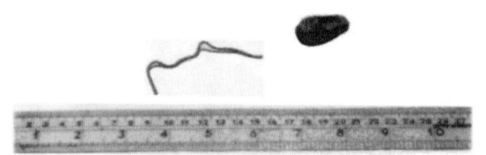

Figure 7   The veterinarian removed a stone and a piece of wire from one of the cow's stomachs. (Reprinted from Day/DelaWarr New World's Beyond the Atom, Figure 46.)

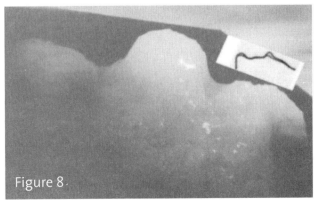

This QuantaGram® of the cow's stomach, created with the Bryce4® Software, clearly reveals the stone and wire, which later were removed by a veterinarian. Close examination reveals the wire's distinctive curvature, an aspect of evaluation that is unavailable through simple 2-D image analysis (see Figure 6)

Figure 8

Figure 9

Past Image

Fetus at 1 month gestation

Past Image

Fetus at 2 months gestation

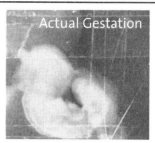

Actual Gestation

Age 3 months

Future Image

6 months gestation

This composite shows images taken of an unborn fetus, using only a sample of the mother's blood, on the same day. Both past images, 1 and 2 months, and a future image, 6 months, could be detected. This demonstrated that whatever energy source DelaWarr had tapped into could create pictures from both the past and the future. The fetus was determined to be actually 3 months when the images were taken (see Figure 13). (Reprinted from Day/DelaWarr New World's Beyond the Atom, Figures 28-31.)

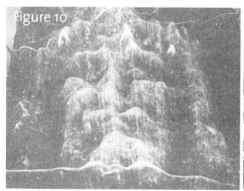

Figure 10

Figure 11

This is a frontal 3-D rendering of the Shroud of Turin face created with Bryce4® Software. Note the clear presence of teeth demonstrating that, whatever created the image, was capable of imaging internal bodily structures.

The same 3-D Shroud face rendered in profile.

(see **Figure 9**). The DelaWarrs told the woman she was three months pregnant, which was later confirmed by her delivery date. What DelaWarr learned from this experience was that both the past and future could be imaged with the camera.

I wondered, was this something we would do by using the Shroud as a "witness" in the camera — take pictures of Jesus from the days when he lived on earth, the day he was resurrected, and possibly even the day he returns? Was I the first to see this possibility and, more importantly, would I also be the first to actually see Jesus again if the camera worked? As the Magdalene before me had been the first to see the risen Christ, was I destined to follow in her footsteps? I could not control my enthusiasm at these possibilities.

I realized something else as I examined the old black and white image of the fetus, which is also found in DelaWarr's first book — it had no umbilical cord. Instead it had a large tube-like protrusion extending from the back of its head. This oddity was unexplainable if one assumed that the photograph was of the fetus' physical body. However, this "tube" was completely consistent if what the DelaWarrs were capturing was not the physical body of the fetus, but rather its soul. Eastern philosophy maintains that the soul is not attached to the mother's body, but to the universal "vital energy," through what is called a "chakra" at the back of the head. Had DelaWarr taken the world's first photograph of a human chakra – without ever knowing it?

Of the 13,000 original images collected at the DelaWarr laboratories over the years, nearly 9,000 of them still remain to be seen, analyzed, and "decoded" today. It was one of these images that I first received from Peter and had analyzed with the VP-8. Since that time, I have decoded nearly three dozen of the DelaWarr originals using a software system — each one containing the same unique and magnificent three-dimensional spatial encoding as the first. All, in essence, were identical to spatial encoding found in the Shroud (see **Figures 10 & 11**).

But what other scientifically-based links were there between the most studied artifact in human history and the DelaWarr images? I discovered that, although disagreements abound regarding the Shroud, most scientists agree on several key points about it's image:

✓ There are no significant traces of paint, pigment, dye, ink or stain
✓ The image is purely superficial, penetrating only the top two microfibrils
✓ No directionality to the image as with brush strokes
✓ No outline to the image as would be necessary for it to be a work of art
✓ No cementing of fibrils as would occur with the application of any liquid substance
✓ Uniform intensity on both front and back images
✓ No variations in density
✓ No particles between the threads, which excludes any kind of powder rubbing

✓ No liquids used to create image except for the blood images
✓ No paint binder
✓ The original is a "negative" capable of producing a photographic positive that appears to be a crucified man.

The question became: how closely did DelaWarr's images match with this description of the Shroud? In order to find out, I took the glass plate that Peter had sent me to The Ohio State University Microscopic and Chemical Analysis Research Center (MARC Lab) on April 19, 2000 to determine the origin and composition of the image. We looked at the image under a light microscope using a variety of amplification settings. The results demonstrated that the silver grains on the surface of the glass plate were bigger in the darker, i.e., more heavily exposed, areas of the image and, subsequently, smaller in the lighter or less intense portions of the image. This is the typical response of a standard photographic material exposed to a light source — a confusing finding since we knew that the DelaWarr images were created in total darkness. There was no added pigment, dye, stain or coloration beyond the silver particles. There was no "directionality" to the image or artist's outline. All identical findings to the Shroud's.

Phase two of our evaluation involved scrapping a sample from the non-image section of the glass plate to determine the chemical composition of the plate itself. After all, perhaps DelaWarr had manufactured some special plates with unique chemical make-ups such that these images would "miraculously" appear. The Cameca SX-50 Scanning Electron Microscope (SEM) was used for this analysis. SEM is capable of performing quantitative chemical microanalysis of major and minor elements in solids, including glass. It is ideal for characterization of surfaces or particles including thin films. The results of this analysis demonstrated that the glass was a standard silicon-based material with no unusual properties.

Phase three included scrapping a sample from the image portion of the glass plate. This would be the real test to determine if DelaWarr had sketched any of his images with some type of artist's tool. Using the same equipment and procedure as for the non-image sample described above, the SEM results revealed a standard silver-based photoemulsion as described by DelaWarr in his book — nothing more, nothing less. The MARC Lab concluded that the images were, most likely, the result of some "high-energy radiation" for which they could not ascertain the origin or energy signature. In essence, the image was identical to that of the Shroud's.

The Shroud of Turin Research Project (STURP) team, which extensively studied the Shroud in 1978, made several public declarations about the Shroud's image (Jumper E, Adler A, Jackson JP, *et al.*, 1984) that lend credence to the theory positing a connection between the DelaWarr images and the Shroud:

- ✓ "...it seems as though the image formation mechanism acted through space, between the body and the cloth, such as for diffusion or radiation. However, these mechanisms must be excluded, because, although they can discolor the cloth at a distance, they cannot form a high resolution, sharp image, such as what we find on the Shroud."

- ✓ "... It thus seems as though we are looking at the internal skeletal structure of the hand imaged through the intervening flesh tissues onto the Shroud cloth." [Also note the teeth in **Figure 10**]

- ✓ "... it follows that whatever mechanism produced the image of the body onto the cloth, it must be a radically different mechanism than any physical mechanisms that have been considered to date. For what process is capable of rendering internal body structure into the image patterns that we see on the Shroud?"

- ✓ "Immediately, we recognize that the image must have been generated by some principle whereby body structure became encoded into varying shades of intensity on the cloth."

Further analysis revealed that, when the body image was generated, the Shroud apparently deformed to a somewhat flatter draping configuration laterally positioning the image of the sides of the face several centimeters inside the bloodstain pattern. The fact that there is a several centimeter discrepancy between the locations of the bloodstains in the hair and the sides of the face are problematic for image-formation theorists who attempt to relate the cloth and body correlation as essential to the image itself (Jumper, Adler, Jackson, *et al.*, 1984). The DelaWarr process eliminates the need for such a correlation between the image and the actual physical body as the images are produced holographically from a portion of the *bioenergetic*, not the physical, body.

Further problems exist for researchers in attempting to explain image intensity discrepancies between the frontal and dorsal images of the Shroud that may be explained by a bioenergetic radiation mechanism. Scientific calculations determined that there should be a nearly two-order of magnitude difference in pressure between frontal and dorsal cloth contact regions. However, this was not reflected in the relief amplitudes, or plateau effects, generated via the VP-8 analyses of the frontal and dorsal images. This unexpected result suggests a pressure-independent mechanism may have created the Shroud image (Jackson, 1991). Clearly, the DelaWarr process, which created what I dubbed QuantaGraphs®, is "pressure independent."

Several other notable similarities exist between the DelaWarr images and the Shroud. First, both were created (putatively in the Shroud's case, definitely in the DelaWarr case) in complete darkness without use of any visible light source. In

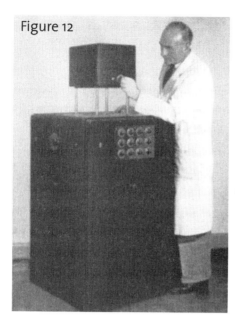

Figure 12

Photograph of one of the earlier versions of the DelaWarr camera. (Reprinted from Day/DelaWarr New World's Beyond the Atom, 1956)

the case of the Shroud, the darkness is implied by the sealed tomb enclosure; whereas, the DelaWarr system is encased in total darkness while the images are produced (see **Figure 12**). Second, the image creation process involves substantial amounts of vibration to the encasement structure around the test object (camera with DelaWarr; tomb with Shroud). The DelaWarr system utilizes a vibrational device during the "exposure" time, which is required in order to obtain a clear image. According to the New Testament (Mt. 28:2) an "earthquake" shook the tomb of Jesus' around the time his tomb was discovered empty. Such an earthquake, if it indeed did occur, may also account for the rolling away of the heavy stone at the entrance to the tomb. Third, the Shroud and the DelaWarr images both required clear human (or perhaps super-human in the Shroud's case) intentionality in order for the images to appear. Finally, both the Shroud image and the DelaWarr images are negatives capable of producing photographic positives. However, according to Italian scientist and Shroud researcher, Giovanni Riggi, this image is not a photographic negative per se but, rather, more closely aligned to a "magnetic negative" (Riggi, 1994).

A "magnetic negative?" Was this something akin to our modern-day Magnetic Resonance Imaging (MRI) medical techniques? Being in the health care field, I knew a little about MRI. It is the most advanced diagnostic imaging system available today. MRI images are formed by the combination of a strong magnetic field and radio waves interacting with, primarily, the hydrogen protons in the body. Patients are enclosed in a magnetic field created by a large magnet, which causes the spinning nuclei of hydrogen atoms within the body to change their axes of rotation. Altering the magnetic field by sending radio waves through it further affects the behavior of the hydrogen protons by causing them to move out of alignment. When the radio signal stops, the protons relax back into alignment and release energy. These changes in excitation and relaxation are recorded by receivers (antenna coils), then mathematicly reconstructed by a sophisticated computer into spatially-encoded two and three-dimensional pictures of the body (see www.picker.com).

Without disclosing their origin, I sent several 3-D reconstructions I had made of the DelaWarr images to MRI expert Dr. Philip Morse, who is also a Professor of Chemistry at Illinois State University (USA). Believing that what he was examining were computer-generated MRI-related renderings, Morse commented, "What it looks like you've done is generate a 3-D image using intensity data as the third dimension with some shading (that is, any given point is represented by X, Y, Z = intensity, intensity . . . the "bones" in the fetus picture are clearly NOT on the surface of the fetus, but are interior (see **Figures 13 & 14**) . . . To get actual 3-D information would require multiple images from different angles and a more complex reconstruction algorithm. It can be done from, for example, MRI slices. . . You have some great images!!!" (via e-mails June 2000)

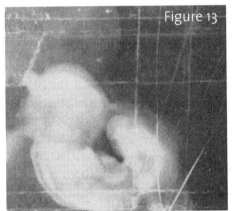

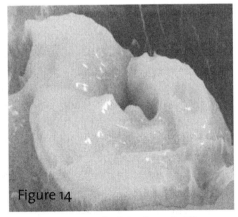

3 month old fetus imaged by DelaWarr in 1951. Note the clarity compared with the past and future images seen in Figure 9 and the "tube" protrusion coming from the back of the head. Notably missing is a prominent umbilical cord, which should be clearly observable in a fetus this age. (Reprinted from Day/DelaWarr <u>New World's Beyond the Atom</u>, Figure 30.)

The QuantaGram® of the fetus in Figure 13 shows remarkable spatial encoding characteristics.

In attempting to explain the DelaWarr technique in terms of the principles of MRI, Morse used the cow's stomach image (see **Figure 6**). He commented, "The object is one dimension (wire) so bends will be reflected in the intensity differences depending on the amount of other material surrounding it. The 2-D image actually encodes the spatial distribution of the object because it is only one-dimensional in the first place, so position (location in the stomach) could be encoded by intensity. . . I'd need to see your (computer) code to figure out what you are doing. I don't see any need at the moment to postulate anything other than graphical manipulation (in the most positive sense) to generate the images you produced. However, if you are using some other method to obtain the image, then..... THAT is interesting!"

Clearly, the images easily passed muster as excellent, if not superior, reconstructions of some type of "MRI" imaging. Undeniably, no computer code or MRI slice compilation was used in capturing, or rendering, any of the fifty-year old DelaWarr images. The connections were certainly intriguing.

After months of study and meditation, I received an important insight into the fundamental principles of what the camera was recording and how it worked. The DelaWarr camera acts to produce what appears to be a "Quantum Hologram" (QH). The theories of a holographically-based universe were originally championed by two of the world's most eminent thinkers: physicist David Bohm, a protégé of Einstein's, and Karl Pribram, a highly-respected neurophysiologist from Stanford University. Their holographic model received dramatic experimental support in 1982 when a research team, led by physicist Alain Aspect in Paris, demonstrated that the web of subatomic particles that compose our physical universe possesses what appears to be an undeniable "holographic" property.

Holographs have a property called "distributedness," which means that any fractional portion of the recorded hologram contains sufficient information to reconstruct the complete original 3-D information pattern. Consequently, it can be theorized that within humans and other animals, the holographic biophysical radiation can be present in blood, sputum, hair and other small subsets of the subject, due to the holographic property of distributedness.

Russian scientists have likely measured this holographic bioenergy without discovering its holographic nature. Their research, which suggests the existence of a previously undetectable subtle radiation linked to physical DNA, may support the hypothesis of an intact energy field containing relevant organismal information capable of being coupled to an optical imaging device (Gariaev PP, Poponin VP *et al.*, 1992; 1995). Was this the "spiritual DNA" that Jesus had told me about, which contained the splendors of our soul?

I sent my theories, papers, 3-D evidence and the DelaWarr books to renowned QH theorist, Edgar Mitchell, Sc.D., former Apollo 14 Astronaut, author, and founder of the Institute of Noetic Sciences. After studying the material, he wrote several detailed e-mails to me. In them he concluded, "There is simply no doubt that what DelaWarr was tapping into was the quantum hologram. He is describing exactly the properties that the formalism suggests should be there. The fact that he was achieving resonance using an array of devices to record acoustic frequencies, magnetic frequencies, visual photographic effects and frequencies is precisely the properties the QH should have, because the information is carried in the phase relationships between the wave forms. The fact that there are preferred polarizations and preferred directions with regard to the Earth's magnetic field for many of the specimens, organs, organisms, conditions, experiments, etc. demonstrates the complex interactions between all levels of chemical, electromagnetic and quantum properties. The fact that a complete mapping can be visually presented in 3-D is also a QH property, as it is a geodesic structure in 3-D and also changes with time. It is also demonstrating that one is dealing with different scales sizes of matter and energy, but not different kinds of stuff. . . It is reasonable that if the Shroud is indeed a human image, that it was deposited by the same type interactions that you propose. . .I really think you are on to something that will advance our knowledge of these issues." (Mitchell/Benford personal correspondence, June 2000).

Perhaps, too, I was led to the DelaWarr work so that it could be "resurrected" and put to use, solving some of today's most profound problems. For instance, it could be easily used to detect Mad Cow disease in individual animals so that entire herds would not be destroyed. It could detect tuberculosis in individual lions to prevent the destruction of entire prides or in people to avoid widespread outbreaks. Even for the early detection and treatment of other diseases in humans, such as AIDS, hepatitis, ulcers, arthritis, depression, cancer, or a whole range of infectious diseases, which scientists are predicting will explode with the continued destruction of our rainforests. And how about using the camera for the discovery of more oil and minerals for future energy needs? The list and implications are endless.

It was starting to become crystal clear — the Shroud was a picture of Jesus' soul, not merely his body as researchers and historians so adamantly believed. Beyond the cloth's tangible blood stains, which revealed the final physical marks of his scourging and crucifixion, the surreal image of a man overlayed on these markings was akin to the quantagraphic DelaWarr images.

Jesus' final lesson while still on Earth, recorded in his Shroud, was unfolding like the petals of a young flower that was being exposed to the light for the very first time. He left us proof that we are more than just a composite of atoms and molecules — finite in dimension and limited in existence. We are what he had been telling me all these years, unique spiritual beings intertwined with one another and every other creature and inert object in the universe. There is no such thing as "non-locality." It is only perceived that way.

Most importantly, I had learned that we alone, among God's creations, could control and manifest with our unique conscious thought the very soul, the very substance of all things. DelaWarr had stumbled upon the very essence of our existence and, in turn, helped Jesus to finally bring forth his final and most profound lesson for humanity.

M. Sue Benford

Chapter Thirty Three

A "Shroud" for the 21st Century

Although the DelaWarr images, and the glass plate, had been an extraordinary example of how Jesus keeps his promises, it still was not enough. A crucial piece of the Shroud puzzle still lurked in the scientific crevices of my mind: the surface image appeared on linen without any modern technology. As dramatic as DelaWarr's accomplishments in obtaining spatially-encoded images on glass plates, the linen-image aspect of the Shroud still loomed unchallenged. Even though one of the Shroud's most noteworthy researchers, the late chemist Dr. Alan Adler, had sent me linen to test in the camera, the current DelaWarr group was unsuccessful in getting any discoloration on it. Although disappointing, the results were not unexpected as no one had mastered the feat of garnering a matching image on linen cloth. Many had tried to paint, draw, etch, dust, burn, irradiate, and photograph a suitable replica, but there was always something amiss either chemically or physically.

I turned my concern over to "the guys," and asked for their help. After all, if Jesus truly wanted me to have the full understanding about his Shroud, he would need to give me a testable image on linen. This seemed to be an impossible task as so many had attempted this very thing — and failed.

One night in meditation, John approached me smiling. He reminded me of a series of experiments I had begun years earlier but had abandoned to pursue the DelaWarr work. Following a consistent series of spiritual "leads," I began my pursuit of this quest with a renewed anticipation. The previous years had taught me how to discern the etheric messages and the subtle indicators in order to unlock well-hidden ancient mysteries.

Surprisingly, my path lead to one of the grandest ancient mysteries of them all: the Great Pyramids. To me this seemed all too strange. The pyramid "fad" had gone out in the 70's and, I assumed, probably for good reason. How could this have anything to do with creating a Shroud image on linen?

As bizarre and unlikely as this all seemed, I decided to test the theory that combined what I had learned about DelaWarr's use of a "test object" coupled with willful intention and the Great Pyramid. I cut a small subsample, 4 x 2.5 cm, from the Adler linen and used this as my "experimental" sample. I then built a small five-inch high, cardboard pyramid "tomb," adhering to specifications described by Czech engineer and inventor Karel Drbal in his 1959 Patent (Republic of Czechoslovakia, Office For Patents And Inventions, Published August, 1959, # 91304). Drbal only received this patent after ten years of disclosures and submissions of experimental data to the patent office proving his claims that the pyramid, matching the geometry of Egypt's Great Pyramid, could in fact sharpen razor blades (Toth and Nielsen, 1974; 114).

Drbal explained the results of his razor-blade research by asserting, "That such an action on the dipole-molecules of water is possible in a resonant cavity, fed with appropriate microwave energy, was proved by the scientists Born and Lertes (see: Archiv. der elektrischen Uebertragung, 1950, Heft 1, s.33-35. 'Der Born-Lertessche Drehfeldeffkt in Dipolflussigkeitn im Gebiet der Zentimeterwellen'). It was found that the microwaves of centimetre-wavelengths and their harmonics can produce an accelerated rotation of the water dipole-molecules, and this effect can have as a result the dehydration process - the 'driving out' of water dipole-molecules from the smallest cavities and projecting them in the open air. This is exactly the process of electromagnetic dehydration."(Toth and Nielsen, 1974; 117). Until quite recently, it was believed that dehydrated cellulose of the Shroud fibrils was the cause of the image, not paint, pigments, or other substances (Schwalbe and Rogers, 1982; 3-49). However, recent research on the Shroud image fibers by Rogers has shown that, in fact, it is not the cellulose itself that is discolored but, rather, the surface starch impurities on the cellulose! (Rogers, 2002). Rogers writes, "The fact that the color resides only on the fiber surfaces leads to the hypothesis that the color formed as a result of chemical reactions involving impurities on the surface. The spectra strongly suggest that the impurities were carbohydrates that dehydrated as a result of the image-formation process." He further emphasizes in his paper that, "The cellulose was not involved in the color-producing chemistry of the image." (Rogers, 2002). Rogers hypothesized that an ancient substance, called *Saponaria officinalis*, and also known as "Soapwort," might also have contributed to the discolorations in the image areas of the Shroud. These observations would prove crucial to my own image formation experiments.

Although not fully understood or accepted by mainstream science, some physicists do believe that the pyramid is not only an accumulator of energies, but also a modifier of these same energies. It is recognized that any object in which energy vibrates is capable of acting as a resonating cavity. It is further speculated that this energy would affect the molecules, or crystals, of any object in the path of the beam of focused energy. Some even equate it to an invisible laser beam, having a different frequency and intensity (Toth and Nielsen, 1974; 133). Of interest is that, according to Stephen Mehler in his article *The Origin of the Word Pyramid*, the Greek word pyramid means "fire in the middle."

All pyramid researchers also acknowledged the importance of the Earth's magnetic field in the various results obtained. Similar to DelaWarr's magnetic focus, magnetism appeared a uniformly key variable in the pyramids as well. DelaWarr had made an additional observation that might be important and testable in light of what I was learning about the energies inside pyramids. He noted, "It also appeared that these phenomena of life were closely connected to that of charged particles, for when some of the photographs described above were examined under a microscope, there were visible the tracks of atomic particles in the emulsion, marks where particles had collided, and so on, as is commonly seen in photographs taken of atomic happenings inside a Wilson Cloud Chamber." (Day/DelaWarr, 1956; 48). I decided that the only way to find out if there was any connection between pyramids, the Shroud and the DelaWarr phenomenon was to do some tests.

On March 5, 2001, I built a pyramid using standard poster quality cardboard. My miniature pyramid measured 10 cm high (about 5 inches) with sides 15.7 cm and a four-sided base of 9.5 cm each. I placed a dull Exacto-knife razor blade on top of fresh, unexposed Kodak Ultra-speed dental film. I decided that the dental film, securely encased in protective coverings, might produce the charged particle tracks that DelaWarr had recognized on his glass plates. I positioned the edge of the razor blade so that it was facing West. The pyramid itself was positioned so that the walls faced true North, South, East and West while the corners aligned with NW, SW, etc.

On March 7, 2001, I added a 3 cm high cardboard box platform in the center of the pyramid. I then placed the X-ray film and razor blade on top of this platform, which was positioned in the center of the pyramid.

According to DelaWarr, "... an ordinary... photograph of a person would act as a 'link' for tuning-in to him, though not such a good link as a blood specimen or a sputum slide." (Day/DelaWarr, 1956; 66). Would it be possible to use a Shroud photograph to get an actual image of the person on the cloth or maybe something else connected to that person? To test this, on March 8, 2001, I decided to build a second pyramid according to the same specs I used on 3/5/01. This time, however, I included a simple 1 by 1.5 inch real looking Shroud-face photograph (the negative version) and laid it on top of clean, dry linen provided to me by the late STURP

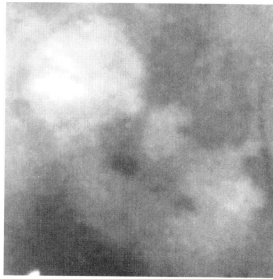

The image of a "fetus" appeared in the lower left hand corner of a dental X-ray that had been left in a pyramid.

Figure 15

The same "fetus" in Figure 15 demonstrated some 3-D characteristics. Note what appears like an umbilical cord coming from the middle region of the image. (Courtesy Robert Kersten, © 2001)

Figure 16

chemist, Al Adler. I put the photograph face down on the cloth then put both (linen and Shroud picture) on top of a fresh, unexposed Kodak Ultra-speed dental film (white, smooth side of plastic film packet against the linen). All three objects - film, linen and picture - were laid on top a 3 cm high cardboard box inside the pyramid.

The Shroud face was aligned to face West. The pyramid was positioned so that the walls faced true North, South, East and West while the corners aligned with NW, SW, etc. The final "ingredient" was to focus intense "thought" on the apparatus demanding that an image appear. After placing the linen in the pyramid, along with the "test object" Shroud face, I had a soul-to-soul talk with "the guys." I told Jesus and John directly that, "this is your chance. If you really want the truth known, and this is what the truth is, then it is all up to you now. Put something on that linen that can be seen, tested and understood." They both agreed that it would be done.

On March 15, 2001, I developed the film underneath the razor blade in the first pyramid. It had been in the pyramid for 10 days and had been undisturbed for 8 of those days. I followed the standard instructions for manual development of dental X-rays, which were included on the packaging sent by Kodak. Incredibly, I could see a faint image of the razor blade in the upper right hand portion of the film. But even more incredibly, I also noticed the image of a strange looking "fetus" in the bottom left corner of film (see **Figure 15**).

Where did this "fetal" image come from? Did it possess any of the known characteristics of a fetus (either a real one or the etheric DelaWarr fetus)? I sent the image of the "fetus" to an optical physicist for his evaluation. I also asked him to determine whether or not the image had any of the 3-D spatial encoding characteristics of the Shroud and the DelaWarr images. He commented that this image looked very similar to the one he had been shown from the DelaWarr book of the 3-month-old fetus. He also noted that this fetus differed from DelaWarr's in that it appeared to have an umbilical cord and placental sac attachment. More astounding, it also had spatial encoding characteristics (see **Figure 16**)

Next, I developed the X-ray from pyramid 2 that was under the Shroud picture. The resultant image had an odd stream of "capillaries" throughout the film. When fully fixed and dried, it looked like the outline of the Shroud picture but with no discernible features. Even more interesting, the linen, which had also in the pyramid for a week, had two small yellowish-brown streaks! The small, darkened areas looked very similar to the discolored fibers on the Shroud itself.

I attempted to replicate the same experimental results with several pieces of linen but, no matter what, I could not get any additional discolorations on the cloth. Dental X-rays left in the pyramids, however, consistently produced what appeared to be some kind of charged particle tracks – similar to what repeatedly appeared on DelaWarr's glass plates. Perhaps these tracks represented the remnants of the "Fundamental energy" described by DelaWarr. All we needed to do was find out exactly "what" particle had created these tracks and we would know what the energy was. Simple enough, I thought, since each nuclear particle leaves its own unique footprints, or tracks, that are identifiable.

In order to find out what particle made these tracks, I sent several X-rays to numerous particle track experts for identification. I purposely did not tell the scientists what I had done to create the tracks so that their reviews would be objective. The "blinded" reviews I obtained came from experts at The Ohio State University Nuclear Engineering department, NASA's Marshall Space Flight Center, Argonne Labs, and the Rochester Institute of Technology (RIT). Dr. Walter Fountain, of NASA writes, "The 'images' on these three X-ray film samples do not have characteristics consistent with nuclear track images in either a macroscopic view or a microscopic view that are familiar to our knowledge and experience . . . We are convinced, after detailed microscopic examinations . . . that the images referred to by you as 'dots' and 'tracks' were not caused by the passage of nuclear particles through the films." (via e-mails 5/9/01 and 5/10/01). The OSU engineers, the Argonne staff and RIT, reached the same conclusions. The tracks I had captured were of an "unknown" origin.

An important observation was made by Dr. Richard Hailstone of RIT who noted, "I have not seen these 'dots' on films before. Since they can be seen without magnification they are much larger than the specks we see in our samples where a transmission electron microscope operating at 7500-10,000 times magnification is needed. As they do not appear in the background we can presume they only appear when the film is exposed and processed." (via correspondence of 5/8/01) Dr. Hailstone explained in a follow-up e-mail that, "If the dots are silver they should be bleached back to silver ions in a [fixing] bath." (via e-mail 5/11/01). This implies that a chemical alteration occurred in the surface emulsion changing the chemical structure of the impacted silver compounds. But this conclusion posed a serious problem to the known laws of physics. After all, what type of non-nuclear energy could actually change the chemical structure of an object?

I took the X-rays to the OSU MARC lab for testing with their high-tech scanning electron microscopic (SEM). The results demonstrated that the exposed region (with dots and tracks) contained trace amounts of sulfur, magnesium and aluminum, whereas, the background region contained only the expected carbon, nitrogen and oxygen. Whatever caused the dots and tracks on the X-rays seems to have also created some differences in the basic chemistry of the emulsion.

But what about the linen – did it also demonstrate any type chemical change where the supposed unseen energy had discolored the linen? I decided to take my little experimental linen sample to the OSU MARC lab on March 27, 2001 to determine the chemical nature of the discolored fibers using the SEM. What the tests showed was that in every instance where discoloration was found on the linen, what appeared to be crystalline calcium deposits also were present. One thought was that these were "phytoliths" (plant stones); however, the literature is noticeably silent in mentioning the production of calcium phytoliths in flax (linen). Another thought was that this was simple surface contamination but this idea was discarded by the OSU scientist who performed the tests and who was an expert in determining surface contaminates from real artifacts. Amazingly, these calcium crystals appeared to be literally "growing" out of the fibers (see **Figure 17**).

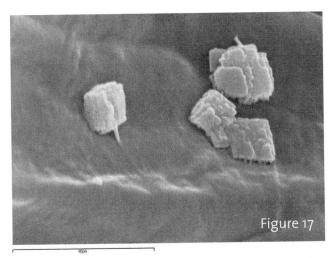

This image demonstrates the presence of calcite crystals in only the discolored areas of the experimental linen sample. Dehydration of surface impurities most likely caused the crystals to precipitate from the cloth. Calcite was also found growing from the Shroud.

Subsequent evaluation of the calcium crystals by a mineralogist at OSU, showed that the crystals were calcite (calcium carbonate). Most likely, the dehydration process had caused the crystals to grow from the surface of the linen. Simple evaporation is a well known catalyst of crystal formation and can be accomplished quite simply. But several questions still remained like why was not the entire surface of the linen discolored?

Finding calcium in the experimental sample's discolored regions is particularly pertinent when considering the Shroud image. Data from the measurements taken of the Shroud in 1978, revealed nearly twice as much surface calcium in the image areas of the Shroud as in the "pristine" area of the cloth (Morris, Schwalbe, London, 1980; 44). Further, a SEM test done by Dr. Walter McCrone and his associates showed that, not only was calcite present on the Shroud, but it also appeared to be "growing" from the surface of the linen (McCrone, 1999)

On March 28, 2001, I began testing another idea whereby the linen was soaked in "sweat" or salt water. I decided to make two new, and bigger, pyramids for this experiment so I constructed two 10-inch tall cardboard pyramids using the same dimensions of the Great Pyramid that I used for the smaller structures.

I cut two small linen samples from the same swatch I received from Adler that I used in my first experiment. I then soaked them in a salt-water solution for 15 minutes. After drying, each linen piece was placed in one of two new bigger pyramids on top of X-ray film. A positive Shroud face (the original version) was placed on top of the linen in the right pyramid while a negative Shroud face (the photographic-looking version) was placed on top of the linen in the left pyramid. After one week, on April 4th, the linen/films were removed. The linen in the left pyramid, with the photographic looking Shroud face, contained the same small, yellowish streak of discoloration as had the earlier linen in the first experiment! The other linen was unchanged. Furthermore, X-rays from both pyramids revealed the same characteristic dots and tracks that were present in the previous experiments.

The implications were enormous. My mind was racing with questions. Had DelaWarr really discovered, as he put it, a "Fundamental radiation?" This Fundamental radiation, he presumed, also was intimately involved with human intention and mind-matter interactions. Could this actually have any truth to it? Could we at some basic level actually influence the very components of matter with our thoughts? Was this something Jesus wanted us to learn about ourselves through understanding how the Shroud image was created – knowledge of our innate power over creation? This last earthly lesson of his certainly would be his grandest.

If, in fact, this preposterous idea had any merit, then it stood to reason that we should be able to create the same dots and tracks on the X-rays WITHOUT the assistance of the pyramids or the DelaWarr camera. I decided to put it to the test with a series of "thought" experiments. Employing Joe and my two children, then ages 7 and 12 years, I asked each person to lightly touch a fresh dental X-ray to his or her forehead while holding a simple thought to "place something on film." They were to keep the thought in their mind for one minute. The experiment was repeated over a dozen times with similar results. In each test, small areas of dots and tracks were produced on the developed films that matched the pyramid tracks (see **Figure 18**). The dots and tracks were not as large or pervasive as those in the pyramid but, nevertheless, they were visible. More importantly, these same dots and tracks could also be found on several of the DelaWarr images (see **Figure 13**) and, amazingly, on the Shroud of Turin (see **Figure 19**). Certainly there was some simple explanation that I was overlooking.

On April 15, 2001, I contacted optical physicist and imaging expert, Dr. Bruce Maccabee, regarding the presence of the various images and tracks seen on the X-rays. Dr. Maccabee was well known for his interpretations of presumed UFO photographs. He was trained to discern the truly unique from the simple mistakes often leading people to wrong interpretations of their photographs. Perhaps

M. Sue Benford

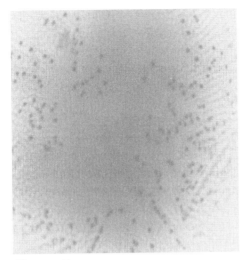

These unidentifiable "dots" and "tracks" appeared in both pyramid experiments and in "thought-only" experiments. Experts could not identify what particle made these tracks on the surface of the dental X-rays. Note the similar "tracks" on the DelaWarr fetal image in Figure 13 and in the Shroud of Turin image in Figure 19.

Figure 18

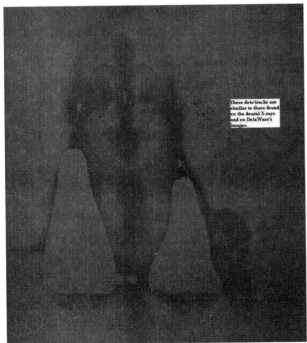

Unidentified tracks appeared in several locations on the Shroud of Turin. They are easy to see in this UV photograph. (Courtesy Vernon Miller, © 1978)

Figure 19

he could shed some light on what the nuclear particle track experts and I were observing so I sent him a detailed description of my results. He responded that, "It seems to me you are reporting images that are similar to those created by Ted Serios many years ago. . . images created without use of optics, as in an ordinary camera . . . A film image is a film image. How it got there is not necessarily determinable from the image itself. You are using dental film. This is black and white, I believe. It would appear that some sort of penetrating radiation is causing the chemical change in the film which allows for 'fixing' of an image (non-chemically changed film chemical is washed away). Have you tried this with Polaroid film? You can get single sheet pieces of film that are used in Polaroid camera back attachments to cameras . . .The film adapter has, built in, a pressure roller system that causes the development of the film to any light, you would NOT pull the thick paper cover from the film, but rather would put the target of interest on or near the film just as you do with the dental film. After the 'exposure' you would simply pull the film piece out of the holder and allow for development." (via e-mail, 4/15/01)

It seemed like what Dr. Maccabee suggested was a good way to test whether or not what I was getting was a real or imagined effect. Thus, during the months of April and May 2001, I purchased a 545 Polaroid film holder that uses single 4 x 5 inch film and several packages of Polypan 53 type film. No camera was involved. I followed Dr. Maccabee's suggested protocol while using an original positive photograph of the Shroud face. The face was placed on top of the film holder, with film inside, while I simply thought about putting the face on the film. Numerous trials by myself produced nothing but, when I asked Joe to help me with the experiments, we were able to produce three faint face-like images. One looked more like the regular Shroud face while one looked like a "Byzantine" coin portrayal of Jesus (see **Figure 20**). The third photo only showed faint eyes and a partial nose. Nevertheless, SOMETHING had indeed occurred!

To get some crucial third-party validation, on May 16, 2001, I sent the most recognizable face photo to imaging specialist Brooks Corl, at the Polaroid corporate headquarters, without disclosing the methodology used or that the face used was the Shroud's. In an e-mail response back to me after his evaluation, he writes, "Yes, I guess I can see the trace of a 'face' you are referring to. Considering even the fully developed image is mottled and not fully saturated, I think we should consider the possibility that your radiation source is either too weak or of a 'marginal' wavelength that it doesn't fully or easily penetrate the 4 x 5 film envelope." (Via e-mail, 5/16/01)

I was astounded – he had most likely hit the nail on the proverbial head without even knowing it. Our untrained and beginner attempts were most certainly "too weak" and, unquestionably, Polaroid film would not necessarily be sensitive to whatever "marginal wavelength" was causing these images, the tracks on the X-

Figure 20

One of the Polaroid "thought" experiments produced an image eerily similar to the portrayal of Jesus found on a Byzantine coin. The mottled and subdued image was judged to be caused by "weak transmission" and use of a "marginal wavelength" of the energy source creating the image.

rays, the discolorations on our linen OR the image on the Shroud of Turin. What if Joe and I had very strong and focused "mind power?" Would we be able to do a better job at creating images – say somewhere in the vicinity of a full Shroud-like body image? Perhaps the DelaWarr camera served as some sort of amplification or assistance device, enabling untrained minds to enhance their innate capabilities. This whole scenario was reminiscent of my weightlifting days. At first, I was weak and untrained but, with lots of practice and perseverance, I became the strongest woman in the world. Was Jesus trying to tell me that this same "strength enhancement" was also possible on a mental or spiritual basis?

One day in late April, I pulled the original experimental linen sample from its secure plastic baggie to observe the discolored fibers. What I noticed startled me – the remaining discolored spots on the front of the sample were now gone but, incredibly, a large "figure 8" discolored area had now materialized on the back of the small sample! (see page 229 **Figure 21**) Where had this come from? The sample had been securely tucked away in total darkness since the testing at OSU a month earlier. No one had touched it nor had it seen the light of day. This discolored area looked even more like the image fibers on the Shroud than had the previous smaller streaks.

But my visual interpretation of a "match" with the Shroud was not nearly good enough. After all, incredible claims require incredible proof. An objective, scientific evaluation of the discolored fibers on my linen sample revealed some remarkable similarities with the image fibers on the Shroud (see page 229 **Figure 22**). In summary, what the scientists found included:

✓ The color distribution in the discolored area looks very much like the surface of the Shroud.
✓ The color is discontinuous and only on the topmost 1 or 2 fibers.
✓ The color does not penetrate the threads.
✓ The color matches the color on the Shroud image fibers.
✓ The discolored region does not fluoresce, just like the Shroud.
✓ At 25X magnification in oblique light and using a petrographic microscope, the discolored region looks nearly identical to the Shroud's image area.
✓ At 100X, the discolored region looks superficially slightly different. The color appears in discrete zones.
✓ There are places where the color descends and ends abruptly on several fibrils simultaneously on a thread that is going under an adjoining thread.
✓ When the discolored fibrils are mounted in 1.515 immersion oil, the color is a close match for the Shroud.
✓ Identical with the Shroud, there is essentially no color in the medullas.
✓ The color does not affect the index of refraction, which means it is an extremely thin layer in the discolored zones. This is also characteristic of the Shroud.
✓ In several instances, the color shows up on only one side of a fibril. This further demonstrates the extreme surface nature of the discoloration.
✓ The depth of the color (ranging from light yellow to brownish) depends on local concentrations of the surface sizing.
✓ The color ends abruptly in some places where the sizing ends or abruptly changes thickness to a much thinner film. However, the sizing is still seen in uncolored parts of the samples. This means that something differentially affected the colored areas of the linen even though the sizing is all over the surface of the linen.
✓ The Shroud color is a result of a surface dehydrated polysaccharide, suggesting something was there and was differentially affected as in the experimental sample.

In conclusion, whatever energy impacted the discolored regions of the cloth was enough to dehydrate the sizing material but not enough to affect the cellulose. This is true also for the Shroud.

I was astounded! It appeared that the main differences between my little sample and the Shroud was in the fabric itself. It was apparent that the surface sizing and dyes played a crucial role in acting as a catalyst to produce the discoloration on my little cloth. In the case of the Shroud, this would equate to the use of the ancient dye known as S*aponaria officinalis* as had been hypothesized by some of the STURP researchers – most recently by Ray Rogers in his published manuscript (Rogers, 2002).

What type energy was in that tiny pyramid and why did I obtain a sizable discoloration when no other similar discolorations have been noted in other pyramid experiments? Why, too, I wondered was I unable to get another large discoloration like the first – only a few discolored threads here and there? The answer was obvious – other key variables had to play a significant role in providing the needed energy capable of producing the observed effect. The only question remaining was — what were they?

M. Sue Benford

Chapter Thirty Four

Timing is everything

I was stumped and frustrated. Why could I not replicate the "figure 8" or, at least, some other sizable discoloration? I built several other pyramids — big ones and small ones — but nothing seemed to work. What was the "secret ingredient" that taunted me from behind a veil of the unseen?

What could have happened inside that simple cardboard pyramid, capable of creating elemental *calcite* in the discolored images as well as all the other macro and micro effects now seen? Most likely, it had to be due to a unique convergence of several events. The first part I already partially understood in relationship to the verified properties of pyramids, magnetic fields, and resonating cavities. But certainly if these types of dramatic physical and chemical changes routinely occurred in homemade, cardboard pyramid structures it would be widely reported in the literature (or at least in the *National Enquirer*). Something must have been unique about this particular experiment to create such an effect that has not since been fully replicated.

I delved into the mystery deeper and discovered some amazing, little known, facts that may hold the key to my results and, possibly, those of the Shroud's. According to engineer Joseph Parr, who has done 25 years of pyramid research, there are certain times of the year when the pyramid is "most active." On March 19th, according to Parr's chart illustrating the Earth's absolute position in space, the Earth is at its most direct position in front of the Sun. Furthermore, according to Parr's research, solar activities, such as sunspots and solar flares occurring on the "Earthside" of the Sun, would be most likely to create effects on the Earth – and enhance activity within the pyramids. What were "sunspots" and "solar flares" and how might they affect pyramids? According to information available from various Internet websites:

"Sunspots are relatively cool areas that appear as dark blemishes on the face of the sun. They are formed when magnetic field lines just below the sun's surface are twisted and poke though the solar photosphere. The twisted magnetic field above sunspots are sites where solar flares are observed to occur, and we are now beginning to understand the <u>connection between solar flares and sunspots</u>. Every 11 years the sun undergoes a period of activity called the 'solar maximum', followed by a period of quiet called the 'solar minimum'. During the solar maximum there are many sunspots, solar flares, and coronal mass ejections, all of which can affect communications and weather here on Earth." (http://www.sunspotcycle.com)

"Scientists classify solar flares according to their X-ray brightness in the wavelength range 1 to 8 Angstroms. There are 3 categories: X-class flares are big; they are major events that can trigger planet-wide radio blackouts and long-lasting radiation storms. M-class flares are medium-sized; they generally cause brief radio blackouts that affect Earth's polar regions. Minor radiation storms sometimes follow an M-class flare. Compared to X- and M-class events, C-class flares are small with few noticeable consequences here on Earth." (<u>http://www.spaceweather.com/glossary/flareclasses.html</u>).

According to Earthside images of magnetic flux observed by the SOHO-MDI group at Stanford University, during the period of March 1 to April 24, 2001, "A very large active region known as AR9393 formed during this time." Further, beginning March 15th, the last day my sample was in the pyramid during its one-week stay, "The region contained the largest spot complex of the cycle (to date)." Also reported during this time period was an X 1.7 flare on March 29th. Associated with the flare, although most likely not from the sunspot itself, was an Earth-directed coronal mass ejection (CME) and an energetic particle event.

Since the large discolored region on my sample did not appear until sometime in April, it stands to reason that the time spent in the pyramid was not the only energetic exposure to affect the sample. Something else - something dramatic - must have occurred to further affect the little piece of linen. What I discovered astounded me. On April 2, 2001, active region 9393 unleashed a major solar flare. "Now reclassified as, at least, an X 20, ***it appears to be the biggest X-ray flare on record.***"[*emphasis added*] (http://soi.stanford.edu/data/farside/index.html). Could a flare of this magnitude have anything to do with providing the energy needed to dehydrate the surface sizing of my linen and, on a grander scale, the *Saponaria* on the surface of the Shroud? My head was spinning with the implications.

In terms of connecting the various points with the hypothesized 1st century Shroud image-formation event, several things seemed to fit. First, few people question that Jesus' body was placed in a closed tomb, which would have made for a resonating cavity capable of intensifying whatever energy source was available.

Second, the Earth's direct position in front of the Sun on March 19th would have made intense solar activities more likely to affect our planet. I wondered — was this close to the date of the crucifixion? Although no one is certain of the actual date of Jesus' crucifixion, most scholars agree it occurred at the time of Passover. This holiday is always in late March or early April so it was indeed possible that it occurred close to, or on, the 19th of March. Third, an interesting point of congruence with the 1st century Shroud event is that if you count backwards the average 11 year peak sunspot cycle from 2000-01 (peak of this cycle) it gives a date of 31-32 AD. Most scholars believe that Jesus was crucified in either 30 or 33 AD (Humphreys & Waddington, 1983) — very close to a potential peak sunspot cycle. Once again, the actual date of the crucifixion is not known nor are the peaks of sunspot cycles known that long ago, but the possibility of the crucifixion occurring during a peak sunspot cycle, or during the influence of a large solar flare, could not be immediately ruled out.

Certainly there must be some way to check for the occurrence of any maximum sunspot activity or major solar flares in the first part of the first century? To ascertain any scientific support for this hypothesis, I contacted physicist and solar cycle expert, Dr. Juerg Beer of Switzerland. Dr. Beer is a leading international expert on interpreting ice core data in relationship to historical solar activities.

Although nothing too dramatic was noted from Dr. Beer's data, he did find that there was a "rather steady decrease in [sunspot] activity from 0 to about 40 AD." (via e-mail 11/8/01). This data, however, does not include solar flares because "the energies of solar protons are too low to significantly contribute to the production rate of 10Be. In fact, we observe the opposite. During an active sun we see a reduced production rate due to the modulation of the galactic cosmic rays by the solar wind." (via e-mail 11/9/01). Could the decreasing sunspot activity, and production of 10Be, from 0 to 40 AD somehow be an indirect indicator of increased solar flare activity? The possibility was intriguing.

It is interesting to note that the discoloration on my linen sample did not appear immediately but, rather, following the April 2nd mega-flare. Did the initial exposure to the dehydrating pyramid "prime the pump" such that the fibers/sizing were more susceptible to the energy fallout from the flare? Is this convergence of the "just right timing" of events the reason my follow-up experiments had been much less successful than the initial sample from March and, perhaps, why the Shroud has not been even "accidentally" replicated yet? Do all the variables have to coincide in just the right proportions, at just the right times, in order to produce these same effects? Was the equation perhaps: resonating cavity + enhanced magnetic field + solar flare + strong human intention + "witness" (body fluid or picture) + unknown energy source = Shroud image — and now my "image?" Is this why, after several years of pursuing the answers to the Shroud mystery, I was told to do the pyramid experiments in March of 2001 and not before or since? And, most importantly, if this hypothesis is NOT correct, then what is?

I wondered about the "unknown energy" source that was supposedly resonating in the pyramids and critical in my equation. Were there any bona fide theories or experiments about such an energy residing in resonating cavities like pyramids? And, if so, were there any links to sunspots, solar flares and, as amazing as it might seem, conscious intention? I had to find out.

My research and insights led to an unlikely source across the cold, vast tundra of what once was communist Russia. Hidden behind the crumbled Berlin wall and buried deep within the inner sanctum of secret Soviet research, lay a newfound wealth of information. The melting of cold war barriers had opened an untapped reservoir for western science. But it was a reservoir so provocative and so astounding that its very nature shook the staunchly held manifolds of materialistic science.

My path ended in, of all places, the prestigious Institute of Physics at the National Academy of Sciences in Kiev. The same scientists, who had once diligently worked on the renowned Mir Space Station and Russia's missile defense system, now turned serious attention to pyramids and the unseen force within their confines. Most notable of these researchers were physicists Drs. Volodymyr Krasnoholovets and Valery Byckov. Their impressive resumes demonstrated that they were not your typical crackpots making unsubstantiated claims publishable only in the *Journal of Irreproducible Results*. Krasnoholovets, earned his doctoral degree in theoretical physics at the Taras Shevchenko Kyiv National University. For the past 20 years, he has worked in the Department of Theoretical Physics at the Institute of Physics, National Academy of Sciences in the Ukraine. He is internationally known for research in the physics of hydrogen-bonded systems.

Byckov is no slouch either. He serves as a research scientist at the Department of Physical Electronics in the Institute of Physics and is internationally recognized as a remarkable experimentalist in the making of sensors based on nanoparticle structures for infrared radiation, temperature, and mechanical strength. Byckov is also an expert in the microanalysis of nanomaterials and nanostructures by use of Transmission Electron Microscopy, Scanning Electron Microscopy and Tunneling Electron Microscopy. Besides these qualifications, he is a specialist in the computer analysis and elaboration of sophisticated experiments. Did these Russians have an advanced understanding of something western scientists had ignored or discarded as impossible?

What Krasnoholovets and Byckov proposed was the existence of an unseen energy, called "inertons." These inertons existed in what western science believed to be merely a vacuum of empty space and were created by the inertia of the Earth's rotation. To prove their hypothesis, the pair did extensive and well-controlled studies, whereby the edges of razor blades were monitored, with high-tech equipment, both inside and outside resonating structures. They demonstrated that the changes to the razor blades, inside the structures, were highly significant under certain conditions, e.g., the blades were aligned with East-West versus North-South. They reported that, " In such a manner, inerton waves should be present in any system consisting of a large number of bound particles. These waves are excited and propagate in space and can influence material objects." (Krasnoholovets and Byckov, 2000; 22) On pyramids, the scientists had this to offer,

"Surprisingly, mankind is familiar with the effect of influence of the Earth inerton waves over a long time. Egyptian pyramids are a glowing example. It is well-known . . . that Egyptian pyramids and their small models possess inexplicable properties: the pyramids provide the mummification of animal remains, depress germination of moistened grains, keep up the razor blades sharp, etc. The base of the pyramid is a square oriented with a high degree of accuracy to the directions of the world. . . .This means that like our resonator, which has the shape of a partly open book, the Egyptian pyramid is a resonator for inerton waves generated by the Earth as well." (Krasnoholovets and Byckov, 2000; 22)

I found the nearly-unknown work of the Russians fascinating. Was there also some link between the hypothesized inertons and heightened solar activity as I had deemed necessary for my equation? Further exploration into their research revealed that in the 1950s, Russian scientist N.A. Kozyrev had observed an unusual astrological effect when the same star was observed at different angles simultaneously. This effect was unexplainable using traditional science. However, at the conference *Gravitation, Cosmology and Relativistic Astrophysics* held in the State Kharkiv University in November 2000 (Kharkiv, Ukraine), Krasnoholovets gave an invited talk on inertons, which stimulated discussion by the attending staff of the Cathedra of Astronomy and Astronomers from the Kharkiv Observatory. The group decided that the effects observed by Kozyrev, and subsequently others, might be reinterpreted in terms of the inerton field. Namely, they hypothesized that stars and planets are indeed able to radiate the inerton field along with the electromagnetic one. Thus, heightened sunspot and solar flare activity, which we already know increases electromagnetic radiation here on Earth, may also stimulate inertons inside pyramids and other resonating cavities, like Jesus' tomb, as well. This finding dumbfounded me, but more was still to come.

One part of my equation still remained a total mystery — the role of conscious intention on the material within the pyramid. This unknown had plagued DelaWarr and, most likely, caused his ultimate downfall and the shelving of his work by mainstream scientists. Although parapsychology, or "psi," research has gained some ground in recent years, it still lags far behind the ranking of tangible data collected under laboratory- controlled conditions. The DelaWarr images, remote viewing, mind reading, bending spoons, spiritual healing, etc., all fall well outside the known scientific boundaries. The missing component among all of them was the "unseen energy" necessary to perform what appears to be works of sheer magic. I wondered — was there any possible connection to the hypothetical inertons? In their article, Krasnoholovets and Byckov, astounded me with the following, "Review of Puthoff and Targ described experiments on transmission of mental information over a distance of hundreds kilometres by extra sensitive participant placed into a special metal room. The room shielded the participant-sender by two metal screens; hence the room was absolutely impenetrable for the electromagnetic field. Nevertheless, the information transmitted via the perceptive channel from one participant to another was received successfully. However, it was pointed out that the transmission was efficient only along the West-East line; but it is this direction that the intensity of inerton waves of the Earth is maximum. It is not ruled out that the inerton field as an informational field plays an important role in other phenomena of parapsychology." (Krasnoholovets and Byckov, 2000; 22)

Could there actually be a link between these "inertons" and the intention of human beings? If so, would some of us be able to hoist more inertons than others? Did this explain why Joe and my attempts at creating the Polariod pictures or the dots on the X-rays was very weak? Was Jesus, then, a world-record holder in the "inerton moving" event? Could we really strive to do "greater things" than this, as he had taught?

Although all of this seemed a tremendous series of affirmations, I was still disappointed that there was no discernible face on my linen. Then, one night while Joe was looking through the microphotographic slides of the experimental sample, he pointed out what appeared to be a face. As implausible as this seems, on the tip of a single fiber, magnified a number of times, a subtle and diffuse Shroud-like facial image could be seen (see page 230 **Figure 23**). Was this, however, simply "cloud zoology" in which daydreamers ardently observe cloud-composed white elephants morphing into their favorite T-Rex?

As most Shroud aficionados will explain, not just any face will suffice to reproduce a true Shroud image. The Shroud is known to possess spatial encoding qualities that permit it to be rendered with 3-D systems that convert image density (lights and darks) into vertical relief (shadows and highlights) as could also be done with the DelaWarr images. The "face" on the single fiber was sent to an optical physicist for rendering (see page 230 **Figure 24**). Although not as clear and distinct as the 3-D renderings of the actual Shroud, the image appeared to contain the basic facial characteristics of the man in the Shroud. Of particular noteworthiness were some distinct matching features between the 3-D version of the thread "face" and the Shroud face. On both images, the eyes appear wide set into the sides of the head, a heightened protrusion exists between the eyes at the top of both noses, the same distinctive jagged blood mark appears on the left side in the hair of both images, both foreheads are foreshortened, and the beards both have missing hair in the middle. Were all these things mere coincidence?

M. Sue Benford

Certainly in these cases, independent verification has to be obtained; thus, an informal study was conducted with staff at The Ohio State University. Each person was independently asked to view the 2-D magnified image and to describe what he or she saw. They were then asked to do the same with the 3-D rendering. Of the 17 people questioned, 14 were able to identify a face, with a few claiming to see "Christ." Some saw more in the 3-D rendering while others saw more in the 2-D image. Only four people declared to see "nothing specific."

I was stunned but still confused — why so small? Why put the face on a single fiber that is only seen by 75% of the people? An insight I received answered the question: no one could accuse us of forging such a micro-image. After all, if the image was visible to the naked eye one could assert that I had somehow managed an original hoax. A second thought was that my mind power was simply too weak.

Although satisfied with this explanation, I still wanted more. I wanted to know for certain that this was Jesus' work and not just our minds playing elaborate tricks. I still had a number of unanswered questions about the enigmatic sideways "figure 8," which mysteriously appeared using only my homemade tiny pyramid. Most disturbing, we knew for certain that the surface sizing that became discolored was all over the modern-linen sample, so why did the image form in a notable figure 8? Why was not the entire surface of the cloth uniformly affected by whatever energy had caused the distinctive yellowing of certain threads? There had to be something about that particular image/shape that I had yet to discover.

As fate would have it, a friend I had worked with in the past stopped over unexpectedly one Sunday. I typically refrained from sharing any of my Shroud research with others, but something compelled me to show her the little linen sample with the odd discolored area. She immediately stated, "Oh, you got an infinity symbol!" A what? "You know, the mystical symbol for God — alpha and omega, never ending, that sort of thing." My mouth dropped. Another now saw what I had interpreted as a sideways figure 8 as a symbol representing God. Was this just a mere irony? Perhaps it was a simple coincidence but, if so, then how did I explain that only this particular portion of the linen surface was discolored and in a distinct pattern? Was this Jesus' way of autographing the linen so to speak?

Other interesting features of the Shroud image compelled me to believe that the image was more in keeping with a QuantaGraph®, projected by Jesus' intention, than with an image produced by the body itself. First, as several researchers have pointed out, the hair on the sides of the Shroud face does not fall about the head as if the image was created when the body was prone. Having shoulder length hair myself, this was easy enough to demonstrate. There were no instances that I could contrive to keep my hair from falling flat when in either a prone or semi-prone position. This would not have been a factor, however, if Jesus had projected the image of himself, such that it appeared, as if he were standing up.

Second, the Shroud face contains much better spatially-encoded information than the rest of the body. I spent hours trying to render both the front and back of the Shroud image with the same software that easily captured the face, but with no luck. The body just does not contain the same variation in intensity, as does the face. Of course, if Jesus had purposely left the image in order to be easily recognized, his intention would have been focused predominantly on his face, which is the most easily recognized human feature.

A third interesting, and yet unexplained, aspect of the Shroud is the perception that there are other identifiable images on the cloth besides the body. Although I cannot verify most of the "images," one is quite clear – a chrysanthemum flower – positioned to the upper right of the frontal image of the head (Whanger and Whanger, 1998; 74). As was seen in the DelaWarr image of the cow's stomach, objects besides the main subject can also be captured in a QuantaGraph®.

Fourth, and perhaps the most interesting, was the mismatched and in-human height of the Shroud body image. As disclosed in the book by Lynn Picknett and Clive Prince entitled, <u>Turin Shroud: In Whose Image</u>?, the authors write,

"We bought a photograph of the entire Shroud from the Holy Shroud Guild (of New York), measured it and, knowing the dimensions of the Shroud itself, scaled up our results accordingly. Our calculations put the height of the man on the Shroud – at the front – at 6ft. 8in (203 cm). Not surprisingly, we blinked and repeated our calculations several times. This had been no mistake: the front image is indeed around the 6ft 8in mark. So what is the height of Shroudman at the back? Curiouser and curiouser – he is 6ft 10in (208 cm). Strangely enough, if you look closely enough at the Shroud literature you will find these calculations in there somewhere, but they are hardly picked out in banner headlines." (Picknett and Prince, 2000; 247)

This certainly had to be a mistake so I decided to do some calculations myself using two different full-length Shroud photos. I also decided to be very conservative in pinpointing where the image started and stopped. With the first photo, not taking into account any shortening of the legs due to bending at the knee, I found that the front image was 6ft 3in tall while the back was 6ft 7in tall. The second larger photo came out to be 6ft 3in tall in front and 6ft 6in tall for the back. Picknett and Prince explained the discrepancy as a result of a photographic projection, which permits the creation of smaller or larger than life size images. Certainly this same characteristic held true for QuantaGraphs® as well since all of the DelaWarr images were either much smaller than the subject at hand, e.g., bodily organs, or much larger, e.g., 1 month old fetuses. In most instances, QuantaGraphic® images seem to fill whatever size "canvas" they are projected onto as can be seen from my small infinity sign, the DelaWarr images done on 4 x 5in glass and later on both film and slides, and now possibly on the large Shroud linen.

It was all starting to come together. Could it be that now I had something to hold in my hand — a "Shroud" for the 21st century?

Figure 21

Scan on May 22nd shows deeper discoloration (note tips)

Scan on April 27th shows beginning discoloration.

Approximately a month after the experimental sample was removed from the pyramid, a noticeable "figure 8" appeared on one side of the cloth. The staff of the OSU MARC lab, who closely examined the cloth in March 2001, had not detected this large discolored area. This photo shows that the image actually darkened from the end of April to the end of May 2001.

Figure 22

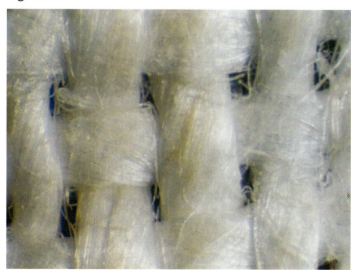

This microphotograph shows the discolored threads of the experimental linen sample under magnification. The fibers were blindly reviewed by several experts. The comparisons to the discolored fibers on the Shroud are remarkable.

Figure 23

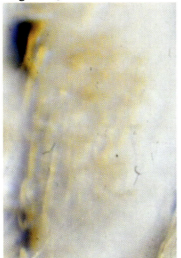

Image appeared on one thread   Actual Shroud face

This "face" was discovered on the tip of a single thread of the experimental linen. Some people see a comparison of this image to the actual Shroud of Turin face on the right.

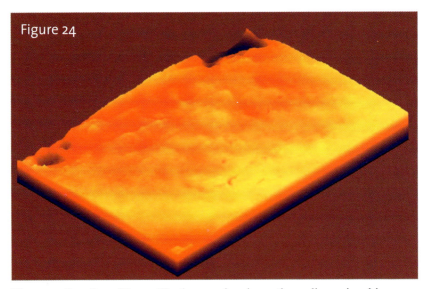

Figure 24

The same face from Figure 23 when rendered as a three-dimensional image. Several overlaps with the actual Shroud face can be seen: eyes extending into the sides of the head, broken nose appearance with bump between eyes (see Figure 11), foreshortened forehead, jagged blood in left side of hair, and V-notch in the center of the beard.

M. Sue Benford

Conclusion

Only the beginning

    Had I been led to all of this for a purpose? Were there possibly some long discarded truths connecting the misunderstood and much maligned DelaWarr research, the hotly-debated Shroud of Turin, and lessons we were all to learn about life in general? Did DelaWarr's "Fundamental Energy" somehow link to the Russian's newly discovered inertons? Was DelaWarr's "Force Field Body" perhaps the Quantum Hologram of current day science or maybe the etheric soul of long held religious beliefs? Perhaps some of DelaWarr's own conclusions answered these questions best – maybe there were still things about the "unseen" that science needed to learn.
    My lifelong questions now seemed much nearer to grasp than in years past. "Who am I?" "Where did I come from?" "Where will I go after I die?" "Will some part of me exist after my death?" No greater or more heart-felt questions have ever been posed by humankind. My dual journeys from weakness into strength had yielded many answers and raised many more questions. Until my life-altering "meetings in the meadow," with my beloved spiritual guides, neither science nor religion had offered definitive answers capable of assuaging the fears we each harbor about our life, its purpose and our final destiny. But it is not for the lack of searching.
    From earliest recorded history, humans have tried to define the "*élan vital*," or vital energy of life. It is this source that is most often associated with the soul, spirit, and mind. Egyptians believed energy centers produced an etheric force, termed "*ka*," that linked the physical body to the spiritual world, while other cultures ranging from Native Americans to Polynesians to Far Eastern cultures envisioned similar

biophysical-spiritual connections, which extend human existence beyond the grave. In fact, there are references made to the phenomenon of the human energy field, or the aura, of the body, in 97 different cultures, according to John White in his book <u>Future Science</u>. Although pervasive in religious and mystical belief systems, the elusive soul still evades the tenacious grasp of scientific discernment. Or does it, I wondered?

Throughout this enormous and profound adventure I call "my life," I had learned that our days in the Earth school never end until the last breath. Undoubtedly, to come my way are both good and bad, significant and insignificant, and easy and hard lessons. But now I am prepared. Now, at least, I understand my purpose as a spiritual being and can rise to the challenge.

And what of the larger consequence of affirming the existence of a soul and the authenticity of the Shroud of Turin? Are we, perhaps, on the verge of demonstrating the unimaginable—humankind's destiny as fledgling "gods"? Like fetuses developing within the mother's womb, our spiritual bodies journey the same ongoing process until, when matured as fully developed "Christ's," we return to our Creator, not as an inferior creation, but as an equal in the light of God. Was this, perhaps, the meaning behind Jesus' teachings when he proclaimed, "Is it not written in your Law 'I have said you are gods?'" (Jn 10:34) After all, he had said we would do greater things than he. What level of strength would we require to break Jesus' spiritual world records? Were we on the verge, perhaps, of obtaining the "Message of the Holy Grail" as DelaWarr had hoped?

As I pondered the scenario, a smile crossed my face as a once familiar scene raced through my mind. The irony was profound and unmistakable. In my mind, I walked up to the powerlifting platform and I saw it—my foe, my demon, my Evil One. Empowered by the force of the world, its very appearance was foreboding. The crowd roared for me to defeat it as David had long ago slain the mighty Goliath. I would have to challenge it with more than just my might. Deep inside stirred a power I was yet to recognize, but one in which I knew was greater than the power of the world.

Grasping the metal bar tightly, I thrust my very being against this old and worthy foe. So many times before I had struggled but failed. But in this constant struggle an unseen strength had arisen and I had grown more worthy than my opponent. My new strength would prove to be the undoing of the Evil One.

Everything around me disappeared. The crowd grew silent in the distance, my own body numbed by the pain. Only a small voice remained, deep inside repeating, "I am always with you." And in this renewed strength I found victory. I had challenged the best—the very forces of the world itself. But I stood not alone as the sole champion.

Behind the roar of the crowd, I heard the angels rejoicing. Their triumphant praises told me that I had come home. Finally, and by the grace of God, I had realized the truth. Where once there had only been a weak and broken body, now dwelled an eternal soul. Where once there had been only weakness, now a Strong Woman for evermore.

References

Adler, Alan, "Updating Recent Studies on the Shroud of Turin." In M.V. Orna (Ed.), *Archaeological Chemistry: Organic, inorganic and biochemical analysis* ACS Symposium Series, vol. 625. Washington, DC: American Chemical Society. 1996; 223-228.

Adler, Alan, "Concerning the Side Strip on the Shroud of Turin," Actes Du III Symposium Scientifique International Du CIELT-Nice, 12-13 May, 1997; 103-105.

Adler, Alan: 1999. Personal Communication, October and November.

Benford MS. Detecting the Soul: Controlled Studies Detect High-Energy Fluctuations During Alternative Healing Therapies. Presented at the International Conference on Religion and Science, Columbus, Ohio, May 3, 1999.

Benford MS. The Two Faces of Adam: When Creation Meets Evolution. The Church Herald. Feb. 1998.

Benford MS, Talnagi J, Burr-Doss D, Boosey S, Arnold LE. Gamma Radiation Fluctuations During Alternative Healing Therapy. Alternative Therapies in Health and Medicine. July 1999, Vol 5, No. 4:51-56.

Benford MS, Schwartz GER, Russek LGS, Boosey S. Exploring the Concept of Energy. In:Clinician's Complete Reference to Complementary & Alternative Medicine. C.V. Mosby Publishing, Feb. 2000.

Benford MS. In Pursuit of the Soul: Examining the Catharsis from Life to After-life. Journal of Religion and Psychical Research. Vol. 23, No. 1 January 2000; 27-38.

Benford MS. Can a theory derived from recent experimental data explain precognition and other mysterious spiritual phenomena? Journal of Religion and Psychical Research. July 2001, Volume 24, number 3, pp. 132-141.

Benford MS. Empirical Evidence Supporting Macro-Scale Quantum Holography in Non-Local Effects. Journal of Theoretics. December 2000, 2 (5); on-line.

Benford, M. Sue, Peter Moscow, Edgar Mitchell and Peter Marcer. QuantaGraphy®: Images from the Quantum Hologram. Presented at the Fifth International Conference on Computing Anticipatory Systems (CASYS'01), Liège, Belgium, August 13-18, 2001.

Benford MS. Probable Axion Detection via Consistent Radiographic Findings after Exposure to a Shpilman Axion Generator. Journal of Theoretics. February/March 2002, 4 (1); on-line.

Benford M. Sue and Marino Joseph. Textile Evidence Supports Skewed Radiocarbon Date of Shroud of Turin, online at www.shroud.com. August 2002.

Benford M. Sue and Marino Joseph. Historical Support of a 16th Century Restoration in the Shroud C-14 Sample Area. online at www.shroud.com. August 2002.

Bonnet-Eymard, Bruno, "The Holy Shroud, Silent Witness: In Preparation for a Centenary (1898-1998)" Catholic Counter Reformation in the 20th Century, April, No.295, 1997; 1-34.

BSTS Newsletter, no. 51, June 2000; 43.

Capra, Fritof, The Tao of Physics, Shambhala Publications, Inc., Boston, MA, 1991

Case, T.W., The Shroud of Turin and The C-14 Dating Fiasco: A Scientific Detective Story, White Horse Press, Cincinnati, OH, 1996; 75-77.

Choquette, Sonia, The Psychic Pathway, Crown Trade Paperbacks, New York, 1995.

Damon, P.E. *et al*. "Radiocarbon Dating of the Shroud of Turin." *Nature*, Vol. 337, 16 February, 1989; 611-615.

Day L. (with DelaWarr G.). New Worlds Beyond the Atom. Vincent Stuart Publishers Ltd., London, 1956.

Day L. (with DelaWarr G.). Matter in the Making. Vincent Stuart Publishers Ltd., London, 1966.

Delorenzi, Enzo, "Observations on the Patches and Darns in the Holy Shroud." In Doyle, E., M. Green, Fr., & V. Ossola (Trans.) Report of Turin Commission on the Holy . Unpublished. Translation of La S. Sindone: Ricerche e studi della Commissione di Esperti nominata dall'Arcivescovo di Torino, Card. Michele Pellegrino, nel. 1976; 108-123.

"Effects of Radio Waves gets Wider Laboratory Study:" 1959. Original print publication in *New York Times*, 6 April. Retrieved 8 June 2000 from the World Wide Web: http://www.newphys.se/elektromagnum/physics/KeelyNet/biology/delaw2.asc

Ferguson & Co., Ltd. (Co. Down, Ireland): 2000. Personal Communication, 6 June.

Fox, Matthew and Sheldrake, Rupert, Natural Grace , Doubleday, New York, 1996.

Fox, Matthew and Sheldrake, Rupert, The Physics of Angels , HarperSanFrancisco, New York, 1996.

Gariaev PP, Grigor'ev KV, Vasil'ev AA, Poponin VP, Shcheglov VA. Investigation of the Fluctuation Dynamics of DNA Solutions by Laser Correlation Spectroscopy. Bulletin of the Lebedev Physics Institute, 1992:11-12;23-30.

Gariaev PP, Poponin VP. Vacuum DNA phantom effect in vitro and its possible rational explanation. Nanobiology 1995 (in press).

Gervasio, Richard, "La Struttura Tessile Della Sindone." In La Sindone: Nuovi studie e richerche, Atti del II Congresso Nazionale di Stuudi sulla Sindone Trani. Milano: Edizione Paoline, 1986. [Privately translated]

Green, Maurus. "Enshrouded in Silence: in Search of the First Millennium of the Holy Shroud. The Ampleforth Journal, Autumn, 74, 1969; 321-45.

Harner, Louise: 2000. Personal Communication, 20 July and 2 August.

Hatfield, Ronald: 2000. Personal Communication, 9 June.

Hawking, Stephen, A Brief History of Time , Bantam Books, New York, 1996.

Heller JH and Adler AD., "A Chemical Investigation of the Shroud of Turin." Can. Soc. Forens. Sci. J., Vol. 14(3), 1981; 81-103.

Hoeller, Stephan A., Jung and the lost Gospels: insights into the Dead Sea Scrolls and the Nag Hammadi library ,Theosophical Publishing House, 1989.

Humphreys, CJ and Waddington, WG. "Dating the Crucifixion." Nature, 306, December 22/29, 1983; 743-746.

Jackson JP, Jumper EJ, Ercoline WR. Correlation of image intensity on the Turin Shroud with the 3-D structure of a human body shape. Applied Optics, July 1984, Vol. 23, No. 14;2244-2269.

Jackson JP. An Unconventional Hypothesis to Explain All Image Characteristics Found on the Shroud Image. IN: Symposium Proceedings: History, Science, Theology and the Shroud. St. Louis. MO, June 22-23, 1991;325-344.

Jumper E, Adler A, Jackson JP, Pellicori S, Heller J, Druzik J. A comprehensive examination of the various stains and images on the Shroud of Turin. ACS Advances in Chemistry 1984:205; 447.

Krasnoholovets, Volodymyr and Byckov, Valery. Real inertons against hypothetical gravitons: Experimental proof of the existence of inertons. Indian Journal of Theoretical Physics, 2000, 48(1); 1-23.

Marino, J., "The Disciples on the Road to Turin." Presented at Holy Shroud Guild Seminar, Esopus, New York, August 23-25, 1996. For the full text of the paper, see (http://www.shroud.com/marino.htm).

Marino JG, Benford MS. The Shroud of Turin: Bridge Between Heaven and Earth. Journal of Religion and Psychical Research. April 1999.

Marino J., Benford MS. Rebirth, Resurrection, and the Millennium. Journal of Religion and Psychical Research. January 2000, 23(1):17-26.

Marino, J. and Benford, M.S. Evidence for the Skewing of the C-14 of the Shroud of Turin Due to Repairs. Presented at Sindone 2000 Worldwide Congress in Orvieto, Italy, 26-28 August 2000.

McCrone, W. Judgement Day for the Shroud of Turin, Prometheus Books, New York, 1999.

Meyer, Marvin W., The Secret Teachings of Jesus: Four Gnostic Gospels, Vintage Books, New York, 1986.

Mitchell, Edgar, The Way of the Explorer, G.P. Putnam's Sons, New York, 1996.

Morris, R.A., Schwalbe L.A., and London, J.R., "X-Ray Fluorescence Investigation of the Shroud of Turin." X-Ray Spectrometry, Vol. 9(2), 1980; 40-47.

Morse, Melvin and Perry, Paul, Transformed by the Light, Villard Books, New York, 1992.

Pagels, Elaine, The Gnostic Gospels, Vintage Books, New York, 1989.

Pagels, Elaine, The Gnostic Paul, Trinity Press International, Philadelphia, 1975.

Pagels, Elaine, The Origin of Satan, Vintage Books, New York, 1996.

Pearson, David: 2000. Personal Communication, 21 June.

Peck, M. Scott, Further Along the Road Less Traveled, Simon & Schuster, New York, 1993.

Personal communications from Edgar Mitchell to M. Sue Benford, via e-mails during June 2000.

Personal communications from Peter Moscow, current owner of the DelaWarr remote imaging system to M. Sue Benford, from April 1999-April 2001.

Petrosillo, Orazio and Marinelli, Emanuela. The Enigma of the Shroud: A Challenge to Science, Enterprises Group, San Gwann, Malta, 1996.

"Radio Waves Found to Affect Cell Behaviour:" 1959. Original print publication in *New York Times,* 30 March. Retrieved 8 June 2000 from the World Wide Web: www.newphys.se/elektromagnum/physics/KeelyNet/biology/delaw1.asc

Raes, Gilbert, "Appendix B – Analysis Report: Pl. II-III—Subject: Examination of the 'Sindone'". In Doyle, E., M. Green, Fr., & V. Ossola (Trans.) Report of Turin Commission on the Holy Shroud (pp. 108-123). Unpublished. Translation of La S. Sindone: Ricerche e studi della Commissione di Esperti nominata dall'Arcivescovo di Torino, Card. Michele Pellegrino, nel., 1976.

Raes, Gilbert, "The History of the Sample taken on 24th November 1973, the Problem of the Sidestrip and Fibres of Cotton found on the Sample delivered to the Oxford Laboratory." Presentation at Paris Symposium, 7-8 September 7-8, 1989.

Riggi, Giovanni, Presentation at University of Indiana—Evansville Shroud Symposium, 12 February 1994.

Riggi di Numana, Giovanni, Rapporto Sindone. Milano: 3M Edizioni. English translation by John D'Arcy (unpublished), 1988.

Rogers, Ray, "Supportive Comments on the Benford-Marino '16th century repairs' hypothesis. " British Society for Turin Shroud (BSTS) Newsletter, Issue 54, November 2001; 28-33, 68.

Rogers, Raymond N. "Scientific Method Applied to the Shroud of Turin: A Review." Online article at www.shroud.com, 2002.

"Rogue fibres found in the Shroud." *Textile Horizons,* December, 1988; 13.

Scavone, Daniel, "Joseph of Arimathea, the Holy Grail and the Turin Shroud." Presented at Holy Shroud Guild Seminar, Esopus, New York, August 23-25, 1996.

For an abstract of the paper, see http://www.shroud.com/scavone2.htm

Schwalbe, Larry and Rogers, Ray, "Physics and Chemistry of the Shroud of Turin: A Summary of the 1978 Investigation," in *Analytica Chimica Acta* 135, 1982; 3-49.

Starbird, Margaret, The woman with the alabaster jar: Mary Magdalen and the Holy Grail , Bear & Company, Inc., 1993.

Steiner, Rudolf, The Spiritual Hierarchies and the Physical World :Reality and Illusion, Anthroposophic Press, 1996.

Tessiore, Giorgio, "Il Prelievo Per Il C14." *Collagemento Pro Sindone,* Settembre-Ottobre, No. 7, pp. 44-47. English translation by Dr. Anna Ottolenghi (unpublished), 1988.

Toth, Max and Neilsen, Greg, Pyramid Power, Vermont: Destiny Books, 1974.
Trenn, Thaddeus, "The Shroud of Turin: A Parable for Modern Times?" Journal of Interdisciplinary Studies, 9(1/2), 1997; 121-140.

Van Haelst, Remi, "Radiocarbon Data Indeed Manipulated." *Shroud News,* December, No. 68, 1991; 5.

Walsh, Bryan, "The 1988 Shroud of Turin Radiocarbon Tests Reconsidered." Retrieved 25 September 1999 from the World Wide Web: http://members.aol.com/turin99/radiocarbon-b.htm

Whanger A. and Whanger M. The Shroud of Turin, Providence House Publishers, Franklin, Tennessee, 1998.

White J, Krippner S, eds. Future Science: Life Energies and the Physics of the Paranormal. Garden City, NY: Anchor/Doubleday, 1977.

Wilson, Ian, The Blood and the Shroud. Free Press, New York, 1998.

[Wilson, I.] "US Meeting is told of Remarkable Experiment." British Society for the Turin Shroud Newsletter, Issue 49, June, 1999; 10-11.

Woodward, K., "2000 Years of Jesus." Newsweek. March 29, 1999; 53-59, 60, 62, 63.

APPENDIX

Concluding chapter from NEW WORLDS BEYOND THE ATOM (1956) by Langston Day with George DelaWarr.

THE FUTURE

> But contemporary science, by the mere fact of having cut itself sharply off from religion and 'mysticism,' i.e., by having set up for itself a definite 'taboo', has become an accidental and unreliable instrument of thought. The constant feeling of this 'taboo' compels it to shut its eyes to a whole series of inexplicable and unintelligible phenomena, deprives it of wholeness and unity, and as a result brings it about that we have no science but the sciences. P.D. Ouspensky in *A New Model of the Universe*.

Some critics while admitting the validity of DelaWarr's claims try to belittle his discoveries by objecting that his instruments are mere mechanical aids to psychic perceptions. This may be so, but no one criticizes the telescope or the microscope because they are mechanical aids to vision. With these and other optical instruments such as the spectroscope we have learned a very great deal about the Universe and the structure of matter, and we have entirely changed our view of this planet's position in the scale of Creation. It is quite possible that in the years to come when these new forms of radiation are better understood we shall think quite differently about such things as the operations of Nature and the inner workings of the human organism.

Science, which reached its point of maximum 'solidification' in the later Victorian period, is already turning towards less grossly materialistic concepts; but these new concepts are far from clear, and as with all solidified systems of thought which begin to break up into hard lumps, there is considerable disintegration. Dualistic thought runs through the sciences like a series of Iron Curtains.

For instance, there is great confusion of thought on the problem of Mind and Matter, Professor Adrian, of Cambridge, has probably done more work on the detection of brain impulses than any other man. He has tapped many thousands of nerve centers in the brain and traced their nerve channels to various parts of the human and animal anatomy, recording the impulses on the electrocephalograph. Yet when lecturing on this subject several years ago in Oxford, he said, "There is no evidence to prove the existence of the mind."

On the other hand, Sherrington has written (in *Man on His Nature*):

The mind is something with such manifold variety, such fleeting changes, such countless nuances, such wealth of combinations, such heights and depths of mood, such sweeps of passion, such vistas of imagination, that the bald submission of some electrical potentials recognizable in nerve centers as correlates to all these may seem to the special student of mind almost derisory. . . .The mental is not examinable as a form of energy. That in brief is the gap, which parts psychiatry and physiology.

These two contrasting views by two most eminent authorities on the subject show clearly the gulf which yawns between men who are still thinking in terms of the old Victorian formula and those who realize that they do not cover the facts.

DelaWarr's discoveries are a step towards bridging this gulf. The human mind, which is capable of modulating an energy-pattern, has a direct connection with physical forces. Universal Mind is able to manifest through an energy-pattern as matter. The DelaWarr Camera connects a purely mental function known as E.S.P. with an image on a photographic plate. And so on. The No Man's Land between psychiatry and physiology narrows down, perhaps eventually to disappear.

This narrowing of the gap is certain to have an effect on medical science which like physics is divided, roughly speaking, into two schools of thought. There are those who believe that all diseases originate in the mind, and others who attribute illnesses to infections, exhaustion of the body, exposure to cold and damp, and other purely physical causes. No doubt both schools of thought are partly right, but a better knowledge of the Force Field Body should bring these differing views into line, and once the new methods of diagnosis and treatment are established, we should have a medical science, which makes less use of crude drugs and relies more on the curative forces of Nature.

The DelaWarr instruments provide us, in effect, with a sixth sense, which is able to penetrate the crust of gross material results and see what is happening a little higher up on the ladder of causation. With such a faculty it should be possible to develop preventive medicine and also resolve many an ancient controversy.

Are homeopathic dilutions really effective in treating diseases? Have herbs the curative properties, which many claim for them? Does X-ray therapy permanently damage the Force Field Body? Is there any virtue in so-called spiritual healing, or the Laying on of Hands? All these things should be capable of scientific verification.

The same thing applies to foods. Apart from discovering by analysis what chemical essentials of diet may be lacking in canned fruits and vegetables, dried and processed foods, etc., it should be possible to test such commodities for vital radiations.

From a nutritional point of view, these food preparations are thought to be of equal value to fresh foods, but is this really true? Is there no difference in the vitalizing effect between canned peaches and peaches just picked from the tree? Has yesterday's milk lost something, which is present in milk warm from the cow? Does the injection of antibiotics into a herd of cows affect the bacterial balance of the animals and detract from the nutritional qualities in the milk yield? Are there stronger radiations in corn grown under natural conditions than in corn grown on land treated with a chemical fertilizer? It may be that we shall soon know the truth about such matters.

We may perhaps venture a few speculations as to where these discoveries may lead in the rather more distant future.

It has often been pointed out that if we possessed eyes, which responded to X-rays or Hertizian waves we should see an entirely new Universe. The new radio telescope enables us to 'see' invisible stars, but compared with the subtle radiations with which this book is concerned radio waves, X-rays and Hertizian waves are extremely clumsy media for observation. With a telescope, which operates, so to speak, in the sub-ether, who can tell what we shall discover? What shall we 'see', for instance, when we train it on Mars? For one thing we should undoubtedly discover whether or not there is life on Mars similar to our own.

These radiations also stretch back into the past. Thus the skeleton of a megalosaurus or of a pterodactyl is in resonance with the creature which lived millions of years ago, and by analyzing the radiations we should be able to discover more about it than can be gleaned from the fossilized bones.

It needs little imagination to realize that vast fields of exploration lie before us and that the knowledge, which can be gathered by these new techniques may radically alter the whole pattern of modern scientific thought.

The discoveries briefly outlined in this book show how the material world rests upon a framework of finer vibrations, which in their turn, have their origin in something still further removed from the material. What lies higher up on the 'Jacob's Ladder' which connects our physical world with the Prime Source we cannot tell, but at least we have a picture of a Universe created and sustained by higher levels of existence.

The dead hand of gross materialistic thought lies too heavily on modern science. Let us hope that the time will soon come when the Message of the Holy Grail is fulfilled: The restraining and hindering work of the materialist, limited as it is by time and space, must wither and pass away like chaff that is sifted from the wheat.